# THE IGBOS AND ISRAEL:
# AN INTER-CULTURAL STUDY OF THE LARGEST JEWISH DIASPORA

by Remy Ilona

Street to Street EpicCenter Stories
Washington, DC
February 2014
ISBN: 978-1-938609-00-8

Text Copyright © 2014 Remy Ilona
Visuals Copyright © 2014 Remy Ilona

All rights reserved under International and Pan-American Copyright Conventions.
Published in the United States by Street to Street Epic Publications, Washington, DC

Kulanu.org
EpicCenterStories.org


Ilona, Remy

Summary:
Jewish Igbo scholar Remy Ilona presents and analyzes Judaic practices and concepts within the Igbo culture of Nigeria.

ISBN: 978-1-938609-00-8

## Table of Contents

**Reviews** ...... 8
   Review of Remy Ilona's *The Igbos and Israel - An Inter-Cultural Study of the Largest Jewish Diaspora*, by Dr. Daniel Lis, Social Anthropologist, University of Basel, Switzerland ...... 8

**Dedication** ...... 14

**Introduction** ...... 15

**CHAPTER ONE: Life Circle Events** ...... 20
   **Rituals Associated With the Birth of Children** ...... 20
      Omugwo (seclusion of mother who just delivered a child) ...... 20
      Ibi ugwu (circumcision) ...... 22
      Iba afa (naming) ...... 23
      Iputa na omugwo (coming out from seclusion) ...... 26
      Child Presentation, Dedication and Redemption ...... 27
   **Initiation Rites** ...... 28
      Ima mmonwu/Iwa akwa (equivalent of undergoing bar mitzvah) ...... 28
      Iru mgbe (equivalent of bat mitzvah) ...... 30
   **Inu Nwanyi (marriage)** ...... 32
      Typical Igbo Marriage ...... 32
      Ime ego (the bride price) Ihu onu nwanyi (fixing of the bride price) ...... 49
      Ima ogodo/igba nkwu (the marriage feast) ...... 53
      Inye okuko (levirate marriage) ...... 54
      Nwanyi inu nwanyi (woman-to-woman marriage) ...... 55
      The Ihachi nwanyi (retaining a daughter to procreate for the family) ...... 56
      Endogamy and Exogamy ...... 56
      Iju Nwanyi / Igba Anukwaghim (Divorce) ...... 58

**CHAPTER TWO: Comparative Study of the Ideas Underlying Omenana and Judaism** ...... 61
   Omenana and Judaism ...... 61
   Igbo Perception of God ...... 67

    Some Important Matters in Omenana ........................... 83

**CHAPTER THREE: Onwu Na Akwamozu** ................... 92
    Rituals Associated With Dying and Death .................... 92
    Ikwa mmadu na ndu (sitting shiva for the living) .... 104

**CHAPTER FOUR: Feasts and Festivals** ...................... 106
    Emume Iri Ji (The New Yam Festival) ......................... 106
    Oriri Achicha (Passover and unleavened bread) ...... 108
    Ima ntu (Sukkot) ............................................................ 109
    Eke Ukwu/Nkwo Oru (Sabbath) ................................. 110

**CHAPTER FIVE: Socio-Religious Customs** ................ 113
    Inye / icho oji na isa asisa oji (offering of kola nut and apologizing for its unavailability) ................................ 113
    Igba Ndu (entering into covenants) ........................... 116
    Ibu Ihu (Tithe) ................................................................ 118

**CHAPTER SIX: Aru (abomination) and Ikpu Aru (purifications)** ....................................................................... 120
    Igbo and Israelite Concept of Abominations ............. 120
    Other Things or Acts that the Igbos Consider Abominations: ................................................................ 124
    Ikpu Aru (to cleanse or purify the land of abomination) .................................................................. 127

**CHAPTER SEVEN: Ichu Aja (Sacrifices and Offerings)** ....................................................................................... 130
    Ways of Igbo Sacrifice .................................................. 130
    Ichu Aja ............................................................................ 134
        Ilo Chi/Mmuo (peace offering) ............................. 134
        Igo mmuo (sin offering) ........................................ 137
        Igbu Aja (Atonement—Yom Kippur) ................... 138
        Ifio egbo: A Ritual Similar to the Kaparot Ritual ......... 139

**CHAPTER EIGHT: Classes Among the Igbos** ........... 142
    Osu .................................................................................... 142
    The Duty of the Osu ...................................................... 143
    Ohu (Slaves and Slavery) ............................................. 146
    Absence of Kings, Queens, Princes and Princesses .. 149

**CHAPTER NINE: The Socio-Religious Personalities and Authorities** ............................................................... **153**
   Igbos Without Kings Historically ................................. 153
      Aka ji ofo ................................................................. 154
      Eze Mmuo/eze ana ................................................ 158
   Nwa Nri/Nri Clans ......................................................... 159
      Nri Clans .................................................................. 162
      Nwa dibia na onye amuma (doctor/seer-prophet) ..... 163

**CHAPTER TEN: Duties, Relationships, and Behaviours** ....................................................................... **167**
   Respect for Elders and Parents ................................... 167
   Children ......................................................................... 169
   Strangers ....................................................................... 172
   Hired Labourers ............................................................ 174
   In-Laws .......................................................................... 175
   Children Towards Parents ............................................ 175
   Less Fortunate Relatives .............................................. 176
   Towards Animals .......................................................... 177

**CHAPTER ELEVEN: Treatment of Crime and Other Offenses** ........................................................................ **181**
   Igbu Ochu (intentional homicide) ................................ 181
   Manslaughter ................................................................ 182
   Ikwu Udo (suicide) ....................................................... 184
   The Witch/Wizard and Witchcraft: Ita Amonsu ......... 185
   Onye Asiri, Igba Asiri (gossiping) ................................. 186
   Insubordination to Parents and Dishonoring of Parents .......................................................................... 187
   Thieves/Armed Robbers ............................................... 188

**CHAPTER TWELVE: Igbo Revulsion for Irresponsible and Unnatural Sexual Behaviours** ............................ **189**
   Adultery ......................................................................... 189
   Premarital Sex .............................................................. 191
   Homosexuality and bestiality ...................................... 195

**CHAPTER THIRTEEN: Land Matters** ....................... **197**
   Igbo-land ....................................................................... 197
   "The Land" and the Feeling of Being in Exile ............. 199

**CHAPTER FOURTEEN: Ritual Cleanliness**............201
   Ikwo aka na isa ihu uchu (washing of the hands and face in the morning)..............201
   Perception of Exposed Faeces as an Eyesore.............202
   Iza Uno Na Iza Ezi (sweeping of the house and compound)..............203
   Washing of The Hands Before Eating...........205
   Nwanyi i No Na Nso (menstrual seclusion)..............206
   Igbo Reaction to Leprosy...........208

**CHAPTER FIFTEEN: Dietary Matters By Remy Ilona and Ehan Ever**............210
   Distinction Between Clean and Unclean Animals.....210
   Nni (Igbo food)..............211
   Igbu Anu (slaughter of animals)..............215

**CHAPTER SIXTEEN: Similarities Between Igbo and Semitic Manners of Dress**............220
   Igbo Attitude to Clothes..............220
   Fringed Garments..............220
   Caps and Wrappers..............221

**CHAPTER SEVENTEEN: Parallels Between the Igbo and the Hebrew Reckoning of Time**............224
   The Igbo Week And Seventh Day Sabbath............224
   Day Begins at Night..............225

**CHAPTER EIGHTEEN: Joining the Igbo and Jewish People and Leaving Them**............227
   Nnabata Na Nsupu (Igbo and Jewish conversion and excommunication)..............227
   Nnabata (conversion)..............229
   Nsupu (excommunication)..............231

**CHAPTER NINETEEN: The Igbo Society**............233
   The Igbo Clan..............233
   The Structures of the Igbo Clans..............237
   How the Igbo Society Works..............240
   The Nuclear Family..............242
   The Extended Family..............243

Women's Representation in Government ............... 247
CHAPTER TWENTY .......................................................269
Not a Conclusion ..........................................................269
   Thought-provoking Phenomena ..................................269
      Igbo Folk-lore ..........................................................269
   Igbo and Israelite farming practices ...........................272
   Family Trees ..................................................................276
An Igbo Rhyme That Is Also a Jewish Rhyme (Had Gadya), Translated from Igbo by the Author .........277
   Igbo Version: What Happened to the Tortoise? ........277
   Jewish Version: *Had Gadya* ..........................................279
Acknowledgments ........................................................280
Words of Praise for the Author ..................................287
   Researcher's Researcher ..............................................293
   Suggested For Further Reading: .................................293
About Remy Ilona ........................................................296
   References .....................................................................300

# Reviews

**Review of Remy Ilona's *The Igbos and Israel - An Inter-Cultural Study of the Largest Jewish Diaspora*, by Dr. Daniel Lis, Social Anthropologist, University of Basel, Switzerland**

Remy Ilona, the Abuja-based Igbo author, lawyer and activist some years ago coined the term "the modern day George Basden" for me. I never completely agreed that I had earned that title since George T. Basden – a Welsh-Anglican Missionary – had lived for 40 years amongst the Igbo and I – after all – had just spent two weeks in Nigeria with Ilona, touring newly established Igbo Jewish communities in Abuja and visiting Nri priests at Agukwu-Nri – a group of people that had already been compared to the Levites of the Israelites in the 19th century by outside observers because of their position in matters of ritual significance to the Igbo society.

Ilona's book is written with the background that a very significant part of the Igbos identify the origin of their customs as emanating from the ancient Israelites, and that Jewish identification has been part of the Igbo experience, as I have argued myself in my recent publications and in my forthcoming book.

This identification intrigued Ilona more than a decade ago. This made him to start his comparative research; studying what others have written earlier on the subject and interviewing some of the eldest priests and others at Nri, and other Igbo locations who all confirmed the Israelite origin of the Igbos in oral interviews.

Make no mistake, it is unlikely that Igbo people before their contact with Western societies were conscious Jews in a rabbinical Jewish sense, and no clear-cut archeological evidence of a large scale Israelite or Jewish migration into Igboland has been found so far.

However, there can be no doubt that the Igbo people have been in existence long before the introduction of a Western type of nation model, and that indeed some of their traditions resemble the customs of the Hebrew patriarchs as described in the Hebrew Bible.

In this inter-cultural study Remy Ilona presents a systematic comparison of Igbo culture to Hebrew and Israelite culture.

In conducting such a comparative study, there exists a methodological difficulty in reconstructing the traditions of a society – like the Igbo – who had no written records – a major difference to Rabbinic Jewish Societies. Cultures are not monolithic and are prone to change over time (and that includes Jewish and Igbo cultures as well). Ilona however, is well aware of those difficulties and he rightfully writes that Igbo culture has interacted and was influenced by many of the surrounding cultures as well and makes convincing arguments in this regard.

A number of Igbo authors have in the last few years attempted to explain the widespread notion of the Igbo that they are Jews, giving linguistic, archeological, genetic and also cultural explanations. However, the argument did not always seem to be based on a careful comparison of the two entities.

Remy Ilona on the other hand has been following the project of cultural comparison intensely for a decade. In addition to a careful study of what earlier authors have written on this subject (a point that I will relate to a bit further down) and his own research - by way of oral interviews and observation - Ilona might be one of the few Igbo authors with a profound knowledge of the Hebrew Bible and its later Jewish commentaries. Ilona has devoured a body of literature on Rabbinic Judaism and has interacted intensely with Western Jews in order to compare the customs of contemporary Rabbinical Jews to those of the Igbo, noting that many Jews – like the Igbo in their own culture – no longer practice what is today defined as Rabbinical Judaism. In addition Ilona highlights that Judaism has undergone changes as well and that there are difficulties in comparing Igbo culture to Rabbinical Judaism.

Judaism since the destruction of the second temple has slowly developed from a sacrifice oriented cult and a life style – indeed with many similarities to a reconstructed Igbo tradition – to a religion of the Book. Rabbinical Judaism for a large part took its present and dominant form in medieval Ashkenaz. Judaism needed a response to the religions surrounding it (Christianity and Islam) in order to survive. Ilona then rightly points out that the modern day Igbo are not Rabbinical Jews (although there's a growing number of them) but that their customs rather resemble Israelite culture as described in the Five Books of Moses.

Ilona is well aware of the few cultural differences that existed and still exist between different Igbo clans but presents those traditions which are common to all Igbos, and which are most close to Israelite culture, as best capturing the core concepts of Igbo culture.

Thereby, Ilona follows in the footsteps of authors that were central in the definition of Igbo culture and I will only name here the works of Olaudah Equiano, Chinua

Achebe and George T. Basden. Especially the latter who is repeatedly quoted in Ilona's book.

And here some words need to be said about Basden not only because Basden was one of the few longtime and early outside observers who looked at the Igbos with the eye of an anthropologist, but also because Basden arrived in Igboland at the turn to the 20th century before Igbo culture began to change in a major way. Although Basden was not the first to write on the similarities of Igbo customs to those of the Israelites – several Igbo and non-Igbo had done it before – Basden did it continuously and even more elaborately, as he became more and more involved with the Igbo. One of Basden's motivations to publish his ethnographic work on the Igbo was to capture and document the traditions of a world that was changing rapidly under the influence of Christian missionaries - like Basden himself - and the colonial regime that the British began to establish in Nigeria at the beginning of the 20th century. Basden viewed it as important that future generations of Igbo would know what the traditions of their forefathers and mothers were. His influence on Igbo society as a chronicler of Igbo traditions, as well as an educator and politician cannot be overstated and his work is still well known even amongst young Igbos.

Few Igbo during the time of Basden would wander around in Igboland before the advent of colonization and think of themselves as Jews in the sense that we understand it today, or at least we have no indication of that. Only in the Igbo Diaspora where Igbo learnt about the Israelites or Rabbinical Jews do we find earlier expressions of such a thought. Being aware of this Ilona however opens up with the conception of what a Jew is and shows a much more inclusive understanding of

Jewish people-hood, a model that is worthwhile to give some thought in my opinion.

For me as an anthropologist who has studied the Igbos' Jewish identification from a historical perspective and from a perspective of contemporary attempts of Igbo in Israel to be recognized as Jews, one of the most interesting aspects of Ilona's book was how an Igbo author of Ilona's standing is looking at his own culture 70 years after Basden published his Niger Ibos. It shows then that those Igbo customs, as described by Basden in their relation to those of the Israelites, have solidified over time as central markers of Igbo traditions.

In his book, Ilona focuses on Igbo rituals during life cycle events (chapter one). Those include the rituals surrounding the birth of children, eight-day circumcision of males, seclusion of newly delivered mother, levirate marriage and so on. Remy also enters the long debate about the Igbo conception of a supreme God, (chapter two); Igbo rituals surrounding death (chapter three); feast and festivals (chapter four); Igbo social organization (chapter five); Igbo understanding of clean/unclean (chapter six); Igbo sacrifices and offerings (chapter seven); Igbo classes (chapter eight); socio-religious customs (chapter nine); Code of moral behaviour (chapter ten); Igbo code for crime and other offenses (chapter eleven); sexual behavior (chapter twelve); the Igbo connection to the land (thirteen); the importance of ritual cleanliness (chapter fourteen); the distinction between clean and unclean food and ritual slaughter (chapter fifteen); similarities between Igbo and Semitic manners of dress, (chapter sixteen); parallels between the Igbo and the Hebrew reckoning of time (chapter seventeen); joining the Igbo and Jewish peoples and leaving them (chapter eighteen), a detailed study of the organization of the Igbo society (chapter nineteen), and concludes (chapter twenty) using lore and Igbo agricultural practices he makes a stronge case that the Igbos might have migrated into what is called Igboland presently, from somewhere drier.and closes with an Igbo rhyme that actually resembles the Jewish *had gadya* sung during the Passover.

Every book of course has its flaws.

Not all comparisons might be equally convincing and some cultural characteristics might be part of all human organizations per se. Also, the author has clearly put the emphasis on commonalities and not differences that do exist.

Coming to a close, I would say that the title of the "Modern Day Basden" rather belongs to Remy Ilona and would recommend the book to anyone interested in a Jewish interpretation of Igbo culture and – speaking with Israeli sociologist Eliezer Ben-Rafael – as for an important example of African Jewry that might well represent one of engines of the Jewish reality in the years to come.

# Dedication

Dedicated to my parents Pauline and Joseph Ilona, and to Ta'gbo Ilona, Ngozi Ilona-Onwumelu, Chukwuma Ilona, Emeka Onwumelu, and Nonye Anona.

# Introduction

Is it believable that there are forty million persons of possible Jewish descent in Nigeria?

This book, which talks about the Igbo people, will try to answer the question. Igbos believe that they are descendants of the biblical, ancient Israelites. Numerous non-Igbos, including Jews, have also stated and/or suggested that Igbo culture seems analogous to Israel's. Some of those suggestions are included in this book, and many in my earlier books. This unique similarity of Igbo culture to the culture of Israel has also been observed by Jews who have visited the Igbos in Nigeria in recent times.

My interest in writing this book began a long time ago. As a child my father could not condone what he felt was a lack of interest in the Igbo-Israel connection on my part. From then on I never lost interest in the subject. {Why? Because his father said something specific?} However I was disappointed that there was no one who understood the subject well enough to present a detailed study of it.

I have compared every Igbo practice in this book with a Jewish equivalent. My primary research methodology into Igbo culture was personal observation. I traveled to many parts of Igbo-land, and discussed the topic extensively with numerous Igbos. In the course of my investigations I observed many Igbo feasts and events personally. I never asked a leading question. I preferred to keep the questions simple so that I would get spontaneous and authentic answers. As I have the advantage of being Igbo I rarely received the sort of answers that a foreigner trying to do what I did might have gotten: what he or she would like to hear.

Mostly I went to the countryside, or what we call the rural areas, because Igbo language and culture are still relatively well preserved in such places.

I interviewed elders while I moved. One such interview session can be viewed now at this location: http://www.youtube.com/watch?v=hTo5u9qb-0I&feature=youtu.be

Of enormous value was my own background. I grew up in Ozubulu, my clan. I sang and listened to the Igbo folk songs. I joined an Igbo singing and dancing group called 'Okiti' in my pre-teens and stayed in it till my adolescence. I participated in the *egwu onwa* (moonlight games). I underwent *ima mmonwu* (the Igbo equivalent of the Jewish *bar mitzvah*). I did all these when I was very young. I still participate in some of the festivities that are part of them today. I accompanied my father to clan and family meetings, and to the elders meetings, when I was very young. I listened to the ethical idioms and wise sayings of the Igbos, which are comparable to the Jewish *Pirkei Avot* (Sayings of the Fathers). For a poignant example, the Igbos say 'onye nje-nje ka onye isi awo ife ama.' The English translation is that there is much learning and knowledge to be gained by traveling. A Jewish source, the book *The Jews of Spain-A History of the Sephardic Experience,* by Jane S. Gerber, says "In the Talmud, too, travel for the sake of learning was commanded." There is this Jewish saying, *"F'il haraka Baraka"* (In mobility there is blessing). All these opportunities gave me information that is not in any library. The Igbos are a people who store and preserve history and information orally. So personal participation, observation, and patient listening are very necessary in studies of this kind.

I also studied what other Igbos have written on the culture of the Igbos. What I discovered was quite revealing. My findings corroborate a lot of things that have been mentioned by other Igbos in their works.

On the Israelite side of my research I studied the Tanach (Hebrew Bible) painstakingly, and found it so meaningful. To gain fuller understanding of Jewish culture I read thousands of Jewish books sent to me by my Jewish supporters whom I recognized in the Acknowledgement section of this book. I love to read and stop and think, and see if I understood what I had read. It gave me much pleasure when I discovered that I could understand the Tanach better because I understood the Igbos and vice versa.

I also perused the works of non-Igbo and non-Jewish authors who had written on the Igbos. Even though their conclusions were mainly not correct because the culture and the language were strange to them, sometimes their descriptions of what they saw were helpful.

As the reader could see, it was essentially a three way relationship. And it was very beneficial to use these many resources.

I wanted my work to be as detailed and as comprehensive as possible. To achieve that I went into so many areas. For example; a typical chapter like the 'Life Circle Events' contains the following: birth rituals-ritual seclusion of the mother after birth, circumcision, naming, the termination of seclusion, child presentation, dedication, and redemption; initiation rites; marriage-bride price, marriage feast, dowry, levirate marriage, and divorce.

I also decided to use a lot of Igbo words and terms, and to explain their meanings in Hebrew and English where it is possible and convenient, so that other persons who would do research in this subject area will benefit from my work in more than one way. Very importantly I discovered that words analysis is a very powerful tool in this kind of research.

Working to get the book ready taught me that no civilization is static. I was struck by how Israelite (Biblical) Judaism transformed into Rabbinic Judaism. The lesson helped me to see and understand Igbo transitions, and to include some of those changes into the many comparisons that I made.

I wrote this book for the Igbos, because even though 99% of the Igbos believe that the Igbos came from Israel, and that Igbo culture is Israelite culture, nobody had adduced sufficient evidence before to make the basis of the belief a fact. Perhaps the Igbos think that belief is the end of the matter. But there is another issue: most Igbos of the present era know only very little about their own, and even less about biblical and rabbinic culture.

This is because the Igbos colonial experience brought about a culture clash and confusion, compounding the difficulties of the Igbos recognizing themselves and the relationships that I have described.

I wrote this book to give Igbo, Jewish and non-Jewish academics, Igbos, Western Jews, Jews from other lands, and the general public much needed information about the Igbos. The book may help scholars like British Scholar of the University of London, Tudor Parfit who seem to be interested in the Igbos in an academic way, but lack information and the necessary tools that will help them to approach the subject, and study it satisfactorily.

I wrote this book to honor other researchers who felt that the Igbos are of Jewish origins, and wanted to prove it, but lacked the relevant tools and resources to see the task through.

I wrote this book to honor my father who felt strongly that I should not forget Israel. And my mother who though she was not a highly educated person (in the Western sense), felt very strongly that the Igbos had committed suicide by the abandonment of Igbo culture by many Igbos.

Lastly I wrote this book for those Jews who believe in the lost Diaspora, such as the members and supporters of Kulanu and more recently many others who believe that it was wise to listen to the story coming out of West Africa: of more than forty million persons of possible Jewish descent.

# CHAPTER ONE: Life Circle Events

## Rituals Associated With the Birth of Children

### *Omugwo (seclusion of mother who just delivered a child)*

I will do very well by starting this discussion from the time an Igbo woman 'muputar' nwa' (gives birth) to a child. From that moment she is in a state that the Igbos refer to as *omugwo*. Her mother or another female relative is summoned immediately. One of the purposes for the hasty summons is to get another capable hand into the house at once, because the new mother is already in seclusion *(omugwo)*. A study of our work on Igbo relationship with women having their menstrual flow will help the reader to understand Igbo thought about a newly delivered mother. She is viewed as 'onye no na nso'. *Nso* can mean sacred in Igbo language. It can also mean 'something ritually impure'. Accordingly the new mother is viewed as one who must be secluded or separated from. Jewish thought is similar. According to Jewish writer, historian, and rabbi, Chaim Potok: "from the ranks of scribes and Pietists, around the start of the Hasmonean revolution, came the first of a new breed of religious teachers who drew their support from the lower classes of the city and countryside . . . Because they held themselves aloof from pagans, and tended to be exceptionally careful in matters of ritual purity, withdrawing from contact with anyone suspected of being ritually defiled-as a result of touching, say, a woman after childbirth[1]."

---

[1] Potok, Chaim, *Wanderings - History of The Jews*, (New York: Fawcett Crest,

From Potok's position we can see that some Jews view a very new mother as being in a special state.

Igbo thought is that because the new mother is in *nso*, another woman, who traditionally should be the mother, or if she could not be available, the aunt or any other close female relative has to be around to do those chores that the newly delivered mother used to do. In this period and state of *omugwo*, the visiting lady has the duty of running the home. She cooks the food, and takes special care of the new mother, who is entitled to choice delicacies during the period.

The separation from her starts as soon as the baby comes out. She and the new child are moved to another house, which is different from her regular house.

Note: In the traditional Igbo society no Igbo couples share rooms or houses. Both live in the same compound, but in different houses. This style appears to be in vogue in Abraham's era, and among his family members, if we go by the following comment: "and the damsel (Rebekah) ran, and told her mother's house according to these words", which according to the commentator means:

"Mother's house, i.e., the part of Bethuel's house (compound) reserved for the women[2]."

As I have already mentioned, she (the new mother) is further secluded by being moved to a new quarter.

To emphasize that that precinct is sacred, it is festooned round with *omu nkwu*[3] (fresh palm fronds). Igbos also tie *omu nkwu* across the entrance of houses where people just died, i.e., where there is a corpse. It is also

---
[2] J. H. Hertz, *The Pentateuch and Haftorahs*, 2nd edition (London: The Soncino Press, 1937) p. 84.
[3] G. T. Basden, *Niger Ibos*, (London: Frank Cass and Co., Ltd., 1966) 417.

tied across the booth where a woman having her menstrual flow stays.

The nearness of Igbo and Israelitic thought on this matter can be seen from the following Biblical position. The Lord commanded Moses thus:

"a newly delivered mother shall be deemed unclean....as if she were in her days of impurity" (menstrual flow)—(Leviticus12).

Furthermore, the *Code of Jewish Law* stated:

"A woman who has given birth to a child is unclean[4]."

### *Ibi ugwu (circumcision)*

An Igbo male must be circumcised on the eighth day. This has been so from immemorial times.

F.C. Ogbalu, an Igbo scholar[5], speculated that Igbo circumcision (on the eighth day) is the binding proof of the Igbo-Israelite relationship.

According to G.T Basden[6], "the rite of circumcision is universally practiced and rigidly regarded, (by the Igbos) but nobody knows why. It has the authority of custom (Omenana)."

He also observed that it is on the eighth day.

It cannot be overstressed that circumcision of male children on the eighth day, i.e., after seven days, is originally Israelite. This rite is to stand as the physical sign of the covenant between God and the Israelites.

---

[4]Ganzfried, Solomon, and Hyman E. Goldin, trans., *Code of Jewish Law and Customs* (*Shulhan Aruch*) (New York: Hebrew Publishing Company, 1961) 32.
[5] Ogbalu, F. C., *Omenala Igbo*, (Lagos: University Publishing Co. Academy Press, 1979) 24.
[6] G. T. Basden, *Niger Ibos* (London: Frank Cass and Co., Ltd., 1966) 176.

If there are forty million Igbos, at least eighteen million are male. We can say confidently that all are circumcised, and on the eighth day. That would make the Igbos the largest body of people who have persons circumcised on the eight day. This rebuts the opinion of American Jewish writer David Klinghoffer that outside of Israel, the U.S circumcises more male children than any other country in the world[7], because besides all the Igbo males that are circumcised on the $8^{th}$ day, millions of non Igbo Nigerians have began to circumcise their sons, in emulation of the Igbos.

## *Iba afa (naming)*

Some scholars have said that the Igbo child is named on the twenty-eighth day after its birth while others have said that it is on the ninth day. Actually an Igbo child may receive a name on the very day that it was born, or on any other date agreed by the family of the new-born.

As with ancient Israelwhere naming of a child was a communal /kindred affair, so is it with the Igbos.

Every family member will endeavour to be present on the agreed date. When all the expected persons are assembled, the happy mother will bring out the child. Both, mother and child, would be resplendently dressed. The mother would hand the child over to the oldest male member of its family who would have already sat down before the family altar, usually armed with the family *ofo* (staff of authority).

By tradition he should give the child a name (the one chosen by the father). The next person to provide a name for the child is its mother. The grandparents will also give the child names. Every person among those

---

[7] Klinghoffer, David, *The Discovery Of God* (New York: Three Leaves Press-- Doubleday, 2004) 208.

that have gathered is also entitled to give the child a name.

When everybody must have given the child a name, the *aka-ji-ofo* (family elder) asks for quiet, and starts praying to Chukwu (Great God). He begs Him to remember and consider the good deeds of the newborn's ancestors and use them to guard and protect the child through life. When he finishes praising, pleading and supplicating, he will seal the prayer by smacking the *ofo* on the ground and everybody will intone or chorus *ihaa* (amen). From this moment feasting and general merry-making starts. The generous will start showering gifts and presents on the newborn and its mother.

Like the Jews the Igbos may give a child a name that connotes an experience that they passed through. For example Hannah called her son Samuel because she had asked him of the Lord. Abraham and Sarah named their son Isaac because God used him to give them laughter (and joy). My son is named Chijindu because we believe that I recovered from an illness that had all but taken my life (made me to undergo a laparatomy procedure, and a colostomy procedure, both of which enabled me to have 100% recovery from what those close to me call my great illness) because we Igbos believe that Chi ji ndu (God is the keeper/preserver of life).

G.T. Basden observed[8]: "A couple (Igbo) who have waited several years for a child will (may) name it 'Ogwalu Onyekwe' (He who is told (of it) will not believe, that is that a child will still come after all these years) or 'Ife-yi-nwa' (there is nothing like a child)."

---

[8] G. T. Basden, *Niger Ibos* (London: Frank Cass and Co., Ltd., 1966) 175.

Also like Moses who named his son Gershom (Exodus 2:22), which signifies 'I have been a stranger in a strange land', Okonkwo (an Igbo man) does the same in Chinua Achebe's *Things Fall Apart*[9] by naming his son born to him in exile Nwofia, which means 'the child born in a strange land.'

In addition the Igbos share a practice with the Jews: Compounding the names of their children with the name of the Supreme Being. A few of such are: Dani-EL, Micha-EL, Nathani-EL, Rapha-EL, Gabri-EL, Samu-EL, Ya-shua, etc. Abram Leon Sacher mentions this in passing; as he discussed King Ahab's relaxation of Israel's rules on rigid monotheism. To Abram Leon Sacher[10],in spite of Ahab's lapses:"He still gave his children names compounded with [God]."

The practice in discussion appears to be widespread in Israel. Even the name Israel is compounded with 'EL' which is a title for the Supreme Being. And there are countless Israelites in the Biblical, post-biblical and present period whose names are compounded with God's name.

As for the Igbos, it is the rule to compound names with the names of God. The writers' parents begot seven children and they are named thus: Ngozichukwuka, Chinonyerem, Chukwudi, Chukwuma, Chukwuaduom, Chukwuka odinaka and Nchedochukwuka. All the names are compounded with Chukwu. Also the writer's favourite niece who came into the world as her mother left the world was named Uchenna, meaning that it is the Father's (God's) will, that made such a sad

---

[9] Achebe, Chinua , *Things Fall Apart*, (Ibadan: Heinemann Educational Books, 1958).115.
[10] Sacher, Abram Leon, *The History of The Jews* (New York: Alfred Knopf, Inc., 1930) 50.

occurrence to happen. My wife and I named our first son Daniel Chijindu Ikechukwu Iddo. Both Igbo names are compounded with the name Chiukwu (Great God). The Igbos address God as Father (Nna) too.

The Igbos name children after departed relatives too. They also name them after their parents. Two of my siblings were named after my father, Joseph and Josephine; while a grand-daughter, my niece, was named after my mother.

### *Iputa na omugwo (coming out from seclusion)*

This ritual-packed feast is so-called because it is the formal end of the seclusion of the new mother. It involves the happy father and mother of the new born babe feasting with their kins-folk and friends, who give them gifts and presents. But before this feast is celebrated the woman must have observed the ritual bath (immersion).

Below is our brief account of Igbo women's ritual bath after seclusion following child birth:

When the period of *omugwo* (seclusion) is over, an Igbo woman is to undergo a ritual bath (immersion) in a flowing stream or river.

Igbo writer Flora Nwapa[11] seems to be hinting at this custom in the following passage: "Soon it was seven market days since Efuru's safe delivery. But before she went out she had to go to the lake and put her feet in the water."

---

[11] Nwapa, Flora, *Efuru* (Ibadan: Heinemann Educational Books, 1966) 33.

From the *Code of Jewish Law and Customs*[12], we find this tradition to be Israelitic too:

"A woman who has borne a (child) is unclean for seven days, after which she must count seven days and then perform the rite of immersion."

F.C. Ogbalu[13] also mentioned this ritual bath among the Igbos. The standard practice among the Igbos is for the new mother to be accompanied by her peers to the stream or river, with an elderly woman who will supervise the ritual.

The above quoted Jewish source (*Code of Jewish Law and Custom*) also mentioned that a supervisor attends the ritual bath. In Igbo tradition feasting follows as soon as they return.

### Child Presentation, Dedication and Redemption

In Igbo-land after the child is weaned it is taken by its mother to the *okwu Chi (ana)* (sanctuary of God), and presented to Chukwu. She goes with gifts of yams and roosters.

Also in Igbo traditions is to be found the child dedication. The parents appear before Chukwu with gifts and pledge that the child will serve Chukwu and the community faithfully all its life.

G.T. Basden would liken the Igbo child presentation, dedication and redemption to the Israelite models[14]. On redemption, he observed; "on the birth of a second son, he also was brought and presented before (Chukwu) . . . the Father followed with a ram (sheep or goat) and the

---

[12]Ganzfried, Solomon, and Hyman E. Goldin, trans., *Code of Jewish Law and Customs* (*Shulhan Aruch*) (New York: Hebrew Publishing Company, 1961) 32.
[13] Ogbalu, F. C., *Omenala Igbo*, (Lagos: University Publishing Co. Academy Press, 1979) 22.
[14] G. T. Basden, *Niger Ibos* (London: Frank Cass and Co., Ltd., 1966) 417.

beast was substituted and thus redemption was wrought for the son."

**Initiation Rites**

### *Ima mmonwu/Iwa akwa (equivalent of undergoing bar mitzvah)*

In discussing *ima mmonwu* I will use how it is done in Ozubulu, my clan, as a case study, even though this custom is generally observed in many other Igbo clans.

It is essentially an induction into manhood of Igbo youths, and the initiation of youths into the Igbo society. During the eve of this event, in the night, the young men would be told the vital secrets of the Igbo people.

These secrets are known by, or are told to, only initiates. Getting initiated is not compulsory. It is only those that wish to know how the Igbos evolved, and what makes the Igbos Igbos that are initiated. But it can't be imagined that some Igbos would decline to be initiated in ancient times or even in the recent past.

The young man that declines to be initiated [nowadays] is derisively called *ogbodu* by his peers who went through the process.

Originally this activity only took place during the months of March to May, the Igbo planting season. Parents and guardians will go to inform the persons who are in charge of *mmonwu* that their sons and wards are ready and want to be inducted into *mmonwu*.

We cannot sincerely say that we know the meaning and etimology of the word *mmonwu*, but presently some *mmonwu* are believed to be masked *spirits*, that the Igbos address as spirits, and in some cases they are also seen as physical embodiments of their ancestors. Their being viewed as spirits enhances their prestige, so that their words can be respected. This is necessary because in ancient times, it was also the *mmonwu* that served as judges when very difficult cases arose[15], and at times, as the secret policemen of the Igbos. As long as the Igbos believed that some of them were the spirits of their ancestors, they were held in awe and respect by the people. Igbo belief is that their ancestors' lives are relevant. Some *mmonwu* are masquerade too. They are used for entertainment.

On the initiation day, the young men accompanied by their guardians will go and pay the prescribed fees. In the evening they will retire to the *Ekwuru* (a special place of assembly).

From the moment the lectures start, music accompanies the teaching. After some lectures the inductees are interrogated about all the misdemeanors they have indulged in, like disobeying their parents, playing pranks, etc. Unsatisfactory answers may earn some a crack of the cane across the back. Meanwhile palm wine will be going around. When the inductees have been taught what the masters feel is enough to put them on the road to be outstanding citizens, they will be asked to start dancing. Their teachers/masters will join them in dancing. Some of their teachers will impress them by displaying acrobatic dexterity, by climbing palm trees without ropes, scaling high fences, etc. These goes on till early in the morning.

Then just before daylight all that they have been taught and told, with more that I can't mention here because they are to be known only by Igbo initiates, are restated to them. All these are encoded in the words *akwukwo*

---

[15] Achebe, Chinua, *Things Fall Apart*, (Ibadan: Heinemann Educational Books, 1958) 62-66.

*mmonwu* (masquerade leaf), and no right-thinking Igbo will reveal them to non-initiates[16].

Henceforth the young men are initiates, who would not have to run into the wilds if they see an *mmonwu* approaching them on the road. The *ima mmonwu* makes me think of the Jewish coming of age rite called *bar mitzvah*.

### Iru mgbe (equivalent of bat mitzvah)

The *iru mgbe* is the equivalent of *ima mmonwu* for Igbo girls. Once a girl goes through the ceremony, she is considered ready for marriage.

The Igbos start the process of *iru mgbe* when the girl is a little child. All the house training the mother makes her go through is part of it. The ceremony is held when she is between fifteen and eighteen years. The parents prepare a great feast for her on the special day. On the morning of the day a proclamation goes forth to remind relatives and friends that the girl is to be inducted into womanhood. Various dancing groups would be invited. Towards mid-day the festivities would start. The elder of the girl's family would make a speech that the girl is now a maiden. Other people would talk too, after which feasting and dancing would start. Merriment continues till evening.

From that day the girl could marry, if she finds a husband, and cohabit with her husband. But it must be noted that this ritual is not compulsory. To do it for a girl is the decision of the parents of the girl.

---

[16] Munonye, John, *The Only Son* (Ibadan: Heinemann Educational Books, 1966) 117.

## Chapter 1: Life Circle Events 31

In these pictures are the *ozoebunu* and *ukwu mmuo mmonwu*; the premier *mmonwu* of Ozubulu clan. Only initiates can join them.

## Inu Nwanyi (marriage)

### Typical Igbo Marriage

The typical Igbo marriage is so similar to the marriage of Isaac and Rebekah, as can be reconstructed from the Bible. But there are obvious dissimilarities too. For example, while Isaac married his very near relative the Igbos would regard doing such as an abomination! This and numerous other things lead me to conclude that the Igbos are familiar with the traditions and the culture that Abraham knew, and also with the one that God introduced through Moses.

Some respected Biblical scholars have said that the Scriptures only gave general rules and guidelines; that on a lot of issues it did not go into details. Those persons add respectfully that the knowledge of the Oral Torah (Talmud and Mishnah) increases the understanding of the Bible, as they give the details which may not have been given in the Bible. In the case of the Igbos, I can say that if all their traditions can be recorded and perfectly extrapolated, the Igbo Talmud and Mishnah would be said to have been codified. I will now proceed to narrate how Igbos conduct and contract marriages.

A comprehensive study of the Igbo marriage would require volumes, and for that, I am not ready yet. So I will seize this opportunity to inform the reader that what I am doing is to try to introduce the Igbo marriage procedures in very broad outlines, and show enough evidence that it is strikingly similar to the marriage that Isaac had, i.e., a Hebraic marriage. I will also adduce enough evidence to show that the Igbo marriage incorporates the ideas in vogue in the times of the

Patriarchs and Matriarchs and those in vogue after the reforms of Moses.

I have mentioned earlier that this is not a comprehensive study of the Igbo marriage, because time and space for that is not available now. And really such a discussion will require much time and space, because there are various types and kinds of Igbo marriages. The monogamous, polygamous, Levirate, etc, marriages. An Igbo woman can also marry a woman, i.e, she can get a wife for the husband just as the matriarchs Rachel and Leah did. For now my aim is to concentrate on marriage between a young Igbo man (*nwa okorobia*-like Isaac) and a young maiden (*nwa agboghobia*—like Rebekah).

The Igbo words 'inu nwanyi' means 'to marry a woman.' Igbos may also use 'inu nwunye' which means to marry a wife. The two phrases may also mean marriage, or the marriage feast itself. However all the above will yield to 'inu di na nwunye' which signifies being in a state of marriage, in nearness to the English word—marriage.

To the Igbos marriage is the primary institution that guarantees the survival of the family, and the society.

Interestingly a non-Igbo author, G.T. Basden, who lived with the Igbos for more than twenty years captured the Igbo attitude to getting married accurately. Summarizing his opinion will mutilate something which is perfect, so I will quote him in *extenso*:

"Marriage is a most important event in the Ibo's life. From the time that boys and girls are capable of thinking for themselves, marriage is set before them as the one object to be attained. During the earlier years it does not assume a serious aspect, but question any boy or girl, and the answer is certain to be that, in due course, they must marry. Celibacy is an impossible prospect. Unmarried persons of either sex, except in special cases, are objects of derision, and to be childless is the greatest calamity that can befall a woman. Hence a very high value is set upon marriage[17]."

The Igbos knew or realized that life is an important affair that needs to be approached with all seriousness. That the problems that come with living can only be solved by men and women doing their own parts. And that since the life of mankind is short, or not permanent, that man needs a replacement to carry on his work when he dies. That for that replacement to be able to carry on the work, that he or she has to be responsible, and thus should be nurtured under the watchful eyes of the pair that brought it into the world.

It was not, and is not, automatic for every human being to perceive or realize the above stated objective. One's sense of perception has to be extra keen for one to feel what Abraham felt, that made him cry: "O Lord God, what wilt Thou give me, seeing I go hence childless" (Genesis 15:2-3). Authentic and traditional Igbo feeling is identical to Abraham's.

Persons who avoid marriage (deliberately) in the Igbo society are scorned. A woman may fall into this category by being over selective (*igba nhodi*), in the choice of a husband. If the person who fails to marry is a man the Igbos will call him an *ofeke* (a not serious person). No Igbo likes to be an *ofeke*, so everybody strives to marry. Adin Steinsaltz provides us with the direct Jewish parallel in *The Essential Jewish Talmud* on page 181. In his words-"Judaism regards the taking of a wife as an important concept, binding on every man Even a man

---

[17] G. T. Basden, *Among The Ibos of Nigeria* (London: University Publishing Company, 1921) 68.

who is no longer capable of fathering children is urged to avoid the celibate life."

But for an Igbo to marry is no mean and easy task. The marriage rituals of the Igbos are so demanding and tasking that an *ofeke* may not be able to marry.

I am going to describe the Igbo marriage ritual henceforth, and I will concentrate on it as it concerns a *nwa okorobia* (young man) of whom it is presumed by Igbo traditions that he should initiate that he wants to get married. Before I start this discussion I must give the hint that *n'ime uno* (privately) both parents may also have been prodding the young man to start getting ready for marriage. But as he is not an infant, the words 'a chor'm inu nwanyi' (I want to get married) has to emanate from him.

The day he declares to his parents that he wants to get married is their happiest day. The reason why tradition requires the young man to take the step is because the same Igbo tradition demands that a man be economically secure to an extent before marrying. To the Igbos marriage is a serious matter. 'O bu ho azu e ji ata aki' (it is not child's play). Some of the ways the Igbos gauge a person's economic viability are:

The person must have a trade or occupation. In traditional Igbo society, some persons are wine-tappers, farmers, basket weavers, prophets, seers, doctors, etc. But one thing is common to all of them. They are all crop and animal farmers too. In addition to having an occupation, a young man intending to marry is also expected to have built his own house. This is mentioned in Chinua Achebe's *Arrow of God*[18], where the second son Obika's new homestead is mentioned.

This house of his means his own personal house and a separate one for his wife. Traditionally the Igbo man and his wife live within the same compound but in different houses. Ancient Semitic practice had that feature also. In Genesis: 24:28, the commentary explains "her mother's house" to mean the part of Bethuel's house reserved for the women[19]. I mentioned this during my discussion on *omugwo*.

Before proceeding I must say that what I have raised could be seen as contradictory. It is that the Igbos expect all adults to be married early; and at the same time expect the males to have acquired financial stability before marrying. One's attention is drawn to the two positions which seem to be conflicting. But they are not in conflict, rather what they do is that they help each other to create balance and harmony in society. Ancient Igbo society laid great stress on balance and harmony.

Typically in traditional Igbo society, by the time young men leave puberty, they were somewhat financially stable.

Igbo tradition also demands emotional stability from a man before he marries. The man is supposed to be a big brother, and somehow a father-figure to the wife. The maturity expected of the man is to the extent that he must have grown to recognize real beauty, which is good character to the Igbos.

---

[18] Achebe, Chinua, *Arrow of God* (Ibadan: Heinemann Educational Books, 1964) 90.
[19] J. H. Hertz, *The Pentateuch and Haftorahs*, 2nd edition (London: The Soncino Press, 1937) 84.

The major ingredient that the Igbos look for in a wife-to-be is good character. I will deal exhaustively with this later. For now I will discuss the primary force that drives the Igbos into marrying. This primary force is the need to have children. This is eloquently expressed in the Igbo saying: 'ife eji anu nwanyi wu maka nwa' (the reason why one marries a wife is to have children).

Igbo writer F.C Ogbalu[20] alluded to this in his work on Igbo childbirth and *omugwo*, where he discussed that there is no expense an Igbo man would hesitate to incur in order to make his wife who just delivered a baby happy and satisfied (because she had enhanced his chances of living into the future).

The Igbo position of having children as the *raison d'etre* of marriage is akin to a Hebrew *raison d'etre* too, as expressed in a Hebrew source, which can be seen in the exchange between Tobias and the angel Raphael:"Then when the third night is past, take the maid to thyself with the fear of the Lord upon thee, moved rather by the hope of begetting children than by the lust of thine. So in the true line of Abraham thou shalt have joy of thy fatherhood[21]."

In the entire story the angel tried to point out that lust (and I personally add 'love' which is in many ways the modern cover for lust) should not be the primary consideration in the quest for marriage, but that the need to procreate should be the primary driving force.

Another Jewish source; Dr. J.H. Hertz, stated that the purpose of marriage is twofold: (a) posterity

---

[20] Ogbalu, F. C., *Omenala Igbo*, (Lagos: University Publishing Co. Academy Press, 1979) 19.
[21] *Book of Tobias*.

(procreation) (b) companionship. He extracted the first from "be fruitful and multiply[22]."

Igbo novelist John Munonye's description of an Igbo's thinking on this subject is a treasure. Extracts from it (Chiaku's thoughts about the marriage of her only son) follow: "But should she not start now to think about having images of him? Yes, she should begin to look for a good girl who would produce his images, sweet restless things whom she could carry in her arms and laps, or hug to her breast, and who would grow up to call her Big Mother[23]."

I will now start a discussion on the practical steps that are to be taken when a young man decides to marry.

He will inform his parents, who will be overjoyed, and who will in turn inform the extended family, every member of which is supposed to join in the search for a suitable bride. The searchers will be on the lookout for: a girl from *ezigbo agburu* (good stock).

John Munonye's work on Igbo insistence on marrying into families with clean records is illustrative. Below is an extract from his book: "What about Odu's daughter?... Ego is her name...she is from good parents.. I am sure about that. The family is *obi*, without doubt.. A family was called *obi* if it possessed not just the physical house, but also a clean history and a reasonably hopeful future[24]."

The Igbos also want to know if the girl's character is exemplary, and if she is industrious. Her domestic,

---

[22] J. H. Hertz, *The Pentateuch and Haftorahs,* 2nd edition (London: The Soncino Press, 1937). 931.
[23] Munonye, John, *The Only Son* (Ibadan: Heinemann Educational Books, 1966) 48.
[24] ibid. p. 21

culinary and other skills are also important to the Igbos. The health profile of the family is important too.

Igbo customs and practices as enunciated above are similar to Hebrew practices in several respects. Just like the Igbos, the Hebrews lay stress on family history (stock), as discovered in an exchange in the Apocryphal book of *Tobias* between Tobias and angel Raphael in the following words: Tobias apologized, "forgive me...for doubting thy lineage, thou comest from good stock indeed." I find the emphasis on stock and lineage very much interesting and Igbo-like.

In Abraham's quest for a wife for Isaac we were not told that he laid emphasis on stock, but it was implied in his message to Eliezer. By insisting that his son's wife must come from his own kinsmen, it is clear that he wanted a girl whose family history he could trust, and could vouch for.

We also saw Rebekah and Isaac inclining towards the same tendency when it was time for Jacob to marry. Even from Esau we saw the realization that by marrying outsiders that he had contravened the traditions, or at least the desires, of his family, and thus earned the disfavour of his parents.

On another criterion that the Igbos consider as very important, the girl's character, we can see definite similarities between the Igbo and Hebrew perceptions. As the Igbos lay emphasis on the girl's character, and even have an emphatic saying, *agwa wu mma nwanyi* (good character is a woman's beauty) underlining it, so do we have a Hebraic/Semitic equivalent on 'character'– J.H. Hertz's explanation being so illustrative. According to him: "it is noteworthy that Eliezer decided to make beauty of character the criterion in his selection of a wife for Isaac[25]."

At this point I must also note that Igbos would never be happy with marriages between Igbos and non-Igbos. Igbo novelist Buchi Emecheta handled the tension and conflict that arose when an Igbo girl consented to a marriage proposal by a Yoruba man so masterfully in her book[26]. (The Yoruba is a Nigerian ethnic group that has traced its origins to the ancient Egyptians. It is against Igbo traditions for Igbos to marry non-Igbos. Israelite women were also specifically barred from marrying non-Israelites, while the men may if they must.

Love is not explicitly set out as one of the things that the Igbos go all out to search for, in other words, the Igbos searching for a wife because a young man wants to marry do not look for a girl that the young man is 'already in love with' because Igbos believe that love grows when the couple begin to live together, and begin to please each other (with their good conducts). The Igbos believe that it is the wife's good conduct that earns her the love of her husband, and vice versa.

Now we head into the marriage rituals proper. As soon as the parents 'receive' the news from their son that he is ready for marriage, they take the driver's seat, that is they start to play a leading role. In fact traditionally it is the duty of a father/parent to sponsor the marriage of his sons. A capable widow may also do so. We find what Abraham did for Isaac closely paralleling the Igbo practice.

---

[25] J. H. Hertz, *The Pentateuch and Haftorahs*, 2nd edition (London: The Soncino Press, 1937) 83. G. T. Basden, *Niger Ibos* (London: Frank Cass and Co., Ltd., 1966) p. 214.

[26] Emecheta, Buchi, *The Joys of Motherhood* (Oxford: Heinemann Educational Books, 1979) 209.

*Icho nwanyi* (to look for a bride) is no easy assignment among the Igbos. The whole extended family is involved. The father of the young man summons his kinsmen, and presents kolanut and wine to them. He informs them that his son is ready to marry. They (the kinsmen) must be informed at a very early stage, because they are part of the family, and the incoming bride will be their relative, so they should make inputs in finding an ideal bride.

As family members they are presumed to be trustworthy, and thus can be relied on as searchers in the coming task of searching for a wife (*icho nwanyi*). The reliance of the Igbos on trusted people is not unlike Abraham's reliance on Eliezer[27].

The kinsmen are joyful at receiving the news, because the Igbos are a people that crave increment in their numbers. They pray to Chukwu to make the mission a success, and they swing into action. The women-folk are all involved. Even the kinsfolk *(ndi ikwu nne)* of the young man's mother may be informed, though informally, and everybody starts *icho nwanyi* (looking for a wife).

A few things are uppermost in the minds of the searchers: *Agwa wu mma nwanyi* (good character is a woman's real beauty) is the premier one. Also they are very careful in order not to enter into negotiations with close relatives, as the Igbos take very seriously the rules forbidding marriage with near relations. Among the Igbos if direct blood relationship can be established between two persons, marriage cannot take place between them.

---

[27] J. H. Hertz, *The Pentateuch and Haftorahs*, 2nd edition (London: The Soncino Press, 1937) p. 82.

G.T. Basden's observation about this is set out in the following passage: "In proper marriage, consanguinity up to eight or ten generations is *nso* (forbidden)....yet at Idah, Dr. Oldfield remarks: "I was conducted by Abboka to Amagdoby, the king's sister, who was also his head wife...The people of Idah (the Igalas) and the Ibos are neighbors, and have had more or less intercourse for generations, yet this sort of union would be regarded with intolerable horror by the latter[28]" (The Igala are a Nigerian ethnic group that lives to the north of the Igbos).

Basden went further by comparing the Igbo and Israelite practices, and observed:"The degrees of affinity in the matter of marriage (among the Igbos) are even more strictly adhered to, or rather, they are more meticulous than those set forth in the Levitical code[29]."

Yet Igbo tradition abhors marriage with non-Igbo people. Only marriages within the clan, or with Igbos from neighbouring Igbo clans, are viewed with approval. And very interestingly people must take extreme care to ensure that they do not marry persons who are related to them by blood. I advise the reader to take a look at the Igbo Society section of this book. I am from the Uruokwe sub-sub clan of Ozubulu. I cannot marry from Uruokwe, nor can I marry any of my mother's near relatives from Amakwa/and anywhere else, nor my father's near relatives from the other parts of Ozubulu or anywhere else for that matter. Besides the two prohibited sections I am encouraged to marry anybody from Ozubulu, save my aunts, nieces, cousins, etc.

---

[28] G. T. Basden, *Niger Igbos* (London: Frank Cass and Co Ltd 1966) p. 215.
[29] ibid. p. 21.

Anybody with a good understanding of the Hebrew Bible will notice that Igbo practices on marriage do in some respects become dissimilar to Hebrew practices in Abraham's era. However I would say that where they don't resemble Hebrew practices in Abraham's era, they seem like what the Hebrews would have started doing after the reforms of Moses. Abraham and his immediate descendants up to Jacob married very close relatives.

When those searching for a bride think of, or see, a suitable girl, a mini meeting is held in which the family is informed about the girl, and a general survey is there and then conducted on her background, to know if she is marriageable. An Igbo novelist, John Munonye[30] shows us Igbo practice in that area by describing how one of the main characters in his book handled the search for her son's wife. When she had found a good girl, she summoned a family meeting. The first girl she had seen, Nwada's daughter was not qualified, because in the words of Oji, her elder brother—, "the girl is our flesh and blood".

The second was qualified because— "she was from good parents, but nevertheless we won't marry only her body: there are other things to consider. Is she strong, obedient and industrious? You should inquire extensively, my sister. He that goes into marriage without the necessary inquiries, let him be ready to have in his house a scoundrelly chatterbox[31]."

In order to make sure doubly sure the family may conduct serious investigation before even sending the first delegation to the prospective bride's home. The young man may not be in the party that pays this first

---

[30] Munonye, John, *The Only Son*, (Ibadan: Heinemann Educational Books, 1966) 48.
[31] ibid. p. 48.

visit. We noticed that Isaac did not accompany Eliezer when he paid the first visit to Bethuel's (Rebekah's) home. Custom demands that the team should go with some *ngwo* or *nkwu enu* (wine, palm wine). It is interesting to note that Eliezer took along some gifts with him when he went on the first visit to Rebekah's home.

When the wife-seeking party gets to the house of the prospective wife's father; after they have been welcomed they will just engage their hosts in small talk. After sometime they will leave small talk and get serious. Here the great Igbo talent for inventiveness comes into play. Euphemistic language is what they will use to introduce their goal. Typically they may aver that there is an orange which they have seen in the host's compound which they are desirous of plucking and going away with. The parents of the girl, who must have been joined by their closest kin by then, will respond evasively too, that they will need some time to find out from the orange whether it is ready to be harvested by their guests. The rule is that they must never be hostile to their guests, even if they are not favourably disposed to the idea of entering into marriage with them.

Meanwhile the wine that the guests came with will be going round, and small talk will also be going on, till dusk, when the guests will take their leave.

At this junction the reader should be aware that there is hardly any other thing that makes Igbo parents happier than seeing their daughters get married. This is because the Igbos believe strongly that 'ugwu nwanyi wu di' (that marriage completes the honour and prestige of a woman). It is also good to note that the maiden will not play any role during the preliminary visits, beyond being summoned from the women's quarter to come and greet the guests, after which she must return there.

Semitic practice was quite similar to Igbo practice. Scripture enlightens us that Bethuel and Laban, the father and brother respectively, of Rebekah, received Eliezer warmly.

Also similarly with Igbo practice, J.H. Hertz[32] explains Semitic practice as noted in Genesis 24:51 to mean: "As is usual in the Orient, the preliminary negotiations in regard to the marriage takes place without consultation with the maiden."

The above is in consonance with Igbo tradition, but also as with Igbo customs, Hebrew or Semitic custom gives the girl the last word as we can see from Genesis 24: 57 where Bethuel's side informed Eliezer that, "we will call the maiden and inquire at her mouth."

With all the foregoing, it is evident that Igbo practices are similar to Semitic practices.

I will now start working from the maiden's angle. Like the ancient Semites from whom Bethuel, Laban and Jacob sprang, the Igbo tradition is that the eldest should marry before the younger. From Genesis 29:26 the reader notices that Laban obeys this custom by tricking Jacob into marrying Leah first, and even stating that it is against his custom for the younger to marry first.

Igbo tradition does not encourage people to casually disregard a marriage proposal. Accordingly if the girl in question is not already betrothed to any other man her family will start their own inquiries (*iju ase*). They will want to find out if the young man is from a good stock

---

[32] J. H. Hertz, *The Pentateuch and Haftorahs*, 2nd edition (London: The Soncino Press, 1937), p 86, (Genesis 24:51).

(*agburu*). They will try to find out if his family members have been thieves, womanizers, have suffered from leprosy, mental illness, etc. In the modern period, they will also try to find out if they are *osu*. I devoted a major section of this book to the *Osu*, who in the Igbo traditions played an important priestly role, that is much like the role of a certain kind of temple workers in the Israelite tradition.

If they get satisfactory results, they will then send word to the young man's family through a middleman who must have been appointed at this stage, that they are free to visit again.

This middleman is called *onye aka ebe*. His role is important. He settles minor quarrels between the husband and the wife if the marriage takes place, and he does this till the marriage is formally over, by death or divorce. Its important to observe that the Igbo marriage is not dissolved by death of the spouses, because when marriage takes place, both families become one in a sense. When the groom-to-be's family gets word that they are free to visit again, the only logical reason they should attach to the invitation is that the girl is not yet betrothed to another man, that both parties do not fall within the prohibited degrees of affinity and consanguinity, etc. It does not mean that their proposal has been accepted. During this next visit the groom-to-be has to come with the members of his own family. Some close friends may come with them. And they will come with palm wine. Even though the groom-to-be will be present, he will not talk much. Most of the talk from the delegation will be from the leader of his team, which in many cases may be his uncle, father or elder brother. After they have been offered hospitality (*oji*), that is kola nut, the visitors will start small talk, and the talk will generally not be about why they are there. As the talking is going on, drinking of palm wine will also be going on. I think that the reason why the prospective groom follows on this visit is for his possible future in-laws to assess him at close range. As before the girl may come into the *obi* to say *nnoo* (welcome) to them.

Before they leave that day one of two things must happen. The first is that if their hosts are interested in exploring the possibility of the union further, they will tell them to visit again, and when to visit. But if they are not interested, they will diplomatically tell them 'you will hear from us.' This is enough signal to the prospective groom's people that they should look elsewhere. But if they are invited to visit again, and given a date, it signifies that the marriage may go ahead, all things being equal.

For the next visit, the groom-to-be's group has to come with a big jar of palm wine. The kinsmen of the prospective bride will also be present in numbers. After praying and sharing of kola nut, discussions of general matters start. The hosts are expected to say less, while the visitors are expected to talk more. After some time will have passed a member of the visiting family will present the wine they came with to their hosts, and drinking will commence. After the men have each had a few cups, the host will summon his wife, and a cup of wine will be handed to her. Tradition demands that she will sip some and hand over the rest to her husband who will drain the cup. After this the prospective bride is summoned, and some wine is poured into a cup and given to her. In olden times, either her mother, or a friend or relative, will be following her, and she will start walking around the people in the *obi* (the family beit Knesset) as if she is searching for someone. But this only happens if she accepts the wine. If she does not accept it, it is taken as enough evidence that she has rejected the marriage proposal. If she accepts the wine, and after walking around and 'searching', and she does not 'see' the groom-to-be, but her father, to whom she hands over the remainder of the wine after sipping some of it, that is also conclusive evidence of rejection of the marriage proposal.

But if she searches out the groom-to-be, genuflects in front of him, sips some wine, and hands over the remainder to him, everybody who had been waiting and watching with bated breath will nod in satisfaction and restrained joy, while the exuberant will clap. She has given her consent! A coconut could also be used to enact this ritual. If the bride-to-be accepts a coconut from the groom-to-be it is taken as consent. In so many respects much of what is described here have Hebrew/Semitic parallels. In the Igbo case, the girl's consent is indispensable.

J.H. Hertz's[33] comment on Genesis: 24:39, shows Hebrew tradition to be very similar: "It is evident that whatever the preliminary negotiation in the 'arrangement' of the marriage, the whole matter was contingent on the consent of the maiden."

Note: what the bride has given at this stage is the pre-betrothal consent. Because she has given her preliminary consent, as the hosts are leaving that day she will go with them for the ritual that is called *ibu na ite mmanya* (to return their empty jar of wine), and *ine ne ana* (to survey, i.e., to enable her to have a preview of life in her prospective new home). She will have the opportunity to interact with all the family members.

---

[33] ibid. 85, (commentary on Genesis 24:39).

The family will also watch her, but there must not be any sexual intimacy between her and the groom. In Igbo tradition it is *aru* (abomination) for the maiden to cohabit sexually with the affianced at this stage, or with another man after this stage (if she eventually gives her consent). When this visit which is supposed to last for sixteen days is over, she is sent back to her parents with gifts, contributed by the groom, his parents, relatives and friends.

It is still possible for her to back out at this stage without any stigmatization. But if she had chosen to get married to the suitor, all that she must do is to inform her parents when she gets home, and they would send word immediately to the family of the groom to come forward on a chosen date for negotiation/fixing of the bride-price. The groom or his family is also free to back out at this stage; by simply ignoring the invitation to come for negotiation over the price of the bride.

But I must note at this stage one feature of the Igbo marriage that is very important: As the reader must have noticed there are three visits with wine to the prospective bride's home. By Igbo tradition if the jar/pot of wine falls down and breaks while the prospective groom's party are on their way to the prospective bride's on any of the three occasions, it is taken as a signal/bad omen that the marriage will not be a good one.

### *Ime ego (the bride price) Ihu onu nwanyi (fixing of the bride price)*

This is usually done in the house of the *onye aka ebe* (middleman). The prospective groom and his kinsmen will visit there with a big jar of palm wine on the agreed date. They may also come with *utaba* (tobacco), *akanwu* (potash), and some money. The girl's side will also select a team which will come to the venue on that same day. The proceedings will commence with prayers, after which the leaders of both delegations will start work. Drinking will be going on during the pricing of the bride. Here euphemisms are also applied. They will act and speak as if they are negotiating for the sale of a goat, because the traditions of the Igbos consider it disrespectful to price a human being as if she were for sale. This negotiation can take a long time. Eventually they will arrive at a position that will be good for both sides, and at that stage the suitor's side will inform the prospective bride's side that they want to come forward soon to pay the bride price. The bride's family chooses a day and communicates with the suitor's family, who are expected to acquiesce.

That day too, the bride's delegation will inform the groom's side about all the minor requirements that they need to fulfill before the marriage is considered sealed. Negotiations are allowed at this stage too.

At the end of the day, the *onye aka ebe* (middleman) gives a minor feast to celebrate a successful *ihu onu nwanyi* (pricing of a bride). When the feast is over, everybody leaves for his own home.

It is my remarkable observation that what the *ime ego nwanyi* (payment of bride price and its accompanying ceremony) stands for to the Igbos, is what the betrothal custom stands for to the Israelites. Once an Igbo man has paid the bride price, and scaled through all the accompanying ritual requirements, he can regard himself as married.

Now I will deal with the *ime ego* and all its rituals.

On the day of *ime ego* (paying of bride price) some booths without walls, covered by canopies and called *okpukpu* in Igbo language are erected. The Igbos use palm fronds and sticks to make them. It is inside them that the parties will sit. And the parties include the friends and relatives of the groom and the bride. Notably the Jewish marriage takes place under the *huppah* (canopy). The groom and his side will come with the required quantity of wine, and the bride's side will prepare a feast.

Prayers by the oldest man in the bride's family starts off the programme. Those with the ability to talk will start wise sayings about successful marriages. After some time, quietness is asked for, and the oldest man from the bride's family who traditionally is the *aka ji ofo* (priest/elder) of that family will start blessing the new couple. He will pray that the bride will have numerous sons and daughters. In Chinua Achebe's *Things Fall Apart*[34], the Igbos rendered this particular blessing thus: "We are giving you our daughter today. She will be a good wife to you. She will bear you nine sons like the mother of our town."

Rebekah was likewise given a similar blessing: "Our sister, be thou the mother of thousands of ten thousands[35]."

Meanwhile feasting and drinking will be going on. After some time elders from both sides will withdraw to an enclosure to carry out the bride price ritual. It is noteworthy that an Igbo girl must never witness either the negotiations for her price, or even know the price

---

[34] Achebe, Chinua, *Things Fall Apart*, (Ibadan: Heinemann Educational Books, 1959) p.82.
[35] J. H. Hertz, *The Pentateuch and Haftorah*s, 2nd edition (London: The Soncino Press, 1937) 87.

that was paid for her. It is also noteworthy that Leah and Rachel did not participate in any of the discussions between their father and Jacob that are equivalent to the discussions of the bride price.

In the enclosure the price money is paid, but never in full, because the Igbos believe that: 'ana ho akwucha ugwo nwanyi akwucha' (the value of a woman can never be fully paid up).

I think that the idea underlying the necessity to pay the bride price is just to help the groom to know that every good thing has, and comes with a price; and that what he has paid is not really the equivalent of the value of the girl. The money is handed over to the girl's father. After that some gifts are handed over to those who negotiated the price, after which feasting and drinking of palm wine intensifies.

Remarkably, the Igbos, like the ancient Semites / Israelites, can pay the bride price in kind, that is by working for their in-laws. If a poor man likes a girl, who in turn likes him, and both families agree that their children can marry, the young man may elect to pay for his bride by working for her family for a number of years. That was what Jacob did for Laban his future father-in-law for seven and seven years for the matriarchs of Israel, Leah and Rachel[36]. Some Igbo oral traditions state that in Igbo traditions that it is also for seven years.

I must mention that during the ritual of *ime ego* (bride price ceremony) the bride's mother gets some gifts from the groom. In some Igbo clans this is called *ndu oku*.

---

[36]Ibid, 108-9. (Genesis 29:19-27).

These are akin to the gifts that Eliezer gave to Rebekah's brother and mother[37].

After the *ime ego* the bride becomes officially the wife of the young man, but before they consummate the marriage the ritual ceremony of *isa ifi* is carried out.

In this ceremony the new wife is asked to confess if she has been having sexual relations with other men since the young man indicated that he wanted to marry her. If she confesses that she has strayed, she must mention the names of the men and they must compensate the husband financially. The husband will not be very happy with her, and will feel ill-disposed towards her parents.

According to Basden besides (unfriendly) words spoken, there will be a curtailment of gifts to the parents and other "in-laws[38]."

In the *Arrow of God* by Chinua Achebe we have a good example of those unfriendly words, when an Igbo discovered that his bride had been unchaste[39].

But if the new wife asserts that she is a virgin, proof is sought in the practice that G.T. Basden describes succinctly: "In due time proof is provided by the use of a cloth as in the case of an Israelitish maid[40]."

### *Ima ogodo/igba nkwu (the marriage feast)*

This ceremony ought to be done before the bride moves into the home of the husband, but I think or speculate that because Igbo tradition recognized that a man may

---

[37] ibid, 86. (Genesis 24:53)
[38] G. T. Basden, *Niger Igbos*. (London: Frank Cass and Company Ltd, 1966) p.214.
[39] ibid, p.214.
[40] Achebe, Chinua, *Arrow of God*, (Ibadan: Heinemann Educational Books, 1959).

have been slowed down somewhat after all the rigours that he must have gone through up to the *ime ego*, therefore the man is allowed to postpone the marriage feast to any time that is convenient for him. In the mean time they can start to grow and develop their family. There are some main features of this ceremony.

Like the *ime ego*, it is done in the home of the bride. As the words 'igba nkwu', which is its name in some Igbo communities, signifies, it is done with much wine. This wine is contributed by the kinsmen of the man. A large goat is to be presented to the kinsmen of the bride, who will slaughter the goat and share its meat among themselves.

Music is an indispensable factor in the ceremony. The celebrating couple will at a point, be called up from the *okpukpu* (canopy or *huppah*) to dance together. There is much merry-making, feasting and drinking. In the *History and Culture of the Igbo People*, Matthew O. Orji, described it as "interwoven with the final marriage ceremonies[41]." It is after this celebration that the bride's family gives her a dowry, that is they *duo ya uno*.

### *Inye okuko (levirate marriage)*
Literally 'inye okuko' means to hand over a fowl. There is a practice or custom among the Igbos that a next of kin of a deceased relative should inherit the wife of the deceased.

This inheritance is done after the funeral ceremonies have been fully observed. The family is assembled together, and the widow will be given a fowl, and she will be instructed to hand it to any of the near kinsmen that she likes. Whoever she chooses will inherit her as a

---

[41] Orji, Matthew O., *The History and Culture of the Igbo People* (Nkpor: Jet Publishers (Nigeria) Ltd, 1999) 94.

wife, and is expected to procreate with her so that children can be raised in the name of the deceased. All that we (Igbos) know of this custom is that 'our fathers observed it.' But a study of it shows that the same reason that motivated the legislation of it in Israel—the Israelite model is to ensure that all Israel survives—also gave rise to it among the Igbos. The Igbos consider it calamitous when someone dies without leaving children behind. Thus names like 'Afamefuna' (let my name survive) 'Obiechina' (let the lineage survive, and not die out), etc, pervade the Igbo landscape. They all remind the Bible student of the ancient cry—"O Lord, the God of Israel, why is this come to pass in Israel, that there should be to-day one tribe lacking in Israel[42]."

Note: Israel started as individuals, before growing into a nation; and the loss of one Israelite is like losing of the whole nation.

### *Nwanyi inu nwanyi (woman-to-woman marriage)*

An Igbo woman who could not produce a child for her husband is permitted by custom to marry a wife who will have conjugal relations with her husband, and the resultant children will also be regarded as her own children (children of the first wife).

Igbo practice combines elements of what Sarah and Rachel did. And when God gives children to the new wife the Igbo woman would be perfectly entitled to declare as Rachel: "Chim (my God) has judged my case, and He has also heard my voice and given me a son[43]."

---

[42] Judges 21:3.
[43] J. H. Hertz, *The Pentateuch and Haftorahs*, 2nd edition (London: The Soncino Press, 1937), 110 (Genesis 30:6).

## The Ihachi nwanyi (retaining a daughter to procreate for the family)

"That we may preserve seed of our father," (Genesis 19:32). The quoted passage is the statement of one of Lot's daughters, about the need to ensure that their father's lineage is preserved; since after the destruction of Sodom and Gomorrah, they felt that everybody in the world, save themselves and their father, had died.

If an Igbo family had only daughters, in order to ensure that their father's lineage continues, one of the daughters may be retained to try and have sons for the family. But unlike the daughters of Lot, who were not Israelite after all, but close relatives, the Igbo case will never entertain the idea of their having sexual relations with their father. Rather, men deemed to be responsible men will be asked to do the job.

## Endogamy and Exogamy

We observed that the Igbo marriage is endogamous in the sense that to the Igbos it is right only when one marries within the clan, since the most ancient time, which reminds one of the words of Moses in Numbers 36:6;"This is the thing which the Lord hath commanded, saying, let them be married to whom they think best, only into the family of the tribe of their father shall they be married[44]."

Even now Igbos still consider it wise if one marries from one's own clan, or at worst from a neighbouring clan. Where one strays outside Igbo-land nobody is happy, because it is taken as if the person had gotten lost.

It is in the respect of endogamy, i.e., marrying inside one's immediate family, that Igbo practices depart from

---

[44] ibid., 723,724, (Numbers 36:6).

Semitic practices in the time of Abraham. While Abraham and the earliest patriarchs married their kith and kin, the Igbos are exogamous. They will marry their kith and kin, but never their very close blood relatives, which was the standard set by Moses in the Sinai wilderness.

**The author drains the cup of palm-wine handed to him by his accepting bride at their betrothal**

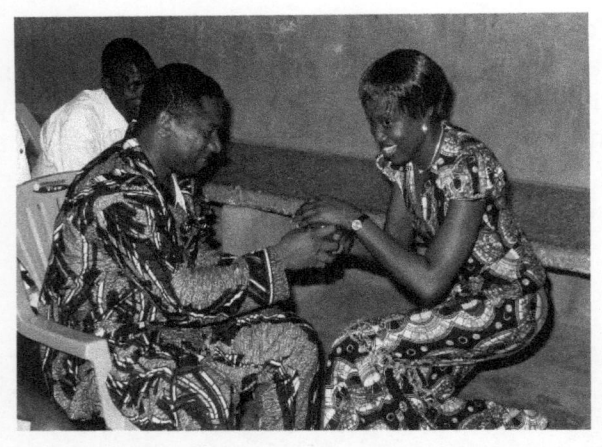

The author receiving palm wine from his bride Irene Ifeyinwa during their betrothal (ime ego), it is the indication that she accepted to be his wife.

The author's father in law Justin Malizu enacting the traditional offering of wine to the author's bride, Irene for onward transmission to the author.

## *Iju Nwanyi / Igba Anukwaghim (Divorce)*

Even in this present era that many different peoples follow what is called the 'popular culture', the Igbo culture when compared with the cultures of other

Nigerian peoples, is deemed to be stable, strong and long lasting. And from what we hear about high divorce rates in the 'civilized world' there is no basis for comparison.

But it must also be noted that there was a time, recently, when the divorce rate among the Igbos was as low as 1 out of perhaps 50,000 couples. When I was growing up in Ozubulu, I knew of only one divorcee, in a clan of population 39,000.

The reason for the almost total absence of divorce in the society could be traced to Igbo marriage traditions, and general Igbo culture. The extensive investigations ensured that persons who are incompatible do not get married to each other. Another factor is that the Igbo people traditionally have what is called *ifere*. Translated this is near in meaning to pride. No decent Igbo family would risk its pride by the opprobrium that would come with the tale that its daughter married and returned, or was returned. The same thing applied also to men. Accordingly wives and husbands learned to live together, despite the inconveniences that come with living together. The Igbos will go to great lengths to avoid divorce, except if adultery on the part of the wife is involved. And from J.H.Hertz we learnt the following: "The very altar weeps for one who divorces the wife of his youth', says the Talmud[45]." This statement conveys the impression that divorce is as repulsive to the Jew as it is to the Igbo.

Among the Igbo divorce is deliberately made difficult in order to discourage it. Unlike the Western marriage which can be dissolved by either party going to court to get a divorce, the Igbo divorce requires that the

---

[45] ibid, p.932

kinsmen of both parties to the marriage should be present to settle the disputes if possible, or to grant divorce if necessary.

An Igbo man is believed to be taking a risk with his life if he condones his wife's adultery The Igbos believe that a man who eats the food prepared by an adulterous wife would fall seriously ill. In the case of the Jews, a husband "is compelled to divorce her [the adulterous wife[46]]." The similarity of both positions is clear.

The Igbo tradition expects a higher level of moral rectitude from the woman because we believe that a woman is the bedrock of the home. We say 'oo nwanyi nwe uno' (a woman owns/makes the home).

---

[46]Ganzfried, Solomon, and Goldin, Hyman E, trans., *Code of Jewish Law and Customs (Shulhan Aruch)* (New York: Hebrew Publishing Company, 1961).

# CHAPTER TWO: Comparative Study of the Ideas Underlying Omenana and Judaism

## Omenana and Judaism

***Omenana*** is the equivalent of Judaism to the Igbo people. The Igbos call their culture Omenana. What I want to do here is to conduct a comparative study of the main idea or ideas underlying *Omenana* and Judaism.

I will proceed by explaining what the phrase *Omenana* means.

**The meaning of *Omenana*** – *Omenana* is a phrase, or a compound word. This phrase or word is hiding much valuable information.

If translated into English language, *Omenana* will give us -- "what to do in the land;" because *Ome* means "what to do in," *n* means "the," and *ana* in the context of *Omenana* means "the land." To the reader the phrase "what to do in the land" would mean nothing until more light is thrown on it. Certain sections of the Torah (the Pentateuch) are very helpful in explaining what "what to do in the land" means.

Chapter 5 of Deuteronomy shows Moses reviewing the Decalogue (Ten Commandments). It also shows him reminding the Israelites of the things that happened when God uttered the 10 *Dvarim* (Commandments) at Mount Sinai. It presents him reminding Israel that after God had accepted their plea that Moses should be the intermediary between Him and them, that God had allowed them to go back to their tents, while He had ordered Moses to wait a while so that, according to Deuteronomy 5:28:

"And I (God) shall speak to you (Moses) the entire commandment, and the decrees, and the ordinances that you shall teach them (the Israelites), and they shall perform (*do*) *in the land* that I give them, to possess it,"(Emphasis mine).

And in Deuteronomy 6:1, we have Moses again stating:

"Now this is the commandment, the statutes, and the ordinances, which the Lord your God commanded to teach you, that ye might *do them in the land* whither ye go over to possess it."

The relationship between God's commandment, statutes, ordinances, and the land is again elegantly presented in Deuteronomy 11:8-9:

"Therefore shall ye keep all the commandment which I command thee this day, that ye may be strong and go in and possess the *land*, whither ye go over to possess it and that ye may prolong your days upon the *land*, which the Lord swore unto your fathers to give unto them and their seed, a land flowing with milk and honey."

In summary, the land is to be kept forever, but only if Israel obeys God and keeps His commandments, i.e., does the things in the Commandment. And should Israel fail to keep the commandments, surely loss of the land (exile) and discomfiture, among other evils, were to follow.

Loss of the land is paramount in the list of evils to come if the laws are disregarded; as we can see from the following Biblical passage:

"When thou shall beget children, and children's children, and ye shall have been long in the land, and shall deal corruptly, and make a graven image, even the form of anything, and shall do that which is evil in the sight of the Lord thy God, to provoke Him; I call heaven and earth to witness against you this day, that ye shall soon utterly perish from off the land where unto ye go over the Jordan to possess it, ye shall not prolong your days upon it, but shall utterly be destroyed. And the Lord shall scatter you among the peoples, and ye shall be left few in number among the nations, whither the Lord shall lead you away. (Deuteronomy 4:25-27)."

Igbos traditionally are obsessed with keeping themselves, their society, and their land free of abomination *(aru)* and sin *(njo)*. They would go to any length to ensure that *aru* is not committed, because in Igbo thought is ingrained the idea that abominations pollute the persons/people who commit them, and makes them unfit to stay on the 'land', lest they also defile the land. In my clan Ozubulu, and in Igbo-land generally we believe and say: 'na ana na atu/na agbo onye mer' aru' (that the land throws out/vomits out persons/people who commit abominations). Because of the consequences that followcommission of abominations Igbos take various measures to ensure that they give *aru* and its commission enough distance.

In the book *Traditional Religion in West Africa*[47], an essay written by S.C. Onwuka, an Igbo who practiced the Igbo religion as a youth, contains the following: "Our .....brothers (in *Omenana*) fear.....the great God. They fear to do evil which will earn them the anger .....of God (*Chineke*) Himself."

And for the Igbos to ensure that they are in the good grace of Chukwu, according to S.C. Onwuka they do the

---

[47] 'Traditional Religion in West Africa' edited by E.A. Ade Adegbola (Ibadan: Sefer Books Ltd, 1998) p.7.

following: "Not feeling sure that they are doing their best towards perfection, they offer several sacrifices, either to obtain mercy or to pacify...At times they feel that their body has been defiled by certain actions. They will kill a fowl and beat it all over the body." All the above describes Igbo efforts to ensure that evil is not committed, so that its consequences would be avoided.

Apart from loss of the land some other consequences of evil-doing in Igbo thought are constant deaths, incurable sicknesses, poverty, suffering, etc. And in Ozubulu, and in Igbo-land generally, the belief is clear and general, that a land where all the aforementioned ills afflict the inhabitants is 'ana na ere oku' (land that is polluted and afire). Igbos believe that the inhabitants of such a land have committed heinous abominations and other evil deeds, and have thus become unfit to stay on the land.

In the traditional Igbo society, i.e., in the era when *Omenana* was more respected, commission of abomination occurred only sparingly, because the Igbos feared [Chukwu] more at that time, and accordingly feared to incur His wrath by committing abominations. Eloquent testimony of my last assertion is established by the fact that in pre-modern Igbo society prostitution and harlotry were nonexistent; because practice of prostitution is *aru* (abominable) to Igbo culture. We find Israelite thought closely paralleling Igbo thought on the matter of prostitution; and this can be deduced from the following: "There shall be no harlot of the daughters of Israel (Deuteronomy 23:18). Because, (in verse 19), they [harlotry] are an abomination unto the Lord God."

Consider the following: As recently as the early 20th century, there were no Igbo prostitutes, because the Igbos knew that prostitution is *aru*, which would defile them, and cause them to lose their land, among other calamities. This was confirmed by an independent observer[48]. In the words of G.T. Basden, a British Anglican missionary who lived and worked among the Igbos for more than twenty years at the end of the 19th and the beginning of the 20th centuries: "harlotry as a profession, was unknown in the Ibo country prior to the impact of Western influences." As well in the Igbo society a mere sixty years ago, *izu ohi* (thievery and armed robbery), and *igbu ochu* (murder) which are also deemed abominable by the Igbos hardly ever occurred.

*Omenana* has been regularly and wrongly addressed or submerged under the misleading terms Ancestral Religion, or African Ancestral Religion, or African Indigenous Religion. Less well informed and less well educated persons, such as European missionaries, and Igbos whom they trained have also identified *Omenana* as paganism, heathenism, or animism. However what *Omenana* is, is becoming clearer because of some good research and other works done on it.

One of such works is the one done by Igbo musician, Ozoemena Nsugbe. In his album entitled 'Omenana na uka' he described *Omenana* as the Igbos own way of life, and religious culture. He enumerated the benefits that accrued to the Igbos when they respected the tenets of *Omenana*. According to him when the Igbos lived fully by *Omenana,* it kept the Igbos clean and safe, and ensured that Igbos lived to ripe old ages. He observed that at present so many Igbos despise and hate *Omenana*. He mentioned that Igbos want to avoid *Omenana* because *Omenana* requires rigorous discipline and holiness. He wondered why the Igbos have failed to realize that they could only make real progress and live

---

[48]Basden, G. T. *Niger Ibos* (London: Frank Cass & Co., Ltd., 1966) 239.

good lives with *Omenana*. He asked the Igbos a rhetorical question: 'kedu ife anyi na anwulu, ana m aju kedu ife anyi na anwulu'(Igbos why are Igbos dying off like flies) now that we have abandoned *Omenana*? He ended his song with the following call: "onye obuna nagharikwa azu mewe kwa *Omenana*" (everybody should go back and start respecting and practicing *Omenana*).

The three terms: Ancestral Religion, or African Ancestral Religion, or African Indigenous Religion mentioned above are misleading because as there is no African people, but African peoples, so is there no African religion, or African ancestral religion or even African indigenous religion, but 'religions'. All the peoples living in Africa were not, and are not homogenous in culture, history, and even physical appearance. As theUrhobo, Igbo, Ibibio, Igala, Idoma and Yoruba of Africa differ from each other, so do the Turk, the Swede, the Hungarian, the Jew, and the English of Europe differ from each other. All the cultural practices and beliefs that I have so far discussed, and those that I will still discuss in this study are uniquely Igbo. Most of them, if not all, are strange to all the other ethnic groups in Nigeria.

To throw more light on the relationship of *Omenana* to the Igbos I will draw an illustration of how Igbos view an Igbo person's reaction and feelings towards *Omenana*.

In the Igbo society, an Igbo who likes, practices, protects and eulogizes the Igbo way of life is called 'onye na eme *Omenana*'. It means one who is living by, and practicing Igbo culture. Such a person is viewed as wise and also as someone whose parents did a good job bringing him or her up. On the other hand, the Igbo who hates, derides, and does not want to practice Igbo culture is viewed as, and derisively referred to as, 'onye na eme omenenu', which simply means that he is a fool; an ignoramus and a ne'er-do-well who acts out of context, and whose parents failed to educate appropriately in Igbo dos and dont's. In recent times Igbos have started referring to them as 'ndi na eme aru' (those who commit abominations), and as 'ndi na emebisi ana Igbo' (those that are desecrating and polluting the land of the Igbos or Igbo-land).

In concluding this study I want to reiterate certain issues that I have mentioned earlier. *Omenana* requires the Igbos to live holy and righteous lives, so that their land will not become afire. So that their well-being on their land will be assured. Deuteronomy which is one of the bedrocks of Judaism made it clear that the Israelites will only enjoy their stay in the land if they are holy and righteous, which they will be by keeping the Commandments of God. It can be seen easily that identical or very similar ideas underlie both systems.

**Igbo Perception of God**

In this section I will give evidence that will prove that the Igbos are indeed very similar to the Israelites in perception of the Deity, i.e., that among other things that they perceived Chukwu, as they call their God, as one indivisible, invisible Being. It must be borne in mind that the most important thing that distinguished the Israelites from the rest of humanity is their struggle to cleave to, and make mankind aware of God, and ethical monotheism. As one writer observed; Israel's career is one long protest against idolatry and polytheism.

As I mentioned above Chukwu, or Chineke as He is alternately addressed, is God, i.e., the Supreme Being to the Igbos. The knowledge of Chukwu or Chineke as God is universal among the Igbos.

To the Igbos Chukwu is also the Supreme Spirit. He is the 'Mmuo ka mmuo' ('the Spirit that is greater than any other spirit'). Being a Spirit to the Igbos, the Igbos know that He cannot be seen with the eyes of man. However, this Being is so close to the Igbos' consciousness that one of the favourite pastimes of the Igbos is to appropriate His names, or rather attributes, to the names of their children. Names such as Uchechi and Udochi i.e., the ones compounded by the *chi* from the name Chineke, and names like Uchechukwu and Udochukwu, i.e., those compounded with Chukwu, are common among the Igbos. I am named Chukwukaodinaka ('everything is in the hands of the great God'). All my six siblings also received names compounded with Chukwu: Ngozi Chukwuka, Chukwunonyelum, Chukwudi, Chukwuma, Chukwuaduom, and Nchedo-Chukwuka. My favorite niece is Uchechukwu.

My briefs here are to show that He (Chukwu) alone is the God of the Igbos, and that the Igbos worshipped only Him, just as by tradition the Jews know and worship only the God of Israel (the Supreme Being).

The Igbos acknowledge that Chukwu can't be fully described, or known, if one takes one of their titles for Him *(Ama ama amasi a masi)* literally. This means- 'He that is known, but can't be known fully'. Nevertheless the Igbos know, and have said a few things about Him and these can be deduced from their names, titles, attributes, etc, of Him.

From the name Chineke it could be seen that the Igbos see Chukwu as the Creator. *Chi na eke*, means 'God that creates,' while from Chukwu it could be seen that we maintain that He is great, almighty and most powerful. We see Him as the overlord, and as beneficent and benevolent. We also believe that He punishes evil doers for their evil deeds, and that He rewards good deeds.

An eminent historian of the Igbos, A. Afigbo[49] acknowledged this in the following words- "The first item in this inner cosmos, and thus in the Igbo mega-cosmos (i.e. the inner cosmos and the outer cosmos) is the being known in English as God. It is the first in having no origin and no ending, in being the creator and ruler of all that has ever existed in the past that exists in the now and that will exist in the future. Continuing, Afigbo avers, "in truth we (the Igbos) do not know its name."

That the Igbos may not know the actual name of the Creator is to be expected. The most God-conscious people, the Hebrews, who are also known as the Israelites or the Jews, the people that God Himself addressed as His first son in Exodus 4:22-23, honestly aver that only Moses was told the actual name of God by God. So in agreeing with Afigbo that the Igbos do not know the actual name of God, I will still be pushing forward a similarity in perception of God that the Igbos share with the Israelites. Even till the present time the Jews do not claim that knowledge of the actual name of God is common. Major segments of the Jewish society aver that the name is unpronounceable. And the Igbos are clear that Chukwu is 'A ma ama a masia amasi' ('He that can't be completely or fully known').

---

[49] Okere, T. I., ed., *Religion in a World of Change: African Ancestral Religion, Islam and Christianity* (Owerri: Assumpta Press, 2003) 175.

Here we have Chinua Achebe, a prominent Igbo novelist, essayist, and historian, reporting a discussion between an Igbo and a Briton; two characters in one of his books:

"... you say that there is one Supreme god who made heaven and earth", said Akunna (an Igbo dignitary) on one of Mr. Brown's visits. "We also believe in Him and call Him Chukwu[50]."

Chinua Achebe further reported his character describing Chukwu: " ... Our fathers knew that Chukwu was the Overlord and that is why many of them gave their children the name Chukwuka ("Chukwu" is Supreme[51])."

We know that human eyes cannot see Him. Thus we have no physical representations of Him, having no idea of how He looks or is. G.T. Basden, the Christian missionary who studied the Igbos for many years, made the following observation: "among the Igbos there is no symbol (image or idol) erected to the Supreme Being[52]."

In this the Igbos are similar to Israel, because to the Israelites what applies is, "When I (God) appeared to you (Israel) at Horeb you saw no form or likeness of God" (Deuteronomy 4:15).

In the *Arrow of God*, by Chinua Achebe, we find an Igbo man making the following comment: "may the great Deity forbid such a thing[53]." I find this very instructive, because from the Igbo man's plea for the great Deity to forbid an act we can see that even though the Igbos do

---

[50] Achebe, Chinua, *Things Fall Apart*, (Ibadan: Heinemann Educational Books, 1958) 126.
[51] ibid, 127.
[52] Basden, G.T., *Niger Ibos* (London: Frank Cass and Co., Ltd., 1966) p. 10.
[53] Achebe, Chinua, *Arrow of God* (Ibadan: Heinemann Educational Books, 1964) 45.

not see God physically, nevertheless they recognize God as the Being that can intervene when the efforts of man have failed.

In the same book, Achebe reported another Igbo man declaring thus: "Aghadike is a great doctor and diviner. But even he cannot carry a battle to the compound of the Great God[54]."

In the above we can discern that the Igbos believe that man is subject to God, and cannot over-rule Him, or win in a fight with Him, no matter the strength of man. These references to Great Deity and Great God in Achebe's book are significant.

As I have stated earlier the Igbo name for the Supreme Being is Chukwu, which means Great God. And as we can see from all the foregoing the Igbos actually see Him as God, and attribute to Him the same or very similar powers, virtues, and characters that the Jews attribute to the God of Israel. However it must be noted that for me to show evidence that will be strong enough to prove that the Igbo perception of God is very similar to the Israelite perception I have to show evidence that the Igbos recognize only Chukwu/Chineke as God. In trying to do so I have tried and striven valiantly to locate other gods among the Igbos, but I failed. I only succeeded in finding Chukwu or Chineke as the God of the Igbos. I tried to see if I could locate the 'gods' from the religious practices of the Igbos, by subjecting some of the entities that some writers have described as 'gods' of the Igbos to the simplest test: i.e., to find out if the Igbos worshipped them. If they had been worshipped that would have been proof that the Igbos viewed them as gods. This is how I carried out the test.

---

[54]ibid, 112.

The Igbo word for worship is *fe*, and to worship is *ife*. If an Igbo wants to go to his place of worship, and he is addressing an Igbo audience about his intentions, he could say to them 'a na m eje na ebe ana efe Chineke (uno uka or obi Chineke) ka m je fee Chukwu'; i.e., I'm going to the *obi* (*beit knesset*) to go and worship God. It struck me forcefully that Igbos only use the word *fe* (worship) when they are referring to worship of Chukwu. The Igbo is yet to be found who would say ka m je fee (anything or anybody) other than Chukwu or Chineke; i.e., we are yet to see Igbos who would say let me, or let us, go and worship anything or anybody other than (Chukwu/Chineke) God.

As the Igbos know, the Supreme Being is Chukwu or Chineke, and as I have explained Chukwu means great God and Chineke means God the creator.

At this point I would have with a clean conscience drawn the curtains on this discussion, with the words that the Igbos know only Chukwu/Chineke as God, and that the Igbos perceive Him as the Jews perceive Him. This is because I have shown evidence that the Igbos would only worship Chukwu/Chineke. They will never worship anything else. They will never even say, 'ka anyi je fee' anything other than Chukwu/Chineke.

However I will still pursue the matter further because this is a good opportunity to clear some issues relating to whether or not the Igbos are monotheists, as the Children of Israel have been since God called out their Patriarch, Abraham.

Certain authors have mentioned that the Igbos have other gods, or have made suggestions that imply that the Igbos are aware of the existence of other gods. I have tried to see if there are grounds for anybody to make such suggestions. I looked at the Igbo language. I did not find a word for 'other gods', or 'small gods', or 'false gods'. As the Igbos know Chukwu as God, which the full meaning of is the 'great God', the best we could achieve at present is to take the word *chi* as the Igbo equivalent of God, because 'ukwu' means great. So, having seen the 'great God', we would be entitled to expect to see *chi ndi ozo* (other gods), *chi obere/nta* (small/little gods), *chi asi/ugha* (false gods) in the Igbo language. But no such ideas/words or names exist in the Igbo language. Reverend Father Dr. R.C. Arazu, an Igbo scholar, recognizes this with the following words, "the gods of Igbo-land can only be said in English or any other European language, but not in Igbo. Igbo language has no words for "gods[55]."

I will now commence to examine the words which some persons have taken to mean 'gods' in Igbo language.

*Arusi*: this is a word the meaning of which is not clear. It could be of foreign origin. *Arusi* may have entered the Igbo language through intercourse between the Igbos who live in the Western sections of Igbo-land and their neighbours who use a cognate word *orissa* for "god" or "gods". However it must be made very clear that when referring to *arusi* that the Igbos never use the word for God, i.e., god beginning with a capital G.

Also besides its use for god or gods, among the Igbos in this modern period strong Igbo men are also addressed as *arusi*.

Research reveals that the word was also used to identify Igbo persons who played very important roles in the lives of the Igbo people, in the remote past. The case of

---

[55] Rev. Dr. Father Martin Arazu, *Our Religion: Past and Present* (Awka: Martin-King Press, 2005) 129.

'Edo Nnewi' is a good example: Edo was an ancestress of the Nnewi people. She led them in war in the remote past. Some Nnewi people would refer to Edo as an *arusi* today.

We do not need to stretch our imaginations too far to understand that the word is a misapplied one. A clue about how the word was misapplied comes our way when we consider that some of the places where the afore-mentioned great men and women of the Igbos lived and were buried, became shrines, like Abraham's, and Rachael's burial places. Some did with time grow to be called *okwu arusi*, and did with passage of time again began to be described as 'shrine of 'god'(in English language) note, god beginning with a small g. The older generations Igbos did not view the sacred places as shrines of gods, because they knew who the personalities associated with the locations were. They knew that they were ordinary men and women who merely performed important functions for their communities. But the modern Igbos may not know this, because of the disconnection between the modern Igbos, and the past of the Igbos. When the missionaries took control of Igbo education, they labeled every Igbo shrine a shrine to 'gods', every Igbo ritual object-a god, and so on and so forth. So the Igbo without a sound knowledge of Igbo history and culture would see the place that his ancestors were buried as a shrine of gods. Also, that wonderously helpful things occur when the remaining adherents of the Igbo religion, pray at the shrines, has also helped to confuse the uninformed more. Recently Nnewi, the afore-mentioned Igbo clan, suffered much torment from kidnappers. Her people were forced to recall the merits of their fathers while praying to God to do something about the kidnapping spree which was ravaging the community. Interestingly the crime spree reduced drastically after the exercise which was called *itu iyi*. Dozie Ikedife, a University of Glasgow trained surgeon who led the exercise, is still alive. Interestingly the Igbos did not call the exercise to 'invoke arusi', but *itu iyi*, which as I have said is simply to recall the merits of their ancestors who lived worthy lives, during prayers to Chukwu. Clearly, Igbos began to think that other gods exist only after they were exposed to cultures, beliefs and doctrines that hold that other gods exist. Igbos also acquired the belief that there are 'gods' after they began to be exposed to religious education that tutored many Igbos to believe that the Igbos had 'gods' too, like the pagans. An old Igbo told me that ancient Igbos regarded the belief that there are other gods beside Chukwu as abomination. And that when some Igbos began to forget the origins and histories of the shrines, and began to think that the personalities associated with them were more than normal humans, their position were described as *aru* (abomination).

Another often misunderstood word is *Mmuo* (Spirit). The afore-mentioned shrines and the persons associated with them have been seen as *mmuo*, and *mmuo* has been wrongly identified as gods. *Mmuo* simply means spirit. Truly Chukwu is a Spirit and is recognized as such by the Igbos, but the Igbos do not just address Chukwu as *mmuo*. They are clearer. For example, He could be addressed as 'Mmuo ka mmuo' (Spirit that is greater than all other spirits), oke Mmuo (great Spirit), etc. When an object or idea is addressed as just 'mmuo' (spirit) by the Igbos, they definitely do not see the object or idea as a deity.

Still another misunderstood word is *agbara*. *Agbara* has been identified with 'other gods' too. In an essay entitled *The Osu Institution-Apartheid among the Igbos*, I wrote the following about it: "The Igbos refer to illustrious personalities; living or departed, as *agbara*. Also, traditionally Igbos have much regard for their ancestors. In some Igbo localities these ancestors are known as *ndi ichie* (honorable people). In some they are known as *agbara*."

The following would also be very helpful: in the Igbo religion (Omenana), the Igbo person/adherent is *onye ogo Mmuo* (worshipper of the Spirit), so there could be no doubt that he did not worship idols/images which clearly have forms, i.e., are physical objects, *and are therefore clearly not spirits*. To the Igbos God has no form, but is *Mmuo* (Spirit). We will get back to this later.

From the foregoing we can see that much has been forgotten, and a lot misunderstood.

If the elusive other 'gods' of the Igbos exist, they would have come under the designation *chi nta* or *chi obere*, i.e., small god, or chi ndi ozo (other gods). But they do not exist in the Igbo language because they are foreign to the Igbos, unlike the Supreme Being Who is present in the Igbo language as Chi ukwu (great God), and as Chi na eke (God that creates).

And what this reminds one of is a similar situation involving the Hebrew Language, which Dr. J.H. Hertz commented on Deuteronomy 4:16 which provides: "lest ye deal corruptly, and make you a graven image, even the form of any figure, the likeness of male or *female*).

While commenting Hertz noted:

"Female. How blasphemous and unnatural such a representation is to Israelite mind can be gathered from the fact that the Hebrew language does not even possess a word for 'goddess': cf. 1 Kings 11: 5, where the Hebrew for goddess is 'god[56]'."

Is it not interesting that as the word goddess could infiltrate the Hebrew mind, only through foreign channels like the English language, so also was a foreign idea — 'small gods' able to infiltrate the Igbo mind through a foreign word/ a foreign language-English. .

At this stage I have to isolate some of the entities and items that have wrongly been addressed as the 'other gods' and the 'small gods' of the Igbos; and explain what they are, or how they came to be misunderstood, or misrepresented.

The *ofo*: I was surprised when I read the work of an Igbo scholar[57], and saw that he had described the *ofo* as a god. The *ofo* is a staff that the elders/priests of the Igbos use as the symbol of authority. Sadly for the writer, as for many Igbos, some of the areas where colonialism succeeded most were in misrepresenting most things about the Igbos, and to a great extent brainwashing many Igbos. One of the ways the colonialists accomplished this was by describing all and every sacred object that they found in the possession of the Igbos as 'gods', 'juju', 'fetish' and 'arusi'. Of course they had an agenda which was to sell their own culture[58], which to their thinking was the most effective way of pacifying a stubborn and stiff-necked people. The colonial agents and colonialists cleverly noticed that the Igbo was, (and still is) obsessively religious; that to the Igbo there was no distinction between the secular

---

[56] Hertz, *The Pentateuch and Haftorahs*, 2nd edition, p.759 (commentary on Deut 4:16).
[57] Munonye, John, *The Only Son* (Ibadan: Heinemann Educational Books, 1966) 58.
[58] Achebe, Chinua, *Things Fall Apart*, (Ibadan: Heinemann Educational Books, 1958) 108.

and the religious, so they set to work to entice and convert them to their own way of life. Their first strategy, preaching about the superiority of their own religion, and the vicarious sacrifice, did not impress the Igbos[59], because central in Igbo theology is the belief that 'ife onye metar' oburu na isi ya' (what you sow, you reap). Having failed to convince the Igbos that they had been in error from time immemorial, they took a decision to ensnare the youths by providing schools[60], which produced graduates who gained employment in the colonial structure. And to pacify and ensnare the adults by opening hospitals, which gave cures to some new diseases. Also the economic model that Western imperialism introduced was alluring to some ambitious Igbos. These moves yielded dividends after many years.

In time the once-rejected tales of the Europeans began to be accepted, even if not understood, and the false claim that every Igbo ritual object stood for a false god began to be accepted among the urban elite. That is why an Igbo could call the *ofo* a god.

Another non-existent but often mentioned 'goddess' of the Igbos is the earth goddess. I have tried so much to find an Igbo community that has or had a goddess called *chi nwanyi ana*, which is the name that that 'goddess' would have had among the Igbos, and I have not succeeded in finding even one such community.

A lot of studies about the Igbos have been conducted with Nri clan as a base for research, because according to some researchers the traditions of the Igbos were or are better preserved there. I worked at Nri for an extended period, and have yet to see *chi nwanyi ana*

---

[59] Afigbo A, *Ropes of Sand* (Ibadan: University Press, Ltd., 1981) 339, 340.
[60] ibid., 340, and Achebe, Chinua., *Arrow Of God*, (Ibadan: Heinemann Educational Books, 1964) 23.

there. My clan Ozubulu, which lies a few kilometers south of Nri, would in my opinion also serve as a good place to conduct a disciplined and systematic study of Igbo traditions. All the core and identifiable Igbo traditions, which interestingly correspond to the traditions of Israel, are to be found in Ozubulu practices, like the *Mgbiri*, (the Jubilee year celebration), *Iri ji* (First fruit offerings) etc. I have found that the Ozubulu people revere Chukwu (the Supreme Being) just as the Israelites, and I have yet to see the faintest evidence that there was a *chi nwanyi ana* (an earth goddess) in Ozubulu.

What has made many persons to have the conviction that the Igbos have an earth goddess is the Igbo belief that abominable acts pollute the person who sins, and that this invites retributions from God Who gave us the land. And as loss of the land is one of the punishments, the fear of the loss of the land, in time got misconstrued as 'worship of the earth'.

An Igbo, Rev. Father (Dr.) Arazu[61], who as I mentioned earlier had observed that there is no word for 'gods' in the Igbo language, had in his quest to prove that the Igbos had other 'gods' made the same mistake that many Igbo researchers made in the past. He relied on the words of an Igbo who had been exposed to so many alien ideas and influences to conclude that Igbos viewed Chukwu as merely one of their gods. Many Igbos in this era think that because other gods exist in other cultures and religions that they must also exist in *Omenana*.

Arazu, using data gotten from a fellow Igbo, compared *ana* which he identified as the 'earth' with Chukwu, and concluded that the Igbos believe that *ana* is a god too.

---

[61] Rev. Dr. Father Martin Arazu, *Our Religion: Past and Present* (Awka: Martin-King Press, 2005) 129.

But it does not seem as if he actually analyzed his information thoroughly.

What, for a start, did Arazu's source see as *ana*? Was it the earth or the land? From Arazu's book we could think that it was the earth. But from this work we would see that the Igbo faith is about behaving ethically on the 'land', i.e., the country. The earth is not directly equivalent to the land.

Also the name of Arazu's source, Ezenwadeyi Izuchukwu, gives us a lot to work with. Izuchukwu means 'counsel of the great God.' It cannot be imagined that an Igbo would name his child 'izu ana' (counsel of the earth).

I would also recommend that serious thought be given to the following: the implications of the Igbo name Ajuruchukwu. This name means 'has one sought the opinion of the Great God?' And also of the Igbo name Uchechukwumee (may God's will prevail). If one delves deeper and deeper one can feel the greatest reverence that the Igbos have for Chukwu in the names.

And one can also see prayers, worship, and appeals in those names. On behalf of no Igbo 'god' (still to be found), including *ana* (the land) were such queries issued, nor was such an opinion expressed. All the entities that Arazu tried to describe as Igbo gods, like *ana, agwunsi, orashi*, etc, remained what they were until their meanings were changed by the Igbos who had left *Omenana*, and modern Igbos who are not well educated on *Omenana*.

Another non-Igbo entity which many think that it is an Igbo deity presently is *eze nwanyi* (*mami-wata or the mermaid*). The Igbos have boundaries with many peoples to their south. These peoples who live close to the shores of the Atlantic, and who are called the riverine peoples in Nigeria believe that there is a goddess that lives inside the water. The neighbouring Itsekiri people call it Umolokun. Among the Yoruba she is Yemanja. All the neighbours of the Igbos who live near the sea believe in this deity. It is this goddess that some persons have identified as the *mami-wata* (mermaid), and presently say that it is in the non-existent Igbo pantheon, probably because some Igbos who interact with the riverine peoples might have borrowed this deity.

But the Igbos have no name for this deity. Contemporary Igbos may think that 'eze nwanyi' means queen. But the word eze which is rendered nze in some Igbo localities actually connotes to 'avoid sin, or evil-doing.' There is an Igbo title called the *ozo* title. Those that take it pledge that they will 'zee' (avoid) 'ime ife ojoo' (doing of evil, sinful things). 'Zee' is the verb of *nze* and *eze*. It is this word that contemporary Igbos have appropriated to king, queen, prince and princess; words that do not have Igbo equivalents, because the Igbos did not have monarchies traditionally. So we can see that *eze nwanyi* which can correspond to queen in contemporary Igbo usage, is a new and borrowed concept, like the goddess herself

A greatly misunderstood word is *chi*. Its misunderstanding has helped to create the myth that the Igbos have other gods, or personal gods, that are distinct from the Supreme Being. *Chi* is the primary Igbo word for God. When *ukwu* is attached to it, the result is then *Chi ukwu*, (great God). Interestingly, this particular name or title is one of those with which Moses / Israel addressed the Supreme Being in Deuteronomy 10:17. As already explained, Chukwu is the Supreme Being

Who created everything. As also stated, there are no such things as *chi nta* or *chi obere*, 'small god' or *chi nke akam* or *chi nkem* 'personal god' in the Igbo language. What writers have misunderstood, misinterpreted and misrepresented as personal god is *Chi m*, meaning 'my God'. Addressing God thus is not peculiar to the Igbos. In Joshua 9:2, Joshua told the deceitful Gibeonites that they would henceforth work in the house of 'my God.'

Nelson Ejinduaka (Show Promoter), an Igbo musician, threw light on this. In one of his songs, a story about an evil man who committed incest with his unwilling daughter, he narrated how the distraught wife of the never-do-well, in anger because of the abominable act, had dragged the husband to the court, where due to a miscarriage of justice he was discharged and acquitted. The sad woman attributed the cause of what happened to her and her daughter, which she viewed as calamitous, to *Chi m* (my God). A person who knows the Tanach (the Hebrew Bible) can't help but think of the Biblical saga of Naomi and Ruth, where Naomi attributed to God both her good and bad times.

Another Nelson story is also helpful. An Igbo woman lost her only child, and had to proceed straight to see Chukwu, because according to Promoter that was in the era that Chukwu was in the world. Is not one's attention drawn to the visits by God to Adam, Abraham, Isaac, Jacob, Moses, and God's call to Samuel? When the woman's mission to bear another child, or to have the deceased one resurrected by Chukwu failed, she cried out 'Chim gburu m,' (my God has killed me).

From the foregoing it is clearer that *Chi* means God, and only the Supreme Being, to the Igbos traditionally and originally.

Another title for the Supreme Being among the Igbos is 'Chukwu Abiama.' It is likely that *Abiama* is an Igbo version of Abraham or Abram. It makes sense to speculate so since *Chi* is the Igbo word for God and we have *Abiama* attached to it sometimes. One would be perfectly reasonable to conjecture that Chukwu Abiama could be God of Abraham in Igbo language. I aver that with all the parallels and similarities between the Igbos and Israel that are presented in this book, even though I can't state absolutely that Abiama is Abraham, yet there exists strong grounds to suppose that both were one and the same name.

In the *Arrow of God,* the sky God (*Chukwu bi n'enu igwe*), whom the Igbos identify with Chukwu (God) was acknowledged as the stabilizer of the world[62].

On getting to this stage I need to summarize all that I have tried to present in the discourse. The Igbos like the Jews believe that 'a Creator created the world. Both peoples know that He is almighty, and all powerful.' In having these attributes and strengths we locate the two Igbo attributes, Chineke and Chukwu, that the Igbos have for Him. The Igbos like the Jews believe that this Being cannot be seen. The Igbos like the Jews believe that there are no other gods.

## Some Important Matters in Omenana

I think that this work will be more complete if I describe some issues in Igbo worship, and some of the objects that are to be seen in Igbo places of worship.

During my field work I started research on the religious practices of the Igbo people. I used Nri Clan which is one

---

[62] Achebe, Chinua, *Arrow of God* (Ibadan: Heinemann Educational Books, 1964) 209.

of the hundreds of Igbo clans as a starting point, because I was impressed by some steps that the Nri people had taken to respect the Igbo religion and traditions. I made several visits to Nri. On the first trip I struck up a friendship with Mazi Nnacheta Obudulu Nwokike and Ichie J.I. Obaegbuna, two Igbo priests of Nri origins. Both men allowed me to witness and investigate what I can now understand to be an equivalent of the peace offerings of the Israelites. See *Ilo Mmuo* in the section on sacrifices and offerings. They gave me full permission to probe all their paraphernalia of worship—the altars, 'idols' and *ofo*.

Their altar is a simple, small rectangular bed-like mound, made from a type of red earth *(aja upa)* that is to be found in Igbo-land. When allowed to be sun-baked it becomes very hard.

Inside Obudulu's *obi* is a small platform on which are numerous graven and carved images.

After reflecting on what I saw I asked both men who the God of the Igbos is? Without hesitation they replied 'Chukwu Abiama/Chukwu okike.' In English both names approximate the great God of Abiama, and the great God that creates. I requested that they should point out His image in the 'pantheon' in front of us. In some kind of shock that anyone could make such a request, both men responded that 'Chukwu wu Mmuo' (God is a spirit), that He can't be seen, that He had no beginning, nor would He have an end. They ended by saying that Chukwu can't even be fully known nor understood. I made a mental note then that I had perhaps gotten close to the reason why the Igbos refer to God as 'A ma ama amasi amasi', which means 'He that can't be fully known or understood.' The summary of their position is that it is absolute folly to reduce God to an image, which to them is even impossible as nobody had seen Him.

Who then do the images ('idols') represent? Their good deceased ancestors, they responded. I demanded to know why they would keep the images of their ancestors in their place of worship. I wanted to know the role their ancestors played in their religious practices. They responded that their deceased ancestors who are now in the spirit world are consequently closer to Chukwu. They added that those who lived good lives could be ideal intercessors for them i.e., that they would be in a better position to attract favours from Chukwu. It was at this stage that I began to see the reason that makes the children of a deceased Igbo woman to hand over one of her photographs to her kinsfolk, after her funeral rites. When my mother passed on in 2006 her kins-folk requested for one of her photographs. I recall asking them why they needed it. They responded that they would hang it on the wall of their *obi*. The communal *obi* is the equivalent of the Jewish synagogue. However what the men of Nri explained really became clearer to me after I observed a similar custom among the Jews. Many synagogues have a board with the names of the departed members. This board is right inside the praying hall. From a knowledgeable Jew I inquired the reason for this practice. He supplied answers that are close to the ones proffered by the men of Nri. The answer that I got from this wise Jew is that the merits of one's holy ancestors definitely place one in good stead before God. The wise man referred me to the Jewish *Amidah* prayer which begins thus: praised are you Lord and God, God of our ancestors, God of Abraham, Isaac and Jacob. Working on this subject exposes one to surprises all the time. What occurred to me at this stage was that the Igbo begins his prayer exactly as the Jew does. He starts like this: 'Chukwu, Chi nke nna nna anyi ha' (Great God, God of our forefathers). After critically analyzing what I found and heard in Obudulu's *obi*, and comparing it with my findings about the Jewish synagogue, and some of the practices, I surmised that in a way the purpose for the Igbos' installation of images of good ancestors close to the *okwu Mmuo* (altar) is similar to what the Jews try to do by having the names of the deceased members of their communities represented in their synagogues. The prayer pattern establishes the similarity. As mentioned, while the Jew acknowledges Abraham, Isaac and Jacob, the Igbo acknowledges *nna nna anyi ha* (our forefathers). The aforementioned Jewish gentlemen were the forefathers of the Jewish people.

Also it is significant that as the Jews start counting their ancestors from Abraham, Isaac and Jacob, their fathers who were distinguished by their adoption of ethical monotheism, so do the Igbos have a recognition that only their 'good' ancestors deserve to be mentioned in prayers, and their images kept in places of worship. The men of Nri were clear that their ancestors who were known to be bad people were not represented in the array of images on the platform.

There is another remarkable similarity that differences in circumstances of the Igbos and Jews have made obscure. The Jewish service in the synagogue is mainly prayers and songs, because of various circumstances that have given rise to major developments in Judaism. But in the Igbo case service includes prayers and other offerings, like the meal offering, etc, that correspond to those mentioned in the Book of Leviticus.

Also remarkable is that I only found profound respect, not worship, for the memories of their ancestors among the Igbos and the Hebrews. I have yet to find other peoples who have a similar degree and type of respect for their ancestors. All the names of the People of Israel are names of their ancestors. Abraham was the 'Hebrew', which is a regular name for ancient and modern Israelites. 'Israel' is the name of the father of the twelve sons who became the twelve tribes. Judah from whose name the word 'Jew' was derived, was one of the twelve sons. In the Igbo case many Igbo clans bear the names of ancestors and ancestresses.

At this point I was reminded of the following observation by Joseph J. Williams, S.J. According to him: "So great was the Hebrew's respect for the memory of his forefathers that it has misled some into believing that ancestor worship actually prevailed among the chosen people[63]."

The above statement was made in respect of the Jews.

From the foregoing it could be seen that the Europeans who tried to interpret Igbo culture and religion could not have done a good job. This is because, beside the fact that they were on a mission to demonize traditions that were not theirs, in order for their own to gain ground, they did not have the skills to begin to understand what they saw. The language was strange to them, and so was the culture. For example, the Igbo requirement that the memories of one's good ancestors should be acknowledged must have seemed other-worldly to the Europeans in whose religious systems there is no such requirement.

I asked the men of Nri about the *ofo*. They told me that the *ofo* is the staff of authority of the oldest Igbo man in

---

[63] Williams, Joseph J. *Hebrewisms of West Africa: From the Nile to the Niger With the Jews* (New York: Biblo and Tanen, 1928) 80.

any Igbo community. We didn't have to spend much time on the *ofo*. My late father Anekwe Joseph Ilona was the *aka ji ofo* of my family for many years. Literally this means the person whose hand is holding the *ofo*. The real essence of the title is that he was the elder/priest of my family.

The gentlemen at Nri did not have shrines or images of the much talked about 'other gods' of the Igbos like Amadioha, Ogwugwu of Okija clan, Akpu, Ndekwuru and Ogwui of Ozubulu, Edo of Nnewi, Agbala of Awka, the afore-mentioned Ana, etc. But however their comments still helped me to understand how those entities which existed only within some clans, or even within sections of some clans, came to be misunderstood and misrepresented as gods by persons who did not have the requisite knowledge to discuss or study Omenana. To the Nri priests certain entities like Ogwui which is a river and some other natural things like lakes, certain trees, etc, were creatures of Chukwu which He had given powers to help maintain equity and balance in the world. They were emphatic that no true adherent of Omenana would take the worship due to Chukwu to any other person or thing. To them to do that is *aru* (abomination).

Some Igbos also made, and brought/imported charms/amulets, mainly from the Bini, and Yoruba peoples from the West, from the Ijaw, Ibibios and Urhobos from the South and the Igala from the North. These charms, some of which were kept in sacred localities were later on described as 'gods' by some persons.

A very good example of what I am talking about is to be found in the following passage extracted from Chinua Achebe's *Arrow of God*:

"He guided himself by running his left hand along one of the side walls. When he got to the end of it he moved a few steps to the right and stood directly in front of the earth mound which represented 'Ulu'[64]."

What the writer was talking about here was the visit of an Igbo chief priest to the shrine of his 'god'Ulu. In the same book the author had told us how the members of the clan of the chief priest had come together to make the charm (which was later misrepresented as a god). The history of the 'deity' was clear, and so was its jurisdiction. Its powers did not extend beyond the village of its makers. In the quoted passage we find its chief priest, who was actually its custodian, going to the 'god's' shrine which was represented by only an 'earth mound'. No images were on the earth mound. Misrepresenting the amulet/charm as a god is equivalent to misrepresenting the guns carried by the security men who guard Jewish synagogues, and the Christian churches in Nigeria against terrorists, as gods. The older generation Igbos had no guns. They deployed amulets because that was what they could procure.

In Ozubulu, my clan, the story is still told about how the clan got together and made the 'deity'(a protective charm) that is installed in one of the quarters of the clan. It is also an Igbo practice to un-make any of the 'gods' (amulets) whenever they got disenchanted with them, probably due to non-performance. In one story Chinua Achebe masterfully describes how the Igbos burnt non-performing "deities[65]," almost like destroying weapons that failed to work.

---

[64] Achebe, Chinua, *Arrow of God* (Ibadan: Heinemann Educational Books, 1964) 28.
[65] ibid. 28.

Some things were also mentioned as 'gods' of the Igbos in pure error. One of such erroneous attributions is to be found in the work of D. Amaury Talbot, a foreign researcher. Talbot had in a section of her book made the following observation: "With the Ibos of Nigeria a female deity is the mother of the highest god, the Thunder god, and of all created things[66]."

This observation is wrong. In Igbo thought no such entity like "nne chi" or "nne nke chukwu" (mother god / mother of god) existed, prior to the advent of Christianity. Until Christianity was brought to them by the European missionaries, who introduced the designation "nne nke Chukwu" (mother of god), the Igbos had no idea that Chukwu Who in fact they believed that He created everything, also had a mother, or could have one. To the Igbo mind that was confusing; as can be seen in *Things Fall Apart,*[67] where Igbos were point out what seems to them an absurdity to the white missionaries who told them about the Trinity, which differed fundamentally from the Igbo idea of a Unitarian Supreme Being.

There is no entity known as *nne chi* or *nne nke chukwu* in Igbo language and thoughts.

I had grave doubts that Talbot had such an incorrect information in her book, partly because I read her observation in another book-*Hebrewisms of West Africa-From the Nile to the Niger with the Jews*[68]. My suspicions proved justifiable when I read another comment

---

[66]Woman's Mysteries of a Primitive People, (London, 1915), p. 8f cited, in Joseph J. Williams, Hebrewisms of West Africa: From the Nile to the Niger With the Jews (New York: Biblo and Tanen, 1928) 79.

[67] Achebe, Chinua, *Things Fall Apart* (Ibadan: Heinemann Educational Books, 1958) 103.

[68] Williams, Joseph J. Hebrewisms of West Africa: From the Nile to the Niger With the Jews (New York: Biblo and Tanen, 1928) 244.

credited to her, mentioning the same female deity, with its name as Eka Abassi (Mother of God). But in the latter comment "she" was situated among the Ibibios, another African (Nigerian) people who live to the south of the Igbos. Eka and Abassi are Ibibio words or names. Also she mentioned the name of her (Eka Abassi's) son as Obumo, and described it as the thunder god, whom she described as the head of the Ibibio pantheon. It is clear that she must have been writing about the Ibibios, but used the word "Ibo" by mistake, as it is similar to Ibibio. Obumo the son of Eka Abassi is a "god" or entity that the Igbos have never heard about, just as his mother is a goddess that no Igbo is aware of.

# CHAPTER THREE: Onwu Na Akwamozu

## Rituals Associated With Dying and Death

It is ideal for me to start the discussion on rituals associated with death from what I call "approaching death," i.e., when an Igbo becomes very sick. The Igbos believe that every sick person deserves care, love and medical attention.

As the patient lies ailing, relatives, friends and neighbours are custom-bound, and free to enter the sick-room.

Personal experience is very enlightening. In 2005-6 when my mother was very sick from the ailment that eventually terminated her life, the members of the Ilona family kept trooping in, to spend time with the sick lady and her distraught children. Occasionally the visitors would say *ndo* (sorry) to the sick.

As a people the Igbos dread and fear death. An Igbo saying aptly described the Igbo peoples' attitude to death: "mpempe ndu ka mpempe onwu mma." Translated into English this means the smallest fragment of life is preferable to the smallest fragment of death. The Igbo that was unarguably one of the greatest Igbos in this era, the Hon. Nnamdi Azikwe was regularly quoted as having said that even with all the promised rewards of heaven, he was not in a hurry to leave this earth that he knows well.

So with this mindset, the Igbos will strive to preserve life, doing everything in their power to ensure that the sick recover. As they apply their medical knowledge, they shower the patient with love and kindness, since they believe that a combination of these can contribute to healing. I find the Jewish attitude and feeling to life, in a presentation by Shmuley Boteach, Jewish rabbi and author[69] very similar to the Igbo attitude to life. Boteach had noted: "Judaism celebrates life to the full and its greatest promise, by the ancient prophets, is that one day all death shall be defeated.' 'And He (God) will destroy on this mountain the shroud that is cast over all peoples, the sheet that is spread over all nations; he will swallow up death forever'[70]."

However, when the Igbos have done all they could, and death persists in coming to claim the sick, the relatives of the sick prepare for the end. Igbo tradition requires that the dying dies in the presence and company of his family members.

Igbos consider it almost *aru* (abomination) for someone to be allowed to die without his family and friends around him.

Jewish practice has a direct parallel to the above as can be seen from the *Shulhan Arukh*[71]. "From the moment a person is in the throes of death, no one is allowed to leave him, in order that his soul may not depart when he is all alone."

Among the Igbos the assembled family members must be quiet. Even sobbing and talking in hushed tones is against custom. But persons may whisper (*igba izu*).

The complete quietness mentioned and required is better understood when read together with an Israelite parallel provision in the *Shulhan Arukh*: "A dying person is to be considered as a living being in all matters, and it

---

[69] Boteach, Shmuley, *Judaism For Everyone*, New York, Basic Books, 2002, 413.
[70] Isaiah 25:7.
[71] Ganzfried, Solomon, and Hyman E.Goldin, trans., *Code of Jewish Law and Customs (Shulhan Aruch)* (New York: Hebrew Publishing Company, 1961) 90.

is forbidden to touch him lest his death be hastened by it . . . still, if there exists an external cause which prevents the departure of the soul, such as the noise of some pounding, that cause may be removed, since this is not a direct deed to hasten the end, but merely the removal of an obstacle without touching the dying person[72]."

The Jewish prohibition against touching the dying is most likely against touching one who has entered into the throes of death.

I think that the same idea underlies the Igbo and Jewish prohibitions of noise in the presence of the dying. Death should not be hastened (induced) or delayed, but should be allowed to creep in and aid the dying unto rest. Also the act of dying should not be treated with levity or disregard.

When the dying has taken his or her last breath, one of the first acts that the Igbos perform is 'imechiya anya', (to close his/her eyes). The male relatives often do this.

From three sources I observed that the Jews do the above too.

Ganzfried-Goldin states: "The eyes of the dead are to be closed. If there are sons, it is done by one of them[73]."

And God Himself assured Jacob (Israel): "And Joseph shall put his hand upon thine eyes," (Genesis 46:4).

And in the Apocryphal bookof *Tobias* we see: "Tenderly he cared for them, and when they died it was he that closed their eyes in death.[74]"

---

[72]ibid; 89.
[73]ibid; 91.
[74]Tobias 14:15.

But what do the womenfolk, and even some men and children, do immediately they are sure that the sick has died? What starts immediately after the death occurred is the beginnings of "ikwa ozu'"(mourning).

Igbos really grieve over death, and Igbos really mourn! In early 2006 my mother died. I was in the bank when I received the message that she had gone. A strong man. That's what I am! But I could not hold back the tears as I rode in the taxi back to my house. The taxi-driver was so moved that he took only half of the fare from me. And when I called my elder brothers in Nigeria and Cape Verde and gave them the news, their reactions were like mine. For some time before her death we somehow knew that she was dying. But we were unwilling to accept that reality, because 'mpempe ndu ka mpempe onwu mma'. Death is never welcome to the Igbos. And on the day that we buried her, my younger sister, and myself, as her youngest son, were the ones that went to the mortuary to collect the body. From the mortuary to my home, a distance of at least six kilometers, we drove. As we progressed through the road that led to my mother's maiden home in Umu Ezike, Amakwa, Ozubulu, all the people, both natives and strangers, that saw the funeral cortege exclaimed 'ewoo nwata nwanyi a anaa!' (ooh this lady has returned home (to her ancestors). All paused temporarily in whatever they were doing, and joined my entourage in grieving. Most Igbos would react as everybody in this story acted. Igbos dread death. A popular Igbo name is Nduka (Life is very dear and important).

I will relate a story of Igbos in mourning which came to us in literature. In Flora Nwapa's *Efuru*, we have a description of the reaction of Efuru when she realized that her daughter who was sick had died:

"She threw herself on the floor of the room and wept hysterically." And shortly after the maid of Efuru reacted thus:'Ogea ran out, put her hands in both ears and shouted: 'Our people come, come: Ogonim is dead[75]."

According to G.T. Basden who observed Igbos in mourning: "It is when the moment of death arrives that the tumult begins. There is an outburst of wailing, the women particularly giving full vent to their grief[76]."

Jewish reaction to death is hardly different. J.H. Hertz' comment on Genesis 23:2, is very revealing[77]: "and Abraham came to mourn for Sarah, and to weep for her." Hertz explains to 'mourn' thus: "The Hebrew word indicates the loud wailing still usual in the East as a manifestation of grief." One needn't go to the 'East' to see what Hertz was referring to. A visit to bereaved Igbos would be enough. Also a visit to modern Jews in modern Israel will be very helpful. According to Martin Van Crevefeld[78], in a story entitled, 'Build a Wall to the Sky', "Week in and week out, Israeli soldiers are photographed weeping over their comrades' graves." Martin Crevefeld contrasted the Israeli soldiers attitudes with the almost celebration of death that is found in some Near Eastern cultures. Something similar is found in many (non Igbo) Nigerian cultures. While the Igbos mourn when their relatives die, many cultures in Nigeria recommend celebration. The Igbo word or phrase for funeral *akwamozu* means 'mourning for the dead'. When for example the Yoruba whose culture has influenced many of the Nigerian cultures that came

---

[75] Nwapa, Flora, *Efuru* (Ibadan: Heinemann Educational Books, 1966) 69.
[76] G. T. Basden, *Niger Ibos* (London: Frank Cass and Co., Ltd., 1966), 270.
[77] J. H. Hertz, *The Pentateuch and Haftorahs, 2nd edition* (London: The Soncino Press, 1937), Genesis 23:2, 80.
[78] Martin Van Crevefeld, "Build a Wall to the Sky," *Newsweek*, April 1, 2002, p.24.

under Christian influence lose a loved one they say that the funeral service is a celebration of life, and during the ceremonies to mark the passing of their loved ones they hold carnival-like festivals in which they distribute souvenirs. In 2010 my room-mate in the hospital in Maiduguri town that I had gone to for some surgeries died. He was Kanuri, barely thirty. Truly his younger brother who came with him to the hospital grieved, but not for more than thirty minutes. I was impelled to make my observations available to one of the surgeons that was treating me. The comment of the doctor who was Igbo was that they (the Kanuri, and their neighbours) mourn, but are more easily consoled than us (the Igbos). The Kanuri is a Nigerian ethnic group that inhabit the extreme north-eastern part of Nigeria.

Among the Igbos as soon as it is certain that the ailing has died the relatives will start turning the mirrors and the photographs in the house, to face the wall. Like a lot of the things the Igbos do, this customary practice of turning photographs and mirrors seemed odd to me, because the Igbos had forgotten the rationale for this practice, until I studied the *Jewish Catalogue* and saw its parallel as a Jewish practice[79].The Jewish practice is also repeated in Rabbi Jacques Cukierkorn's, *Accessible Judaism*[80], and he gives the reason for the practice: "The mirror is a symbol of human vanity which is out of place in a house of mourning."

It is an Igbo requirement that all the close kin of the deceased should start gathering as soon as death occurs. In the Igbo case this includes all the family members. I think that Israel in Genesis 25:9 told us

---

[79] Siegal, Richard, Strassfeld, Sharon, Strassfeld, Michael, *The First Jewish Catalogue* (Philadelphia: The Jewish Publication Society of America, 1999) 174.
[80] Cukierkon, Jacques, *Accessible Judaism* (Booksjustbooks.com, in cooperation with Solving Light Books, 2004) 100.

what I just mentioned as an Igbo practice, in the following statement "... and Isaac and Ishmael his sons buried him, ...." i.e., that the family has to gather to mourn and bury its dead. The Igbo family is more like the Hebrew family, and is much bigger than the 'family' in many other cultures. It includes even the in-laws of the deceased. Informants would be sent out to inform everybody that is related to the deceased and his/her family.

When the informants get to the persons concerned, they use diversionary and soft words/statements like- 'the sick person is not getting better', to prepare the recipients for the main news which would still be delivered with soft deliberative words like 'onye di otua a hapu na' (such a person (the sick person) has departed). An Igbo would not go and announce 'onye a anwuo na'(this person has died). Alfred J. Kolatch presents Jewish custom as parallelizing Igbo practice on this subject. In his words:"The very word and expressions for death and dying used throughout Jewish literature–from the Bible onward–reflect the Jewish desire to soften the shock and trauma experienced by the mourner. Pleasant words are substituted for harsh ones....When Jacob died, the Bible recounts, he "drew his feet into the bed and breathing his last, was gathered to his people[81]."

Meanwhile the relatives who were present when the death occurred will commence the washing of the body. Igbo belief is that a person who participates in the washing of a corpse of a relative has done an honourable and loving thing. Quite a lot of Igbo beliefs are locked up in Igbo sayings. The good Igbo who has decent filial feelings is sometimes referred to as *nwanne*

---

[81] Kolatch J, Alfred. (New York: Jonathan David Publishers Inc, 1996) pp.1-2.

*ozu na aghu ozu ahu*, which means the relative of the deceased that washes his or her corpse. This saying expresses the high regard which the Igbos have for whoever performed the act, and the high esteem in which she is held.

G.T. Basden's observations gives us an idea of how some Igbos washed corpses in earlier times: "Two 'adas' (*ada* in the Igbo system mean close female relatives) are then commanded to bring two small pots of water. They stand one on the right and the other on the left of the corpse. They dip their hands into the water and make passes over the face and continue right down the body to the feet. This is repeated until it has been done four times[82]."

Basden continued:"Camwood dye is next taken and a fourfold passing over the face and body is made similarly to that done with the water. Then follows a fourfold passing with razors ('aguba'). The whole constitutes the symbolical form of: 1. Washing; 2. Anointing; 3. Shaving, and all combined together, ceremonial cleansing. The first two are in general practice; the third is omitted in some parts[83]."

*The Jewish Catalogue* states: "The practice of *taharah*, the ritual washing of the body, is an absolute requirement of Jewish law[84]."

Ganzfried and Goldin contributed the following: "The purification of the body is done as follows. The entire

---

[82] G. T. Basden *Niger Ibos* (London: Frank Cass and Co., Ltd., 1966) 271-2.
[83] ibid. 272.
[84] Siegal, Richard, Strassfeld, Sharon, Strassfeld, Michael, *The First Jewish Catalogue* (Philadelphia: The Jewish Publication Society of America, 1999) 174.

body, including the head, is washed with warm water[85]."

It needn't be emphasized that the Igbo and Israelite practices are very similar on the subject of the washing of the body. The similarity is very clear.

After the corpse has been cleaned, it is dressed up in the best from the deceased's wardrobe.

It is then enshrouded in a mat, and laid on a bed for some period. The *umuokpu* (daughters) of the family will sit around the corpse in a ritual ceremony called *ida abani* singing mourning and funeral dirges.

As the time for burial approaches, -most likely half a day, or slightly more- after the death occurred, for some people a simple coffin made from reeds—*ute ekwere*—is procured, and the body is put inside it. Meanwhile the mourning will be going on. Relatives and friends will be trooping in to commiserate with the immediate kin: The members of the beveaved's extended family have the duty to come with food for the principal mourners, and for feeding visitors, so that their mourning relatives will concentrate on mourning. The male relatives of the dead will be receiving sympathizers where they will sit apart in the front of the *obi*, in an *owoko* (mourning canopy/tent). And from the women relatives, where they sit in the women's quarters, loud wailing will inevitably be issuing, while in the men's area, talk will be going on in subdued tones.

Basic Igbo tradition is that a body must be buried as soon as possible. So while friends and relatives are walking in, and commiserating with the bereaved, depositing cloths, some of which may be buried with the

---

[85] Ganzfried, Solomon, and Hyman E.Goldin, trans., *Code of Jewish Law and Customs (Shulhan Aruch)* (New York: Hebrew Publishing Company, 1961) 105.

deceased, young men from the kindred of the deceased will be digging the grave.

Igbo custom demands that no grave digger must hand over the digging implement to another. When a digger gets tired he will drop the implement on the ground, and another will pick it up and continue. They will continue until the grave is at least six feet or seven feet deep, then the body is brought out in its shroud or coffin and kept beside the grave.

The oldest man in the deceased's family, who by Igbo tradition plays priestly roles, takes charge from that moment. He will bring out his *ofo* (stick or rod akin to the staff of Aaron), and will pray that the deceased should be guided by Chukwu in his journey to his fathers. The body is then lowered into the grave, buried and covered firmly with earth.

It is remarkable that the Igbos view anybody who touched a corpse as deserving to be ritually cleansed. Mathew O. Orji wrote: "Those who carried the dead body were not allowed to enter any dwelling house until water was carried outside for them to bathe. It was after taking their bath during which they washed out all their contact with the dead that they could be allowed to mingle with the living[86]."

In my clan Ozubulu those that touched a corpse will in addition to the ritual bath, also have their hands cleansed with *akwukwo oji* (the leaves of the kola nut tree).

There are different stages of mourning. The immediate family of the deceased must compulsorily be in a state of sobriety for one year, during which they will dress in

---

[86] Orji, Mathew O, *The History & Culture Of The Igbo People* (Nkpor: Jet Publishers (Nig.), Ltd., 1999) p. 36.

mourning clothes. For some days they must not work, i.e., during the period of intense mourning which is seven days. After twenty-eight or thirty days, which include the seven days- counting from the day of death, friends and relatives will come for what is called *izu ozuzu*. I can't really say that I understood what this tradition stood for until I saw its equivalent in Jewish tradition.

However the foregoing having been taken note of, I will go ahead and point out some remarkable features of the Igbo burial custom which are similar to Israel's.

A thing no Igbo family would like to even contemplate is burial of their loved one in a strange land. And in this case what the Igbo consider to be a strange land is anywhere outside the deceased's *ana obi* (his share of his ancestral land in his clan). We saw Jacob in Genesis 47:29-30 and Joseph in Genesis 50:25 emphasizing that they would prefer their remains to be finally interred in their own land (Canaan/Israel). I mentioned that the Igbos would not hand over an implement to another during the grave-digging. Remarkably this custom is found to be Jewish too. Ganzfried and Goldin expresses:"It is the prevailing custom not to take from the hand of another, a shovel or pickaxe, with which the burial was performed; but the one who used it lays it down and the other takes it up[87]."

Igbos would not leave uncovered a freshly dug grave. Also graves must not be prepared in readiness for the ailing. But when a person has died and a grave is dug for him, that grave must be covered with *igu nkwu* (palm fronds) if the relatives must wait till morning before interring him, as the Igbos don't bury the dead at night.

---

[87] Ganzfried, Solomon, and Goldin, Hyman E., trans., *Code of Jewish Law and Customs (Shulhan Aruch)* (New York: Hebrew Publishing Company, 1961) 105.

Jewish Law in the *Shulhan Arukh*, translated by Ganzfried and Goldin states: "A freshly dug grave must not be left open over night[88]."

The Igbo mourning period corresponds roughly to the Jewish. The first seven days after death, the period that Jews call those of sitting *shiva* the Igbos will not engage in any kind of work. Twenty-eight to thirty days will still elapse after the burial before the *izu ozuzu* ceremony is held. After this ceremony, which is a sort of ending of serious mourning, the relatives can return to semi-normal life. From Rabbi Jacques Cukierkorn I got the information that opened up what has become a formal and lifeless ritual to the Igbos: Cukierkorn wrote:"The first month after death is known as *'sh'loshim'*, the thirty days of mourning (which includes the seven days of *shiva*). During this period, the mourners return to work, but abstain from attending festive occasions; they are not to visit places of amusement and they are to avoid listening to music[89].

Among the Igbos it would be deemed utter irresponsibility for a person whose relative died to be seen engaging in normal activities before the *izu ozuzu*. From the facts available, this period of *sh'loshim* is the same as the period before *izu ozuzu* to the Igbos.

I am from Ozubulu, an Igbo clan. Ozubulu still observes Igbo funeral traditions. My mother died on the thirteenth of March 2006. When we held her funeral we observed all the rites for her, including the *izu ozuzu*.

As I have mentioned before, this study is not about the whole funeral practices of the Igbos. The study on that

---

[88] ibid, p.105.
[89] Cukierkorn, Jacques, *Accessible Judaism* (Booksjustbooks.com, in cooperation with Solving Light Books, 2004) 101.

has been started in *The Igbos: Jews In Africa? Vol 1.* This exercise is the study of the basic traditions of the Igbos and a comparison of them with the traditions of Israel.

Anyone really interested in feeling Igbo mourning without attending an Igbo funeral, has to listen to a song by an Igbo musician called Show Promoter[90]. In this song entitled *Celestine Ukwu*, which is about how two young Igbo men, Celestine Ukwu (a great Igbo musician) and Edmund nwa Osumenyi (a Maiduguri-based businessman), who died in car crashes were mourned. A promoter, whose real name was Nelson Ejinduaka captured the Igbo mourning mood very wonderfully. He got it to the basic details. You must listen to the song to feel it, to feel the power expressed in a simple statement like "boys a na ebe akwa" (young men were crying).

**Ikwa mmadu na ndu (sitting shiva for the living)**

The Igbos and the Jews share the custom of holding funerals for those who are still alive, i.e., they mourn the living as if they have died. They do this for persons who commit very heinous offences, i.e, for persons who have died spiritually.

In Igbo-land a person who commits "ife ana na aso nso'"(what the land forbids), i.e abominable things could merit this fate. And after his compatriots have mourned him they would have no further dealings with him. As far as they are concerned he is dead.

American Jewish writer Stephen Dubner in his book *Turbulent Souls* described very vividly how a wounded father sat *shiva* for his offending son.

---

[90] Show Promoter, (Nelson Ejinduaka), Igbo musician.

Some of the author's kinsmen, of the Umu Ezeanyaezughu kindred group, observing the *izu ozuzu* (shloshim) - the memorial after thirty days of death for the author's mother, Pauline Ilona, in 2006, at the Joseph Ilona homestead in Ugwuoye, Ozubulu.

# CHAPTER FOUR: Feasts and Festivals

### Emume Iri Ji (The New Yam Festival)

This is the feast during which the Igbos thank Chukwu (the Great God) for blessing them with good harvests. Its similarities with the Biblical feast mentioned in Exodus 23:16, which was called the feast of harvest are too numerous to be overlooked. The Igbo model like the Israelite model specifies "and none shall appear before Me (God) empty (handed)."

It has relatively few rituals. All adult members of a clan will dig up a few choice yams from their farms, and go to the *okwu chi/ana* (central shrine) of their clan to deposit them.

They may also come with chickens. On the day of the feast, the *Eze Mmuo* (Chief Priest) of the clan will offer prayers to Chukwu, for giving the community a good yield in crops. He will also slaughter a few of the chickens, sprinkle their blood on the altar at the *okwu chi/ana*. He will also gum the feathers of the roosters on the blood.

Once he finishes, the feasting can start. All the slaughtered animals will be collected and cooked together with a good number of yams. This meal will be eaten by the entire community together.

As soon as the eating is over, real merriment takes over. The men will start displaying their masquerades, while the maidens will start dancing. The merriment and feasting can continue for a day or two. After that the people can be free to start digging up their yams to eat, when they feel like.

In the words of Igbo writer Mathew O. Orji[91], "after the feast, women and girls formed separate circles, and danced in groups." This is revealing. According to Joseph J. Williams, S.J; quoting Edward Scott, he offered:

"Among the Jews dancing was always regarded as a becoming expression of religious fervor and joyful emotion: The Jews in early times, like the Greeks and Egyptians, introduced dancing in all their great religious festivals. For instance, at the festival of the first-fruits the whole population of a town would turn out. A procession was formed, headed by flute players, and the virgins danced to the music as they went along. At the feast of Tabernacles or of Ingathering, also, the young people danced around the altar, which was decorated with bunches of poplar osiers[92]".

Matthew O. Orji[93] states that the Igbos knew when to celebrate the feast by the appearance of the new moon. In his words:

"The first person to see the new moon would shout with joy and say: look at the sky-the moon for the new yam festival is out."

He also wrote that once this new moon, known as *onwa asato* (eight month) by the Igbos appears then the festival will be 12 days away.

Another Igbo scholar[94] also mentioned the *onwa asato*. I have no way of finding out at the present time if they referred to the native Igbo lunar-solar calendar or the

---

[91] Orji, Mathew O., *The History & Culture Of The Igbo People* (Nkpor: Jet Publishers (Nig.), Ltd., 1999). 63.
[92] Williams, Joseph J, S.J, *Hebrewisms of West*, p.50.
[93] Orji, Mathew O., *The History & Culture Of The Igbo People* (Nkpor: Jet Publishers (Nig.), Ltd., 1999), 58.
[94] Ogbalu, F. C., *Omenala Igbo*, (Lagos: University Publishing Co. Academy Press, 1979).

Julian calendar. But I can say that the feast is generally done when the new yams are due for harvesting.

### Oriri Achicha (Passover and unleavened bread)

At a particular time of the year the various Igbo clans celebrate a feast that is akin to the Biblical feast of Passover and Unleavened Bread. But unlike the New Yam festival its celebration is no longer widespread. Only few Igbo clans still commemorate it. One such clan is Item in the present-day Abia state of Nigeria. Obadiah Agbai, who heads the famous Igbo-Jewish synagogue; Gihon, Abuja, a retired civil servant and an indigene of Item recalls that no more than five years ago, that he participated in this feast, which is called *oriri achicha kpor' nku* (feast of dried bread).

According to him, in the days preceding this feast his clansmen ate only *achicha kpor' nku* (dried bread). Igbos understand *achicha* to mean dried bread, i.e., bread that is not leavened. According to Agbai, in his community cocoyam is used to make this *achicha*. He said that what is used as seasoning for the feast is *utazi* (the leaf of a bitter herb) that is strangely and uniquely important in the Igbo diet. This bitter leaf recalls the bitter herbs eaten in the Passover seder,

Agbai said that on the last day of this feast, the entire clan congregated in the centre of the clan, and with the chief priest and the elders leading, the whole congregation started walking into the bush/wilds at a fast clip. He said that the walk lasted for up to one hour. He said that when they were well clear of the clan, that they paused, and the chief priest spoke certain words which he couldn't recall, and then turned. The whole clan followed suit, and leisurely everybody started walking back. I think that the fast walk into the bush/forest is akin to the Israelites escape from Egypt. Several persons from other Igbo clans, particularly clans from the Afikpo area of Igbo-land, remember what could be traces of this feast.

Revealingly also, the most popular Jewish Passover *seder* song about the one kid (Had Gadya) has an Igbo variant which I presented in Chapter 20.

### Ima ntu (Sukkot)

For this particular feast, during which the Igbos make small booths of palm fronds and straw, and dwell in them for a number of days; we don't have some of the problems that we have with the *oriri achicha*. This is because a very important Igbo clan still observes it annually.

*Ntu* means booth in the dialect of Umuoji(the Igbo clan that observes it) so *uno ntu* means booth- house. After the construction of these booths, many of the men will move to the booths, and dwell in them for some days. Food will be prepared by the women-folk, and brought to the booths for the feeding of the in-mates of the *uno ntu*. This lasts for some days. On the last day of the feast, the people stage masquerade fiestas, and in play they destroy the booths. There is much eating, drinking and inevitably dancing, of the sort mentioned in the section on new yam festival.

Umuoji is a clan in Idemili Local Government Area of Anambra State, Igbo territory, Nigeria. A visitor to this clan around the last months of the year will likely witness this feast which reminds one of the Biblical call on the children of Israel to dwell in booths for seven days every year so that they will remember where they dwelt as the God of Israel transported them from Egypt to Israel.

## Eke Ukwu/Nkwo Oru (Sabbath)

The Igbo people observe a day of rest, that generally comes around every seven[95] to eight days. This day is one of much feasting and rejoicing. In ancient times when farming was the main occupation of most Igbos some had farms around their compounds, while some had farms in outlying districts. What this means is that some leave their homes for extended periods occasionally, in order to be near their farms. But on certain days, one thing is noticeable, those at home will start preparing for a feast as the sun starts to go down, while those who were in the farms outside the inhabited areas of the clan would be seen rushing back to join in the preparations for the feast. In my clan Ozubulu the feast in question is akin to the Jewish Sabbath. In the Egbema sub-clan it was celebrated on Nkwo oru days; while in the Eziora sub-clan it is celebrated on the Eke ukwu days. Egbema is no longer strict about the feast, that is why I mentioned its observance of Nkwo oru in the past tense. But it is still remembered vividly in Egbema that people just feast and rest on Nkwo oru days.

In this chapter I will concentrate on Eziora, and its observance of Eke ukwu as a day of rest.

The Igbo day starts from sunset, and ends on the next sunset. Quoting an Igbo scholar on this would be helpful: "Before the white man came to Igbo-land with his clock, a new day began at sun-set in Igbo-land. It was also observed like that by the Israelis. Even today for an example, the Sabbath day in Israel is observed on

---

[95] Williams, Joseph J. *Hebrewisms of West Africa: From the Nile to the Niger with the Jews.* (New York: Biblo and Tanem, 1928).

Saturday. But its observance begins on the evening of Friday[96]."

A discussion of the Igbo week and its structure is a must if any headway can be made in understanding how the Eke ukwu day in Eziora is approximate to the seventh-day Sabbath of Israel. Every Igbo clan has what we call market days. These market days are called Orie, Afor, Nkwo and Eke. Markets are held on these four days. It is these market days that some persons call the Igbo week., but as we will see shortly, these four days do not make an Igbo week.The first four days is designated by the Igbos as *izu nta*- the real meaning of this term is not clear, but in this modern era, some persons say it means 'small week'. The next four days is the *izu ukwu*— which we shall take to mean big 'week'[97] here, but which may mean something else. In Eziora, the first *eke* day, i.e., the one in the *izu nta* is an ordinary day, but the second *eke*, i.e., the one in the *izu ukwu*, is a day that the Eziora sub-clan of Ozubulu would never do any kind of work on. Funerals are not held, and marriages are also not celebrated. The people just rest. And till the present time, perhaps no Eziora man can go beyond stating that it is a tradition handed down by our fathers, as the reason for its observance.

In Eziora the indigenes would not work, and they would also prohibit non indigenes from working on Eke ukwu days.

Research shows that many of the neigbours of the Igbos, such as the Edo, Igala, Idoma, Ibibio, Urhobo, etc, have four days weekly arrangements, and some even have a set apart day in each of the weeks, which shouldn't be

---

[96] Orji, Mathew O., *The History & Culture Of The Igbo People* (Nkpor: Jet Publishers (Nig.), Ltd., 1999) 8.
[97] G. T. Basden, *Niger Ibos*, (London: Frank Cass and Co., Ltd., 1966) 151.

too strange as traces of a set apart day were also found in ancient Egyptian practices; i.e., it wasn't exclusively Hebraic to have a set-apart day, but none of the aforementioned groups had any of their days of rest falling on the seventh/eighth day, as that of the Igbos does. Also their set apart days were not for rest.

Remarkably Israel's Sabbath is on the seventh day.

# CHAPTER FIVE: Socio-Religious Customs

## Inye / icho oji na isa asisa oji (offering of kola nut and apologizing for its unavailability)

By Igbo custom a visitor must be given kola nut. Or more appropriately kola nut must be shared with visitors. And when and if the host can't fulfill his obligation to offer a kola nut to his visitor, he has to apologize for his failure to do so.

The kola nut which is a product of the *sterculia acuminata* and *macro carpa* is a small roundish nut which is always almost bitter in taste. It is a common plant in most parts of West Africa. The Igbos call the species that is found in Igbo-land *oji Igbo* (Igbo kola).

Igbos don't just bring out the kola nut, offer it to visitors, and then begin to eat. Sharing the nut with visitors is an exercise filled with rituals.

The nut is first offered to the visitor who returns it to his host with a small speech of appreciation. Rabbi Howard Gorin, an American Jewish rabbi who used to visit Igbo-land frequently, visited the Abia State University in 2008. His experience with the - was quite fascinating and was carried by the ibo-benei-yisrael@yahoogroups.com web discussion group, and the Kulanu newsletter. When Gorin accepted the kola nut, and handed it back to the vice chancellor of the university, with the right words: "oji eze di eze na aka" (the kola nut has gone back to the host), the Igbos who were gathered were happy.

Prayers always accompany the sharing of kola nuts. In my part of Igbo-land, it is the prerogative of the host to say the prayer and break the nut, which is then carried to the visitor/visitors by the youngest person around.

The kola nut offering tells us a lot of important, but now obscure things about Igbo culture.

In gatherings, in my clan, if all the persons who are present are descendants of the legendary four sons of the founder of Ozubulu, then the oldest descendant of Amakwa, the oldest son of Ozubulu, will pray and break the kola nut. And the youngest descendant of Nza, the youngest son of Ozubulu, will share the nuts. However if the gathering is in the territory of any of the other sub-clans of Ozubulu, then that sub-clan may waive their right as host to the eldest (Amakwa), or they may chose to exercise their right.

The area that I want to concentrate on in this study is the kola nut as evidence that being hospitable is religious in spirit with the Igbos, and that the Igbos have the belief that material blessings have to be shared.

G.T. Basden wrote thus of the custom:

"The ancient custom of sharing kola nut is a typical instance. This was always observed when a visitor called at a house, whether a humble one or a palace. If the owner was too poor, or for some other reason unable to offer the nut, he would always apologize for the seeming lack of courtesy. He would make the visitor feel that he was genuinely sorry for his inability to fulfil the time honoured custom. The welcome is not complete without the sharing of the nut. When circumstances prevent fulfillment, the owner apologizes. The Ibo are a friendly people[98]." To the Igbos sharing of kola nut with visitors symbolizes good will, friendship and a spirit of hospitality.

Very careful analysis reveals that the ideas underlying the ritual are that a visitor must be received with friendliness, and must be given refreshment too. To the Igbos, a man or woman who may have traveled from somewhere, maybe far, under the sun, parched, hungry and thirsty, deserves succor, and not merely in words, but in substance.

The life of Abraham the Hebrew Patriarch parallels the Igbo model in hospitality. All visitors that passed his dwellings were welcomed warmly and offered refreshments. The Hebrews did not just welcome their visitors verbally; they gave them food. Some persons have argued that modern Jews who descended from Abraham do not know about kola nut, and do not offer them to visitors, but in the same vein I argue too that Abraham did not know of, nor did he offer lager beer to his visitors as some modern Jews such as myself do (in this era). To the Igbo the kola nut represents the first course in the meal, which will surely follow the verbal welcome. Also some writers have postulated that offering succor to passers-by and visitors was common to all Eastern peoples. Even though it is not easy to determine what they mean by Eastern peoples, I hold that that is not true. The peoples of Sodom and Gomorrah were Eastern peoples, but they were not known to be hospitable and friendly to strangers. From the studies that I have conducted, I have arrived at the conclusion that exercising hospitality the way that I have described is unique to the Hebrews. Accordingly

---

[98] G. T. Basden, *Among The Ibos of Nigeria* (London: University Publishing Company, 1921) 161.

any 'Eastern people' who show hospitality the way I described may have cultural connections with the Hebrews. In Nigeria only among the Igbos is hospitality to the stranger observed as I have described it, i.e., as a compulsory obligation. Thus an honest conclusion that can be drawn on this subject is that hospitality is a Hebraic religious tradition. Among the Igbos it is considered ethical for someone to 'ikpo oku nni', i.e., to invite any nearby person to join him while he is eating. A person who does not invite his neighbours to eat with him is deemed to be unethical.

The offering of kola nut to visitors is one of the customs of the Igbos that the real rationale for their observance have been lost with time. But as I have written elsewhere in this book, old habits die hard. Quite a lot of the basic Igbo traditions keep on being observed, albeit automatically and mechanically. For example the observance of the one in question impelled G. T. Basden to note: "the Ibo is very hospitable[99]."

Igbo author F. C. Ogbalu opines that *inye oji* (being hospitable) is one of the evidences that many persons cite as evidence that Igbos and Jews came from one stock[100].

## Igba Ndu (entering into covenants)

If two or more Igbos have dealings, or had dealings, and one or more of them develop fear that due to ill-feelings arising out of their transaction that any of the parties nurses grudges, and that that may cause the party to think or plan to harm or hurt the others, the

---

[99] G. T. Basden, *Niger Ibos*, (London: Frank Cass and Co., Ltd., 1966) 43.
[100] Ogbalu, F. C., *Omenala Igbo*, (Lagos: University Publishing Co. Academy Press, 1979) 24.

apprehensive party may call for them to enter into what the Igbos call *igba ndu* (covenant).

J.U.T. Nzeako, a scholar of Igbo religion and traditions, describes *igba ndu* thus: "Igba ndu bu mmeko, nriko na njiko mmadu abuo, m o karia otu ahu ka onye obula ghara itu onye ozo ujo, bo onye ozo ebubo, ma eleghi anya, malite iche echiche ojoo[101]."

Translated the above means:

Covenant (*Igba ndu*) is an agreement between two or more persons that they will not think of, or take actions that could be harmful to one another.

Among the Igbos *igba ndu* involves the following:

The parties that want to enter into this ritual covenant will gather or assemble before the *okwu ana* (community shrine) of their clan. In ancient times most Igbo dealings were within clans or families, so most likely the parties would be from the same clan. But if they are from the same family they would then assemble before their *okwu Mmuo* (family shrine).

If they gather at the *okwu ana*, the chief priest or *eze Mmuo /eze ana* (chief priest) of the clan would supervise, but if it is before the *okwu Mmuo*, the *aka ji ofo* or family elder will supervise.

The ceremony is a simple one. The supervising person will make the following declaration:

"If I think ill of you, or about you, or for you, or try to harm you by any means, may I die." The parties to the covenant will repeat it in turns. When they finish repeating it, kola nut will be broken, and they will eat it. In time some communities added the practice of getting

---

[101] Nzeako, Tagbo, *Omenala Ndi Igbo* (Lagos: Longman Nigeria PLC, 1972) 64.

the parties to prick their skins hard enough to draw blood, smearing the kola nut with the blood which will be allowed to inter-mingle and getting all the covenantors to eat the nuts.

What Jacob and Laban did as we see in Genesis 31:44, is similar:

Laban started thus: "And now come, let us make a covenant, I and thou."

And in verse 52 of the same chapter: Laban declared:

"This heap be witness ... that I will not pass over this heap to thee and that thou shalt not pass over this heap to me for harm."

The similarity also extends to the scene of the covenant. The Igbo *igba ndu* is done before the *okwu Mmuo* and *okwu ana*, which are really heaps or mounds of earth, and Jacob and Laban did theirs over or near a heap of stones.

**Ibu Ihu (Tithe)**

Translating *ibu ihu* to English will help us only a little, because while *ibu* will be translated to 'to carry', I cannot find the meaning of *ihu* in contemporary Igbo language in the context in discussion. But this is not to say that some Igbos may not know the meaning of the word which is pronounced '*nghru*' in some Igbo clans.

I will resort to a graphic description of it as a means of studying and understanding it.

In my clan Ozubulu, after the harvest of crops, heads of families will start coming to visit the overall heads of their families (*aka ji ofo*) with baskets of yams, roosters and goats. When they arrive they will declare that they have come with their *ihu*. These offerings are brought to the *aka-ji-ofo*, in trust, and his responsibility is to share them.

The following is from my recollection of what I witnessed when my late father was the *aka-ji-ofo* (kindred/family elder-priest) of the Ilona household. Some relatives arrived with baskets of yams and roosters, most of which were cooked and eaten communally. But a few were reserved for my father. The fore-arm of the animal *(aka anu)* was always reserved for him.

This tradition started to make sense to me after I had read and re-read Deuteronomy 14: 22-28, which stipulates that the most important tithe, in food form, should be brought to a place of worship of the Lord, where it should be eaten by the contributor and his household, the poor, the widows, the orphans, and the Levite.

In the Igbo case the *Umu Nri* (some Igbos who are very much like the Levites) who had settled in many Igbo clans/families benefitted from this offering.

# CHAPTER SIX: Aru (abomination) and Ikpu Aru (purifications)

**Igbo and Israelite Concept of Abominations**

I observed that the Igbo and Israelite minds react similarly to some ideas and events. Typically both peoples are particularly horrified and revolted by evils that are heinous enough to be identified as *aru* (abomination).

The English word that most closely approximates the Igbo term *aru* in meaning is abomination.

To the Igbos *aru* or *alu* is any evil that is so abhorrent that it should not even be heard by the ears. Interestingly an Ashkenazi Jew, Jack Zeller, who founded and headed the Jewish organization Kulanu Inc', asked the author the following question about abomination, and made the accompanying comment: "I wonder if you have ever heard the Hebrew word for abomination blurted out? When blurted out it has a unique and harsh deep throat sound[102]!"

The harshness of the word for abomination *(aru)* in Hebrew certainly correlates with the Igbo idea that an *aru* (abominable doing) is something that is so bad that it should not even be heard by the ear. Because as the word is harsh in Hebrew, it would do what harsh things or words do to the ear: it would hurt it. Igbos habitually and instinctively try to keep *aru* at arms and ears length by expressing 'k am wer' uriom gbapu aru n'aka'(let me use my fingers to totally repudiate abomination). Then the person 'a gbaa uriom'(join the thumbs and middle

---

[102]Personal communication with Jack Zeller, first president, Kulanu Inc.

fingers of both hands together, bring both to the back of the head, cirle the head, and snap the joined fingers. Igbos would also plug their ears when they hear abominable things being uttered.

The following illustrates some of the things that the Igbos saw as abominable, and how they tried to react to some of them.

The Igbos would see the act of a child rebelling against the parents as *aru kwo nwa* (double abomination).

In an Igbo historical story which came to us as literature, an Igbo described the early mission school thus:"The evil gathering which heaven forbid and the earth abhors[103]."

The example in the story which is reproduced below; about some tactics deployed by the officials of the schools opened by Christian missionaries during the colonization of the Igbos, and their attitudes to their hosts (the Igbos) is quite illustrative, and it moved the Igbos to see the institutions as abominable: The story which will follow shortly is about the arbitrariness deployed by a missionary school master against his host (the Igbos). The following lines tell the story: "His father came to the school to remove him, and master ordered us to drive the old pagan out[104]."

This is about a boy whose uncle took to the mission school against the wishes of his father, and when the distraught father went to the school in protest, the above-quoted lines described what happened. The school masters referred to the Igbos (their hosts) as pagans, and taught the Igbos that followed them to view

---

[103] Munonye, John, *The Only Son*, (Ibadan: Heinemann Educational Books, 1966) 58.
[104] ibid. 85.

the entire Igbo people as such, and themselves, as redeemed pagans.

G.T. Basden was absolutely right in stating that contact with education and civilization caused age-old valid customs like respect for elders to start disappearing.[105]

An Igbo musician, Show Promoter, in his song entitled *Chukwuemeka* also gave us an idea of what the Igbos consider to be *aru*. In the story, the chief of Umuaka clan connived in miscarriage of justice, and Promoter sang "Chief Umuaka mer' aru" (the chief of Umuaka clan had committed abomination). In another song which which was about a man that forcefully had carnal knowledge of his own daughter, Promoter presented the girl protesting "oo aru!" (it is abomination!).

This section reminds me of my mother who died in March 2006 (I wrote this in August 2006). When I was young I always heard her saying 'oo aru!' (it is abomination) whenever reports came in that somebody had done something that was really bad.

When Igbos started to settle outside Igbo-land, they began to join the religious and social organizations of other peoples. Inevitably in time their adherence to *Omenana* weakened, and 'ime aru'(to commit abomination) gradually ceased to be unthinkable to the city dwelling Igbos. In other words they began to emulate the peoples that they lived with, and began to behave and think like them. With time they began to commit abominations.

An Igbo writer, Edmund Ilogu (1974) stated:

"For Igbos *aru* (and its commission) includes the connotation of contravention of *Omenani*.[106]"

---

[105] Basden, G. T., *Niger Ibos*, (London: Frank Cass and Co., Ltd., 1966) 421.

## Chapter 6: Abomination and Purifications    123

The reader may need to reflect on what Omenana is, i.e,. the significance and importance of Omenana to the Igbos by comparing it to the Israelite commandment, statutes and laws of God. The suggested reflection will help the reader to understand why the Igbos have absolute revulsion for *aru* (abomination) and anything or any institution that seemed to be propagating it.

I will mention a few infractions of the rules that stand out as *aru* among the Igbos.

I read the following recently: "Everybody in this village and in the entire Nawfia town had condemned him and dissociated themselves from his atrocious act, saying he committed abomination[107]."

The fellow who was referred to had demolished the house of the person that made the speech, a widow.

I will analyze the quoted statement carefully. The accusing lady mentioned 'atrocious act' and 'abomination.' The Igbo people do not mention abomination lightly. In fact in Igbo society we have two classes of offences, *aru* (abomination) and *arurumana* (minor misdemeanors). *Arurumana* could be farting during meal-times, defecating in a sowed field, etc. But *aru* is as I have alluded to it, those things that the ears should not even hear; those things the law of the land forbid.

So in effect the lady was saying that the man had polluted and defiled himself and the land by committing an abomination. And the Igbos know that abominations are not normal doings. We can deduce this from the words of an Igbo dignitary who commented on the case:

---

[106] Adegbola, Ade E. A. *Traditional Religion in West Africa* (Ibadan: Sefer Books, 1983) 19.
[107] *Saturday Sun,* November 19, 2005, p. 9.

"You know in Igbo-land when you see this kind of thing there, you know what it means ... We as custodians of the town can't leave this thing to go like that[108]."

The offence is identical to the offence of oppressing widows, that Deuteronomy 24:17-21, which recommends that thou must be kind and considerate to the widow, seeks to forestall.

**Other Things or Acts that the Igbos Consider Abominations:**

A man having carnal knowledge of his mother, sister or his father's wives.

And the parallel to the Igbo position is found in Israel. Jacob notably took Reuben's (his eldest son's) wife in violation of this rule against having carnal knowledge of one's father's wife very seriously, and practically withdrew the privileges of the first-born son from him because of it (Genesis 49:3-4).

A man committing adultery with his brother's wife or the wife of a member of the family with whom there is blood relationship.

*Ikwu udo* (suicide by hanging). This point deserves a little commentary. The Igbos regard someone who committed suicide as a prime sinner against God. To the Igbos, he should be denied the honour of a decent burial. His corpse is thrown away, in the wilds. This practice is still very much in vogue in much of Igbo-land. It is noteworthy that the Biblical position on the suicide parallels the Igbo position. Deuteronomy 21:23 provides: "for a hanged man is accursed by God". To the Igbos his body is a defiled, profane object which can

---

[108] ibid. 9.

only be handled after certain rituals have been done, and the handlers must be purified after.

The explanation of Alfred J. Kolatch, a Jewish author, somehow echoes the Igbo position. According to him, "since honest words of praise cannot be spoken for those who have taken their own lives, the Talmud and Code of Jewish Law forbid eulogizing suicides[109]."

Kolatch also notes; "Those who were known to be fully aware of their action (suicide) are buried at a distance of at least six feet (four amot) from other graves . . . Among the Falashas (Beta Israel) of Ethiopia, suicides were traditionally not buried in the Jewish cemetery[110]."

G.T. Basden added major misdeeds against Native law and custom as things that are abominations to the Igbos[111]:

Having sexual intercourse with animals.

Having sexual intercourse with a woman who is having her menstrual flow[112].

Very interestingly, the Bible regards all these acts as abominations before the Lord.

The similarities between Igbo traditions and the Biblical laws become very clear when one considers that indulging in any of the proscribed sexual practices in Leviticus 18, amounts to abominations before God.

---

[109] Kolatch, Alfred., *The Jewish Mourners Book of Why* (New York: Jonathan David Publishers, Inc., 1993/96) 75.
[110] ibid. 97.
[111] Basden, G. T., *Niger Ibos* (London: Frank Cass and Co., Ltd., 1966) 60.
[112] Adegbola, Ade, E. A., *Traditional Religion in West Africa* (Ibadan: Sefer Books, 1983) 19.

Leviticus 18:27 succinctly expresses: "For all these abominations have the men of the land done, that were before you, and the land is defiled."

And in the expression that abominations defile the land another parallel between the Igbo and Israelite system is established.

E.A. Ade Adegbola made some interesting comparisons between the Igbo *aru*, and its equivalent in the Hebrew language. In order to present his position lucidly I will quote him *in extenso*:

Abomination and filth.

Onitsha Igbo *lu* is "to be abominable or horrible, to defile, be spoiled" (Owerri Igbo—*ru*).

*Melu* is "to defile, desecrate" (- me—*lu*) "make abominable."

*Alu* is "abomination: pollution, harmful, obnoxious thing, taboo" (Owerri Igbo *aru*).

*Me alu* is "to commit abomination, to break a taboo, to do something traditionally forbidden."

*lu alu* shows the cognate verb *lu* and means " to be defiled, corrupt- to commit an abomination."

Igbo *alu* is cognate with Hebrew hol "profaneness, commonness"—the opposite of holiness (Leviticus 10:10).

The cognate Hebrew verb is *halal /hallel* "to be polluted/"pollute, defile, profane[113]."

---

[113] Adegbola, Ade E. A., *Traditional Religion in West Africa* (Ibadan: Sefer Books, 1983) 18.

## Ikpu Aru (to cleanse or purify the land of abomination)

As I have mentioned repeatedly in this work the Igbos believe that abominations defile the land, renders it uninhabitable and that ultimately it vomits out the sinful inhabitants. To prevent the occurrence of the above the Igbos engage in cleansing or purification whenever abomination occurs.

It must be noted that this exercise is never performed secretly or in private.

Before proceeding I must make a point. Traditionally the Igbos believe that a community's fate is bound together. What 'A' does is believed to be capable of having an effect on the entire community, so 'B' and 'C' and others will not hesitate to raise an alarm when 'A' is committing an abomination. The essence of the idea is captured by the Igbo saying: 'ofu aka ruta mmanu ozuo oha', which means: if one finger is soiled by palm oil, it soils the other fingers in no time.

Edmund Ilogu has a similar opinion: Hereinafter is his opinion:"Another useful point of introduction which we must mention is that all forms of Igbo traditional religion, being 'folk religion', are basically community-oriented, as opposed to the Christian reformed emphasis on religion which is principally the affair of the individual and his God[114]."

The notion that salvation is personal is completely foreign to the Igbos. The Igbos say 'onye gbanahuru /nanahuru ejide nwanne ya, abuho ezigbo mgbanahu/nnanahu'; this means: even though you

---

[114] ibid.138.

managed to escape but your brother was caught, your escape is therefore meaningless.

In some respects this traditional Igbo thought about the society and religion resembles the Israelite model. All Israel, and even some Egyptians who were more comfortable with the Israelites were liberated, or to use the more common word 'saved' by God from Pharaoh's house of bondage.

Also all the nation of Israel heard the voice of the God of Israel at Sinai; not only Moses or a select few heard God's voice.

In addition, repeatedly we see in the Bible admonitions that all Israel must be holy. The requirement of holiness was never restricted only to a section.

So whenever *aru* (abomination) occurred in any Igbo community, the community quickly insists that *na aya akpu aru* (that purification must be done[115]).

In my part of Igbo-land if the offence is a grievous one the people who are generally invited to carry out the rituals are *Umu Nri*, i.e., Nri men or people.

*Ikpu aru* entails sacrifices which are prescribed by the *Nwa Nri* (Nri person). The distinctive feature of *ikpu aru* is that an animal would be dragged through the streets[116]. Edmund Ilogu described the ritual thus:"The dragging of the sacrificial animal through various parts of the locale involved is a symbolism that is religious as well as sociological[117]."

He went on to reiterate what I mentioned earlier. "Inasmuch as by the misdeeds of the one, the many

---

[115] Basden, G. T., *Niger Ibos* (London: Frank Cass and Co., Ltd., 1966) 61.
[116] Ade Adegbola, E. A. *Traditional Religion in West Africa* (Ibadan: Sefer Books, 1983) 140.
[117] ibid.140.

suffer. A member does not only refrain from antisocial behaviour but he also keeps sufficiently vigilant to ensure that his neighbours do not suffer unhappiness and disorder as a result of his behaviour because he does not care for the values and norms of the society[118]."

---

[118] ibid.140.

# CHAPTER SEVEN: Ichu Aja (Sacrifices and Offerings)

### Ways of Igbo Sacrifice

It would be quite expedient if I describe the various ways the Igbos offer sacrifice, and the places those sacrifices are offered. That way we can understand much about sacrifice and offerings in the Igbo religion.

In *Omenana* every Igbo household had one *okwu Chi/Mmuo* (family shrine/altar), while some have in addition an *ogirisi* tree, an *akwali omumu*, and an *ogbu chi*. The the last three items I mentioned cannot be easily translated to English, so I will describe them very well, and from the descriptions we will get to know more about them.

Igbo clans have *okwu Chi/ /ana* (community shrine/altar)for the entire community.

An Igbo *okwu Mmuo*, i.e, the altar in the shrine is strikingly similar to the altar that God spoke about to Moses in Exodus 22:21, and I will do well to quote the Scripture in some detail:

"An 'altar of earth' thou shalt make unto Me, and shalt sacrifice thereon thy burnt offerings, and thy peace offerings, thy sheep, and thine oxen; in every place where I cause my name to be mentioned I will come unto thee and bless thee."

To make an *okwu Mmuo*, Igbos dig up the earth, and get a substantial quantity of the red soil, called *aja upa*. This red earth is mixed with water, and used to make an altar *(okwu Chi/Mmuo)*. In fact an *okwu Mmuo* is a small rectangular platform, with a small hole in the middle.

This altar is then burnt dry by the sun. As already mentioned, every Igbo family used to have one.

An *okwu Mmuo* is the altar that sacrifices and offerings are placed on. In Omenana it is just the mound.. The only things to be found on it are residues of dried blood, roosters feathers, and flour mixed with soup. These are items used for sacrifices and offerings. See the photograph in this chapter, of an *okwu Mmuo* with the author squatting beside it in the album. G.T. Basden indirectly attests that *an okwu Mmuo* does not contain graven images; when he mentioned that: "No *'alusi'* (graven image of a god) is ever used for the observance of *'ichu aja'* (sacrifice)[119]."

As Igbo sacrifice *(ichu aja)* is principally offered on the *okwu Chi/Mmuo,* G.T. Basden was saying in effect that no graven images *(alusi)* were found on the *okwu Chi/Mmuo* (altar). In all my investigations I have never seen an image on an *okwu Chi/Mmuo*.

I have mentioned before that the Igbo altar is akin to the one mentioned in Exodus 22:21. I will proceed to show that both served the same or similar purposes.

The book of Leviticus starts with a detailed description of how the Israelites are to make offerings on the (altar).

Though Leviticus does not specify the slash across the throat with a very sharp knife, it is known to be the only legal way Jews slaughter animals.

The Igbos would ensure that the knife is extra sharp, and would kill the animal with just one slash across the throat, and would sprinkle the blood on the altar. If the

---

[119] G. T. Basden, *Niger Ibos* (London: Frank Cass and Co., Ltd., 1966) 57.

sacrificial animal is a fowl, the Igbos would remove some feathers and gum them on the blood.

Going even by the Leviticus position which is by no means detailed, at least in the English translations of the Bible, we can see some obvious similarities. In Leviticus 1:14-16, we have the following "And if his offering… is of fowls. He shall pinch off its head. And the blood shall be drained out on the side of the altar. And he shall take away its crop with the feathers thereof, and cast it beside the altar."

Sacrifice of larger animals among the Igbos proceeds along similar lines too. Igbos also make offerings of *utara ji* and *utara akpu* (yam/cassava flour) and *ofe* (soup) at the *okwu Mmuo*.

Igbos ensure that their *ofe* (soup) contains enough salt and oil.

They make offerings of this *utara* mixed together with *ofe* to God every morning; and it is placed on the *okwu Mmuo*.

The second chapter of Leviticus, starting from verse 1, and ending on verse 11, deals extensively with how the Israelites were to offer the flour and oil offering on the altar. Verse 13 of chapter 2, mentions that the offering must contain enough salt. Interestingly *nnu na mmanu* (salt and oil) are the primary ingredients in the Igbo soup, and here we have Leviticus recommending that there be enough salt in the offering that also includes oil.

The Igbo drink offering is also typically reminiscent of Israel's. It is not done regularly like offering of *utara* and *ofe* (flour mixed with oil) offering. Part of the first cup of wine is always poured on the *okwu Mmuo*, with a prayer.

I see this offering in Genesis 35:14, and Numbers 15, performed by Israelites, and recommended as an offering to be performed.

At this stage I must mention that it is the head of the family/household who performs all these offerings.

Only the use of the *okwu Chi/Mmuo* is wide spread throughout Igbo-land. Some Igbos also owned other receptacles or bases for sacrifice, but the *okwu Chi/Mmuo* was owned by every responsible Igbo man/family.

Worthy of mention are the *ogirisi* tree, and the *ogbu chi* (fig tree). The *ogirisi* tree was to be found beside some Igbos' *okwu Mmuo*. The *ogbu chi* was normally in the middle of the space in front of the women's quarters. The *ogirisi* tree of the Igbos who possessed them which was almost always beside their altars, also received a share of the blood, feathers, flour and oil, and drink offerings.

Every Igbo clan possesses an *okwu Chi/ana* (community shrine/altar). It is a most sacred and holy place to the Igbos. It is reminiscent of places like the religious sites at Bethel, and Shiloh where Eli and Samuel superintended, before the rise of Jerusalem and the Temple. The *okwu Chi/ana* are in many cases situated in *agbo* (tree groves).

The *okwu Chi/ana* is an earthen mound, much like the *okwu Chi/Mmuo*, but much bigger and as I mentioned earlier it is regularly sited within the precincts of an *agbo* (tree grove). The *eze Mmuo/Eze Ana* (head or chief priest) of the clan performs all the above-mentioned offerings and sacrifices there, on behalf of the clan.

All the foregoing are my brief sketches of the objects on which the Igbos made offerings, the materials they used as offerings and who made the offerings. Now I can move to the discussion of the major sacrifices and offerings which the Igbos perform.

**Ichu Aja**

*Ichu aja* is the Igbo phrase which is most representative of the English words sacrifice and offerings. To the Igbos *ichu* can mean drive away, or to clean or wash. Some Igbo clans may say *ichuchu ya azu,* meaning scrubbing or washing his /her back. Some may say *ichu eze* (cleaning of the teeth); and to the Igbos *aja* means sacrifice or offering.

We find sin offering connoting much the same in Hebrew thought, if we go by the definition by J.H.Hertz which is set out below:"a sin offering. Heb. Its real meaning is something that will purge, purify and wash away the sin[120]."

The Igbos have two major offerings in their religious traditions: *Igo Mmuo* and *Ilo Mmuo*. We will start with *Ilo Mmuo*; and treat *Igo Mmuo* later.

### Ilo Chi/Mmuo (peace offering)

I described the *ilo Chi/Mmuo* offering, which some Igbos also call 'Alomchi' as a 'reconciling with God' offering in my last book[121]. But further research has shown that reconciliation with God is just part of the purpose of *ilo Mmuo.* Another purpose is to bring good fellowship in the kindred group. In other words *ilo Mmuo* is to create amity between man and Chukwu and between man and his fellow man.

---

[120] J. H. Hertz, *The Pentateuch and Haftorahs, 2nd edition* (London: The Soncino Press, 1937). 417.
[121] Ilona, Remy and Eliyahu, Ehav, *The Igbos: Jews In Africa? Vol 1* (Abuja: Mega Press, 2005,) 72.

The *ilo Chi/Mmuo* is a family offering.

Among the Igbos the offering is performed the following way.

The family decides on a day within the year, because the offering must be done every year. Three days before the chosen day, the head of the family, who is the family priest, announces with his horn /trumpet that the *ilo Mmuo* is to be on the chosen date. This message must get to all the family, including the daughters who have married *(umu okpu)*.

As soon as the announcement is received by any member of the family, that member of the family starts proceeding 'home', and the married daughters are expected to come with their children. They will also come with goats and chickens. This will be their contribution to the offering.

On the actual day of the offering, the head of the family will proceed to the *okwu Chi/Mmuo,* and taking a seat before it, he will bring out the family *ofo,* and start praying for peace and goodwill between Chukwu and the family, and within the family itself. At the conclusion of the prayers, he will bring down the *ofo* on the ground and simultaneously the members that are present will chant *ihaa/iyaa* (amen).

Then he will start the offerings. A family member will start handing the animals to him and he will be slaughtering them by cutting their throats, and sprinkling their blood on the *okwu Chi/Mmuo*. This applies to both the goats and the chickens. In the case of the chickens, some of their feathers will be gummed on the blood. When all the animals have been slaughtered and offered, the young men that are present will gather all the dung and bury them deeply before the *okwu Chi/Mmuo*.

Meanwhile the women folk will be busy cooking (*ana esi na ahosi*). The preferred foods for that day and occasion are pounded yam with soup, and yam porridge. The family head gives instruction that all the carcasses of the slaughtered animals should be taken to the women folk to be used in cooking the festive meal. The entire family shares this meal, after which merriment and dancing starts. Before the close of the day, the men folk would bring out their presents for their daughters *(umu okpu)*, who are actually their sisters that have married into other families.

The similarities between the Igbo *ilo Mmuo* and the Israelite peace offering is so striking but becomes manifest only with careful analysis. Consider Leviticus 10:14, 15:

Verse 14 was specific that the offering in question was a peace offering. Specific mention was also made about the breast and thigh of the animal used in the offering and that they were to be partaken of by all in the family. In Igbo traditions *obi anu* (the breast) and the *aka anu* (the thigh) are the exclusive portions of the head of the family, who by tradition is the family priest, but during *ilo Chi/Mmuo* he shares everything with the family, just as Aaron and his sons were to do with their sons and daughters.

I made reference in a section of this book that in the early period of Israel's existence, that the first-born sons very likely played the roles that the Levites and the sons of Aaron were later assigned to play. I will still provide further information on *ilo Chi/Mmuo* by closing off with the position of Igbo author Mathew Okoli

Orji[122]. "The above festival (*ilo Mmuo*) was interesting because it used to serve as a unifying factor for all the members of the family and their grand children. At least once a year all the members of the extended family came together and embraced themselves. They made further introductions as the family continued to extend (grow). They also recounted in common their gains and losses, their individual progress and handicaps."

### *Igo mmuo (sin offering)*

While we can see more easily that the *Ilo Mmuo* approximated the Biblical-Israelite peace offering, we can only suggest strongly that the *igo Mmuo* offering of the Igbos is equivalent to the Biblical-Israelite sin offering.

The real motive behind the *igo Mmuo* can be gotten by understanding that the Igbo term for making sacrifices *(ichu aja)* denotes, as mentioned, to get rid of sin or abomination. Although animals are sacrificed the same way in the *igoMmuo as* during *ilo Mmuo*, in the *igoMmuo* the offerings are not eaten, nor is there any accompanying feasting and merriment. Rather everything is burnt. This is because the person guilty of sin or abomination ought not to start feasting.

I noticed *igo Mmuo* as a daily offering of some Igbos. What I think is that this particular sacrifice contributed immensely to the much talked about holiness of pre modern Igbo society, because people would naturally shrink away from sin if they know that they would spend money on sacrifices if they sin, and that they would not get compensation by even eating the meat of the sacrificial animal.

---

[122] Orji, Matthew O., (Nkpor: *Jet Star Publishers (Nig.) Ltd.*, 1999) 80.

### Igbu Aja (Atonement—Yom Kippur)

If we are to try to find the meaning of *igbu aja* from the words —*igbu* and *aja,* we may encounter considerable difficulties, because they provide very scanty information:

*Igbu* can only mean 'kill' or 'to kill' in contemporary Igbo language, but *igbu* may also connote to extirpate, to remove, to eliminate and even to annihilate. So one can infer that the sacrifice of *igbu aja* is the sacrifice to kill, remove, eliminate or annihilate (abomination).

The above is the maximum I can do in my efforts to discover what *igbu aja* sacrifice means, from its name.

*Igbu aja* is strictly a communal offering. i.e., it is done on behalf of the clan /community.

G.T. Basden described what he saw the Igbos do in older times:

"For the actual sacrifice, two goats, herbs, roots, and other offerings are provided in accordance with instructions from the 'dibia' who, by the by, for this ceremony, must be a stranger hired to come from another town to minister on behalf of the afflicted community. The preliminaries consist in much gesticulating and shouting, which continue until the real ceremony is taken in hand. Some of the victims are slain and burnt, then a bundle is bound up containing portions of the sacrificial offerings. In this sacrifice nothing may be eaten; not even by the priest. The bundle is placed upon a man or woman, who starts on a perambulation of the town followed by the 'dibia' and the whole assembly. When the circuit has been completed, the 'dibia' rushes about shouting and the followers imitate him. All then move off to a spot situated at some distance from the village where the remaining rites are performed. The idea is that *aja* has gone round absorbing all impurities, iniquities and abominations. The first goat having been slain as an atoning sacrifice, the second goat is now loaded with all the reproach and stigma as the sin-bearer; its face is turned towards the 'bush' and it is driven away and allowed to run wild, in belief it is the scapegoat[123]."

We find Basden's descriptions useful, even though due to his lack of adequate knowledge of Igbo culture, and inability to understand Igbo language perfectly he did not give adequate explanation of what he witnessed, but that he affirmed that the events occurred, and are thus Igbo practices carries some weight. What Basden witnessed was a variant of the Israelite Yom Kippur. When I toured Igbo-land with Swiss-Israeli anthropologist, Daniel Lis, who visited Igbo-land in the last week of June 2006 for field-work for his doctoral programme I showed him several goats that have been used for this purpose in my clan Ozubulu. In many parts of Igbo-land this goat is known as 'mkpi mmuo' (goat of the spirit).

### *Ifio egbo: A Ritual Similar to the Kaparot Ritual*

I should not close the subject of sacrifices without recounting what I witnessed at Nri clan in Anambra state, Nigeria.

As I was starting this research, at the prompting of my associate and friend Ehav Ever, I visited Nri clan, and interviewed several elders. To cut this story short, after the elders and I had talked for over four hours, with all our talk videotaped and recorded, I requested the elders to perform some Igbo sacrifices for my benefit.

---

[123] G. T. Basden, *Niger Ibos* (London: Frank Cass and Co., Ltd., 1966) 60.

They requested for a rooster. I purchased one, and a bottle of gin. They procured kola nut. We proceeded to a makeshift altar. Chairs were placed before the altar, and the three priests sat facing the altar, The eldest, Onwa, who was the oldest man in Nri then, commenced the sacrifice with prayers to Chukwu. He ended with thanks to Chukwu. He poured the drink offering, placed a lobe of kola nut on the altar. The second second-eldest Chituo was given the rooster for the actual sacrifice. At over eighty-six years then, he displayed surprising strength for a man his age. He slaughtered the rooster by cutting its throat, and sprinkled the blood liberally on the altar. Next, he started plucking feathers from the rooster, and started gumming the feather on the blood. At a point he removed some from the crop, and waved his hand with the feathers in his fingers around his head, and threw the feathers away. I requested particularly for this sacrifice, because of a story they told me. They told me that when a group of Israeli visitors who visited before me saw that sacrifice, that they all jumped very high into the air and yelled 'this is Israel!'

I wrote about this in *The Igbos: Jews In Africa? Vol 1,* which I published in 2005. The book has being circulating in Nigeria, Israel, America, Canada and Europe. Sometime in 2006, an old friend visited me and showed me a newspaper clipping that had a story about an ultra Orthodox Israeli Jew waving a rooster around his son's head in a ritual called *kaparot*. I then understood why the Israelis had yelled 'this is Israel'.

The author squatting beside an Igbo okwu Mmuo (family altar), and listening to Obudulu Nwokike, an Nri priest, in 2002.

# CHAPTER EIGHT: Classes Among the Igbos

### Osu

Interestingly though much knowledge about the origins of the *osus*, and what they stood for have been forgotten by many Igbos yet the experience of the *osu*-- a class of Igbo priests and their descendants --provides clear similarities and parallels between the cultures of the Igbos and the Jews.

The word *osu* is not very helpful in our quest to find out the origins of the *osu*, which presently is a hereditary underclass in Igbo society. *Osu* as a word has no meaning in contemporary Igbo language; so I have to rely on an avid description of the *osus*, their functions, and how the Igbos relate to them, in order to possibly find out much about the *osu*.

Among the Igbos an *osu* is someone who is dedicated to Chukwu. He transfers his status to his descendants. He or his sons and daughters can expect to marry only fellow *osus* in this contemporary era. Even in this current year (2013) an *osu* cannot expect to marry a fellow clan' person who is not an *osu* (the so called free born). Also as I learnt recently, the Igbos would not make an *osu*, an *nze* (a member of an elite Igbo club).

G.T. Basden[124] described the *osus* as "slaves devoted to the service of an *alusi*." I agree with him only to the extent that the *osu* were 'devoted' to......... but where Basden saw the *osu* devoted to an *alusi* I saw him devoted to Chukwu, Who is the Person to whom he or

---

[124] Basden, G. T., *Niger Ibos*, (London: Frank Cass and Co., Ltd., 1966) 242.

she was actually devoted to. Basden's research has shortcomings. He noticed that the Igbos knew the Supreme Being[125]; Chukwu or Chineke, to use his own words. He mistakenly assumed that Igbos have other or lesser gods too, known as *alusi*. Because he was not Igbo, and did not know the Igbo culture and language well enough, he did not see the alien-ness of worship of what he assumed to be 'gods'(the *alusis*) in the Igbo religion.

From the work the *osus* did I can get at who they were, and what they stood for.

**The Duty of the Osu**

They clean the *okwu Mmuo* or *okwu anas* and their environs, which; they lived in its precincts anyway. They may also eat portions of the sacrificial animals.

An *osu* most likely may remain one for life, and his descendents are most likely to continue in his /her role.

I found a similar and parallel institution in Israelite history and culture. The study of the Israelite model may help us by throwing light on the Igbo model.

In Joshua 9: 4, we have a detailed account of how the Gibeonites tricked Joshua and Israel, and thus a war between the cunning Gibeonites and Israel was avoided. When their deceit was discovered, Israel declared to them:"And there shall never fail to be of you bondmen, both hewers of wood and drawers of water for the house of my God (God of Israel[126])."

The Biblical position which shows Joshua indenturing the Gibeonites for ever as servants of God clearly

---

[125] ibid., 242.
[126] Joshua 9.

parallelizes the Igbo practice of 'igo mmadu na Mmuo or Chukwu' (dedicating somebody to the service of God for life). A major illustration is necessary here. The Igbos believe that some Igbos became *osus* because their ancestors were, to use the popular words [dedicated or consecrated to God]. The Igbos believe that the victims were forcefully given to the Deity as slaves. It is reasonable to surmise that what some Igbos must have done to some fellow Igbos was a version of what Joshua did to the Gibeonites.

The similarity of the Igbo and Israelite positions can't be overemphasized. In both systems perpetual servitude is involved. And the servitude is to the Deity.

Very important also is the point that the Gibeonites got that status instead of being killed in a war with Israel. They got immunity.

Till the present time no right right-thinking Igbo person would deliberately cause physical hurt or injury to an *osu* (his descendants), i.e., *imepu ya obara* (shedding the *osus'* blood). They may not even be insulted verbally.

About the Igbos G.T. Basden wrote thus[127]: "A man or women, labouring under the impression that he or she was in danger, could flee to the shrine and seek protection."

My observations, and Basden's observations bring us to the second avenue through which a person could become an *osu*. I call this route –'becoming an *osu* voluntarily.' An ancient Israelite law grants immunity from persecution, retribution, etc, to anyone who fled into the sanctuary. Joab, David's army chief tried unsuccessfully to benefit from that law (1 Kings 2:28).

---

[127] Basden, G. T., *Niger Ibos*, (London: Frank Cass and Co., Ltd., 1966) 247.

Some Igbos became *osus* when they tried to benefit from a similar situation. Igbo custom and practice is that anyone became *osu* if the person entered the precincts of an *okwu Chi/ana* (the communal shrine/sanctuary) for refuge. This immunity among the Igbos is forever. The *osus* must never be harmed physically. In fact to shed their blood or that of their descendants is a heinous and abominable offence as far as the Igbos are concerned. It is partly the fear of hurting, harming, or shedding the blood of the *osus* by the Igbos, which developed and progressed into avoidance of most contacts, including marriage with them. The other reason that made Igbos to shun inter-marriage with the *osu* was, the Igbos prefer to marry people they know very well, especially in olden times. As most *osu* were from other clans, the Igbos did not know them well enough, and did not feel free enough to inter-marry with them.

In some ways the Igbo *osu* is similar to the Israelite slave. In ancient Israel the slave who rejects his freedom shall have the following treatment meted out to him:

"And it shall be, if he say unto thee I will not go out from thee; because he loveth thee and thy house, because he fareth well with thee, then thou shalt take an awl, and thrust it through his ear, and into the door, and he shall be thy bondman for ever" (Exodus 21: 5-6).

As my childhood memory recollects, jocular references to *nti osu* (the *osu's* ear) used to be in vogue even in the middle of the twentieth century.

For the Igbo *osu* who was also in perpetual service G.T. Basden reporting what he saw said: "(and formerly human '*osus*' are marked by a small slit cut in the lobe of the ear[128]."

Mba Idika, an Igbo author[129] also favourably did the following comparison. "While the ear of the *osu* was cut off at the ceremony of his dedication, the ear of the Hebrew slave who preferred continued servitude to freedom in the sabbatical year was to be nailed to the door post as a symbol that he could no longer leave the service of that household."

The study and comparisons speak for themselves. What is found in Igbo-land closely resembles what was found in ancient Israel.

## Ohu (Slaves and Slavery)

Any study of slavery among the Igbos will touch the related institution of *osu* which we just finished discussing.

A strong case can be made that slavery arose among the Igbos as a consequence of pawning. A pawn is a bond or a security for a loan. When a man is in need of money for some specific purpose, and he can find no other way to meet the demand, he could resort to the custom of pawning. Such a man is also free to pawn his children or his person.

Very interestingly and remarkably we are met by a direct Hebrew parallel.

"If thy brother, a Hebrew man, or a Hebrew woman, be sold unto thee, he shall serve thee six years, and in the seventh year thou shall let him go free from thee" (Deuteronomy 15: 12).

---

[128] Basden, G. T., *Niger Ibos*, (London: Frank Cass and Co., Ltd., 1966) 247.
[129] Adegbola, Ade E. A. *Traditional Religion in West Africa* (Ibadan: Sefer Books, 1983) 25.

Vestiges of this custom survive. But probably I am the only Igbo who recognizes it as the modern version of the *ohu* (slavery) institution of the Igbos.

A system exists among the Igbos called *igba odibo* (being a servant, cum apprentice) to a master *(oga)* for a period. The period in this modern era is negotiable, but it is usually for seven years. An indigent Igbo family may hand over one of their sons to a kinsman, to serve the kinsman who will teach him a trade. When the agreed period is over, the master will give the young man what the Igbos call 'freedom' and he will *duo ya uno* (give him some money and goods as a settlement for services rendered). These can only remind one of:

"And when thou lettest him go free from thee thou shall furnish him liberally out of thy flock, and out of thy threshing floor, and out of thy winepress; of that where with the Lord thy God hath blessed thee thou shalt give with him" (Deuteronomy 15: 13).

It is *igba odibo* which made it possible for millions of Igbos who would otherwise have been languishing in unemployment and poverty to get capital, and good starts in life.

I will conclude this section by narrating how neutral observers, saw the relationships between the Igbos and their slaves, and the Igbo society and slavery:

According to Basden: "The great majority of slaves accepted their conditions philosophically. They mingled with the rest of the villagers, and except that they were slaves, and were barred from the privileges of the free-folk, they passed their days in fair contentment. Master and slave were frequently the closest of friends, the latter becoming the confidential companion of the former (much like Abraham and Eliezer) trusted with affairs which could be successfully negotiated only by a faithful, trustworthy servant[130]."

And between the society and its slaves: "This assimilation of strangers also applied to slaves brought into the town to labour on the farms. In time they would be given land and if they prospered and founded their own extended families they would take up a place in the clan[131]."

What resonates in all these is: "And if thy brother be waxen poor with thee, and sell himself unto thee, thou shalt not make him to serve as a bondservant. And as a hired servant, and as a settler he shall be with thee,' (Leviticus 25:39-40). 'Thou shalt not rule over him with rigour' (Leviticus 25:43)."

The similarities between the Igbo and Israelite systems of slavery is certainly very remarkable, and more so when we consider the following dispassionately: According to a Jewish writer Joseph Telushkin "... the fourth of the Ten Commandments, which mandates the Sabbath, prohibits a master from employing a slave for work on the Sabbath (Exodus 20:10). I am not familiar with any other legal system that legislated a weekly rest day for slaves[132]."

But I say, except the Igbo legal system, where:"For these personal affairs he (the slave) is granted the free use of one day in four (the Ibo market 'week'[133])."

---

[130] Basden, G. T., *Niger Ibos* (London: Frank Cass and Co., Ltd., 1966) 244.
[131] Webster, J. B.The Growth of African Civilization: The Revolutionary Years Since 1800 to the Present Day, (Bucks: 1967) 178.
[132] Telushkin, Joseph, *Biblical Literacy* (New York: Harper Collins Publishers, Inc., 1977) 441.
[133] Basden, G. T., *Among The Ibos of Nigeria* (London: University Publishing Company, 1921) 109.

This point which I just mentioned effectively sets Igbo and Israelite slavery on one side, and sets slavery among other ancient, and for that matter modern, societies on another side.

## Absence of Kings, Queens, Princes and Princesses

There are no places for kings in basic Igbo tradition[134]. Thus the presence of the Igbo sayings: Igbo *ama eze*, and Igbo *enwe eze*, which mean Igbos did not know of kings nor did they recognize kings, and Igbos do not have kings, respectively, in the Igbo lexicon. Isichei echoed this Igbo saying in the following lines:

Village democracy was so typical of Igbo-land that it became a proverb, "the Igbo have no kings[135]."

But the Igbos not only did not know of, nor recognized kings, they also positively feel revulsion for the idea that anybody should receive some of the deference that should be due to *Chukwu* (God) alone.

Understood in its traditional sense, and even in the modern sense, a king is a human being who is set apart from his fellow humans, is almost worshipped, and treated with utmost courtesy, deference and reverence.

All the mentioned treatments rendered to a king, who is born like any other human being would not trigger off positive feelings in the Igbos because in the basic culture of the Igbos is the idea that every man or woman who came out of the womb of a woman is equal. J.B. Webster, A. A. Boahen and H.O. Idowu, put it succinctly thus: "The Ibo were individualistic and egalitarian, every man considering himself as good as

---

[134] Achebe, Chinua, *Arrow of God* (Ibadan: Heinemann Educational Books, 1964) 28.
[135] Isichei, Elizabeth, *History of West Africa Since 1800* (London: Macmillan Education, Ltd., 1977) 110.

everyone else and demanding a voice in his local affairs[136]."

Another quality or attribute of kings; their rights to be in leading positions because of accidents of birth will equally repel the Igbos, who by tradition believe that birth does not confer advantages on anybody. In the entire length and breadth of Igbo-land, all the Igbo people are the governors and kings of the Igbo people.

The only society that I know that closely parallels the Igbo society is ancient Israel. Thus knowledge of Israel's history and experience can help the interested to find a way through the maze that Igbo history appears to be, at present. In some cases authentic Igbo practices have been submerged under alien practices, but those practices of the Igbos still float to the surface occasionally, to be seen by the avid scholar.

The afore-mentioned scholars described the organization of the Igbo society thus:

"In segmentary societies stable government is achieved by balancing small equal groups against each other and by the ties of clan ship, marriage and religious association[137]."

They offered the foregoing description while comparing the structure of the segmentary political system, such as that of the Igbos, with the types of government that was mainly found in pre-colonial Africa, and which they described as:

---

[136] J.B.Webster, A.A.Boahen, and H.O.Idowu, The Growth of African Civilization-- The Revolutionary Years Since 1800 to the Present Day( Bucks: Longman, 1967) 174.
[137] ibid., 175.

"(Typically characterized by the presence of) a central government ... (which) was usually headed by a single person (king, emperor, sultan, almami, etc[138])."

But among the Igbos there existed some clans which possessed very much abridged versions of some of the systems or institutions that were mentioned in the quoted passage; as can be gleaned from the following:

"Possibly through the influence of Benin and Igala the Ibo living on the rivers as well as at Nri near Awka had kings who were in some ways considered godlike[139]."

It is doubtful that the non-Igbo writers whom I quoted really presented authentic and accurate Igbo practices, i.e., about the kings in those domains actually been godlike, but the fact is that some of the mentioned communities actually had what is called village monarchies at a recent period in their history.

However we must add that their monarchs could not have been godlike because all the structures that could have precluded such a development existed and still exist there, as in the rest of Igbo-land, but even if there was a tendency towards reverencing of men it could be understood as a resultant effect of Igbo imitating of Bini, Yoruba, Igala and other influences.

Also like the Igbos, the ancient Israelites, as modern Israelis, must have seemed an oddity to all their neighbours. Strangely, all the great and important peers of Abraham were kings and potentates; while he was more or less like a priest. And in the era of his grandsons; Esau and Jacob, Scripture tells us in Genesis 36:31-43 that before Israel even thought about having kings that the Edomites (descendants of Esau) had

---

[138] ibid., 175.
[139] ibid., 175.

already had kings for many generations. Notably Genesis: 36:31 used the word 'reigned' which is very instructive, when the Edomite kings were discussed. Nobody reigned in Israel, if the word is interpreted strictly. In Saul's era, Samuel provided a balance, as Nathan did in David's era, while Ahijah the prophet regulated King Solomon. Ahab never wished to run into Elijah, and Ahaz listened to Isaiah and so forth.

And in this modern era, Israel is distinguished in the Middle East, by its democracy which was described by Dr. Tashbih Sayyed as:

"... a better system than the American Republican representative system—which is really a representation of power and special interests. In the U.S you get democracy for the few. In Israel you have a democracy for everyone[140]."

Even though it is not my brief to find out when the people of Israel developed the trait to live in freedom (democracy), a Biblical passage taken from Leviticus 25: 42, declares: "The Israelites know no master but Me (God).Their rescuer from Egypt", gives us the clue that would make the Israelites to disdain human authoritarianism. As they are the subjects of the divine King, the God of Israel, they would not willingly and knowledgeably subject themselves to human rule. My finding is that the Igbos lived under God as their King too, but in time they nearly forgot Him, but as old habits die hard, they keep on rejecting rule by humans.

I think that the case is sufficiently made that by tradition the Igbos knew not about kings. And are habitual democrats, like the Israelites.

---

[140] Dr. Tashbih Sayyed, *A Muslim in a Jewish Land*, 13 Kislev 5766 (14th December 2005), downloaded from Aish.com.

# CHAPTER NINE: The Socio-Religious Personalities and Authorities

## Igbos Without Kings Historically

Although the Igbos have never had real kings, in any sense of the word, nevertheless they have always had some persons who presided over their affairs. Those persons' positions derived from their religious roles.

The following helps to explain the place of religion in the lives of the Igbos:

The passage quoted below which was culled from Chinua Achebe's book was an Igbo clan's answer when asked about their clan's king by European colonial officers: ... the villagers told them that there was no king.

"We have men of high title and the chief priests and elders, they said[141]."

The leaders are in fact little more than the spokesmen[142].

It is beyond doubt that the priesthood has to do with religion. Among the Igbos one does not just wake up and become a priest. Certain conditions are met before one becomes a priest. Age/seniority is one of them, among others.

We will see some of those other conditions as we progress, and as I describe the leaders of the Igbos and their functions.

---

[141] Achebe, Chinua, *Things Fall Apart* (Ibadan: Heinemann Educational Books, 1958) 105.
[142] J. B. Webster and A. A. Boahen, with H.O.Idowu, *The Revolutionary Years in West Africa Since 1800* (Bucks: Longman, 1967) 263.

But before I start work on this section I must draw the reader's attention to the Igbo Society section of this book which we will meet as we progress, and which contains a lot of related information, which will help one to understand this section more. That having been said I will now proceed to a concise study of the socio-religious personalities and authorities of the Igbos.

### Aka ji ofo

Simply defined, *aka ji ofo* is the oldest man in an Igbo family, kindred or clan. He must be a bona fide member of that unit, i.e., he must not be of *osu* and *ohu* origins. Also from his father's side of his family he must have a link to the progenitor of the group. In addition he must not have settled among the members of that unit. This last case applies to Igbos from the Nri and Aro clans who resettled in other Igbo clans. Here I must note that for a more detailed understanding of some of the terms which I rendered in Igbo language, the reader needs to study the entire book.

Another important point I must make is that I was faced with a dilemma here. For me to write anything worthwhile on *aka ji ofo* I need to discuss *ofo*.

If I take the credit for being the first modern Igbo to discover the meaning of the *ofo*, I would certainly not be challenged by any Igbo. Until I realized its real meaning, and documented it[143], many Igbos had misunderstood, misinterpreted and misrepresented it[144]. Narrated below is an account of such misrepresentation found in the Igbo novel *The Only Son*: "From their skin bags they

---

[143] Ilona, Remy and Eliyahu, Ehav, *The Igbos: Jews in Africa? Vol. 1* (Abuja: Mega Press, 2005) 77.
[144] Munonye, John, *The Only Son* (Ibadan: Heinemann Education Books, 1966) 58.

brought out their pocket-size idols. Then the oldest one among them prayed.

"Let the gods wipe out this thing that has come into the land in our time!"

"Ofo!" they chorused, simultaneous with the word, they touched the object (*ofo* pocket-sized idols lightly on the ground."

By the time I saw myself as a member of the Igbo society no Igbo viewed the *ofo* as an idol or 'gods', even if they did not remember exactly what it is. Igbos universally believed that it is a symbol of authority which the oldest male member of a family holds on behalf of, and in trust for, the family, but in the above-quoted text we still saw an Igbo describing it as idol/gods. For that mistake/error I can only recommend patient, careful and sympathetic consideration of the past and even present of the Igbos. In the period that the writer who made the mistake worked in, the Europeans had just conquered the Igbos, but had not subdued nor emasculated them. The best tools for achieving that was conversion of the Igbos into the European's religion. And the most efficient and effective way to do that was to label every Igbo object and institution as 'idol', 'gods' and 'pagan', and teach Igbo children who were taken into the mission schools so. I still do not know how the Europeans discovered so quickly that the Igbos are an idolatry-fearing people. And that they the Igbos would feel guilty perpetually if they were convinced that they were pagans, and would thus see themselves as indebted to the missionaries for showing them 'light.'

The writer, like most Igbos, was a pupil/graduate of the mission schools, where the above and similar things were taught.

Interestingly G.T. Basden, a foreigner, was quite contemplative in his study and description of *ofo*. To him, *ofo*, which is a stick obtained from the *ofo* tree, and which becomes effective only after consecration is regarded as "a mediator between the spirits of this, and the underworld[145]."

An Igbo Christian theologian and scholar R.C. Arazu described *ofo* as "... used to make contact with the ancestors and benevolent spirits[146]."

In my first book[147] I described *ofo* as a messenger of the Supreme Being. That is not correct exactly. But I correctly likened it to the Israelite rod of Aaron. In the book of Numbers 17:17, God commanded Moses thus: "Speak unto the children of Israel, and take of them rods, one for each fathers' house, of all their princes according to their father's houses."

In the Igbo term *umunna* which literally means children of the father, but which means family or kindred in the real sense, we can identify the idea underlying the Israelite/Biblical usage 'fathers house' that is in the above quoted passage.

Another Igbo phrase *'be nna'* which can mean father's house, can also mean family if used in the following way *'o be nna ya di ifea'* (this is his father's house).

---

[145] Basden, G. T. Basden, *Niger Ibos* (London: Frank Cass and Co., Ltd., 1966) 57.
[146] Rev Fr. Raymond Arazu,*Our Religion-Past and Present* (Awka: Martin-King Press, 2005) 132.
[147] Ilona, Remy and Eliyahu, Ehav, *The Igbos: Jews in Africa? Vol.1* (Abuja: Mega Press, 2005) 77.

Now as to how Aaron's rod became special in Israel. My conjecture is that originally each Israelite family had a rod which its eldest member held. And that each family viewed itself as a leader in all matters. But that that stance led to incessant bickering, recriminations and 'murmuring.' That to check that, a spiritual leader had to be chosen, and that was done when Aaron's rod was chosen. As had been noted in this book, the oldest male member of an Igbo family also performed priestly duties for his family, in other words he is a priest, and the staff of his authority is the *ofo*.

In Israelite or Hebrew society we saw the same.

Dr. J.H. Hertz noted that:

"On closer examination, however, we learn that the privileges of the birthright so coveted by Jacob were purely spiritual. In primitive times, the head of the clan or the first born acted as the priest[148]."

My opinion is that it was the rod that the Semitic/Hebrew firstborn- priests had from ancient times, that was submitted to God for testing, and Aaron's budded, i.e., was chosen, and he, and his sons became the primary priests (*Kohanim*) of the Israelites.

Among the Igbos we find all the first born sons holding this rod or stick, which comes to them by patrilineal devolution.

The Igbos call these first sons *aka ji ofo*, which literally means the hand that holds the *ofo*. Traditionally they perform religious functions for Igbo families, and still do so even now, even though in many cases, many of

---

[148] J. H. Hertz, *The Pentateuch and Haftorahs, 2nd edition* (London: The Soncino Press, 1937) 94, Commentary 31.

them do not know that what they are performing are religious functions.

During Igbo marriages *(ime ego* and *ima ogodo/igba nkwu)* the *aka ji ofo* prays. He receives *ihu* (tithe) for distribution to the poor, he prays at all gatherings of the Igbos. It is his right and prerogative as the oldest person present. I observed that the Jews who assembled for the first Zionist Congress at Basle respected this tradition. Theodore Herzl the founder of modern Zionism called on Dr. Lippe of Jassy who was the oldest man present at the Congress to offer a benediction[149]. Among the Igbos the *aka ji ofo* still do their job.

### Eze Mmuo/eze ana

The meaning of the Igbo word *eze* is not very clear to the modern Igbo. In contemporary Igbo it is taken to stand for king, priest, leader or chief. But it actually means the same thing with *nze*. Nze is someone who shuns evil-doing. The words *eze* and *nze* are the nouns of the Igbo verbs *ize* and *zee*. These mean to shun, to avoid, etc. The Igbo *Ozo* title holders are addressed as *nze* or *eze*. They do everything humanly possible to avoid sin, filth, and corruption. In olden times, the standard of decency required of them was high to the extent that they carried bells when moving about, so that people would be forewarned of their approach, and not say sinful or corrupt things to their hearing. My great-grandfather was Eze Anyaezughu. My grandfather was Eze Ofido. Interestingly as the words *eze* and *nze* are close to the Jewish *nazir* in spellings, so are they also close in meaning. In the Hebrew community the *nazir* is a holy man who is set apart to the extent that he doesn't eat normal foods. Samson the great Israelite

---

[149] Dunner, Joseph, *The Republic Of Israel*, (New York: Whittlesey House, 1950) 23.

leader, judge, and warrior was a Nazirite. In former times an Igbo *nze/eze* ate only in his house.

*Mmuo* stands for spirit. So in the context in discussion *Eze Mmuo* means chief, priest or leader for the spirit (Chukwu). Interestingly the priest in ancient Israel was also the 'chief man among his people'-(Leviticus 21:4).We can eliminate king, because by tradition the Igbo hadn't the institution of kingship (monarchy), though the Igbos knew about it. Some of the most popular and enduring Igbo sayings are 'Igbo ama eze' and 'Igbo enwe eze' (Igbos don't respect kings and Igbos have no kings). We have priests, and leaders, but had no kings so our assertion is correct.

The title *Eze Mmuo* is sometimes exchanged *with Eze ana. Ana* here means the land, ie, the community. In Igbo tradition the *Eze Mmuo/ /Eze Ana* is the chief priest. In my clan for example which is made up of several families, the central place of worship is known as *okwu ana.* It is also known as *okwu chi* (God's altar/sanctuary). One man known as *Eze Ana/EzeMmuo* serves as the priest at the *okwu chi/ /ana.* He is in charge of the place. He makes offerings to the Spirit (Chukwu) at the sanctuary.

His position is hereditary, but at times he may be chosen from another family, like Samuel and his succession to Eli.

## Nwa Nri/Nri Clans

The Ilona, ie., my family is one of the families that make up the Ozubulu clan; an Igbo clan.

As I was growing up I noticed that the Ilona family has an integral part/member called the Iketalu. They are part of the family known as Ilona, yet they don't use the Ilona surname like other Ilona. They rather go by the name Iketalu. My curiosity was aroused. I asked my father why that branch of the family answered a different name. My father told me a story which I have never forgotten.

In the distant past, which may be one hundred and eighty to two hundred years ago, the man Ilona met an Nri man who had traveled to Ozubulu, and was looking for a good place to settle. When Ilona heard his story, and of his need, he quickly welcomed him, and assigned a portion of his own land to him, enough to live on, and to farm. And they became one family. And even up till the present day they (their descendants) are still living together, as brothers.

My mind is drawn to the following Israelite provisions, when I think of how Ilona welcomed Iketalu the Nri man, and gave him land to reside on, and farm:

"And the Lord spoke to Moses in the plains of Moab by the Jordan at Jericho, saying command the children of Israel, that they give unto the Levites of the inheritance of their possession cities to dwell in, and open land round about the cities shall ye give unto the Levites. And the cities shall they have to dwell in, and the opening land shall be for their cattle, and for all their substance, and for all their beasts"- (Numbers 35: 1-3, 8).

Clearly the Israelites were to accommodate their brother Levites.

From Deuteronomy 18; we understand that the Levites were to move around in Israel; in the course of their religious and spiritual work. And they were to be provided for by fellow Israelites wherever they went.

## Chapter 9: Personalities and Authorities 161

Very interestingly Nri men had benign monopoly on the performance of certain religious rites among the Igbos. One of such rites is *ikpu aru* (purification); which they are invited to come and perform in various parts of Igbo-land.

In very ancient times the Igbo clans though autonomously administered, co-operated in certain religious affairs. This is seen from a story that is connected to the *ofo*. The Igbo clan called Nri believes that by tradition that they are the holders of the *ofo* of the Igbo people. Some Igbos that are not from Nri agree that this claim is true. The Nri priests performed important spiritual and religious functions for the Igbos, like purification of the land when major abominations are committed. My research shows them as being very close to the Igbos as the Levites are to the Israelites. The Scriptures as we can see in Leviticus 3:40, gave the Levites religious supremacy in Israel. I can also say that the Nri are superior to other Igbos in certain areas of *Omenana*, such as the one mentioned above. But on routine matters, even religious ones, the *aka ji ofo* of the various Igbo families take precedence over the Nri men that are among them. So far we can see that the Nri are akin to the Levites and the *aka ji ofo*, akin to the Israelite Reubenites (descendants of Reuben, Israel's first son). We can also see that the *aka ji ofos* do not concede totally to the Nri, just as the Reubenites found it difficult to concede to the Levites. This is discernible from the Korah, Dathan and Abiram revolt against Moses and Aaron. Abiram was a Reubenite.

According to J.H.Hertz: "These (the rebels) were led by Dathan and Abiram, of the tribe of Reuben, the tribe that once possessed but lost the 'birthright in Israel, and was it seems, chafing for the recovery of that primacy[150]."

## Nri Clans

I am a regular visitor to the Agukwu Nri Clan and the Nri outpost in Oraeri clan. Both clans which are typical Igbo clans exist in Anambra State, Igbo-land, in present Nigeria.

Very interestingly the Nri people are uncannily like the Levites of Israel. Like the Levites whom Jacob vowed 'to scatter in Israel'(Genesis 49:7) the Nri are scattered among the Igbos. The premier clan of the Nri bears the tell tale name *Nri-enwelani* which means 'the Nri have no land.' The Levites were specifically to have no designated land in Israel but were to be accommodated in all Israel.

A. E. Afigbo, a most prominent Igbo historian in referring to Nri, the major settlement of the Nri group; specifically called it:

"... Nri, the Holy City[151] ..."

An outspoken Jew made a thought-provoking comment one day on the Ibo-benei-yisrael@yahoogroups.com web list. He wondered what the Levites among the Igbos were doing when the Igbo people began to assimilate the cultural and religious practices of their neighbours and the Europeans. I told him, and the reading public what I learnt at Nri; that the Nri did their job to the best of their ability, but that the Igbos just couldn't withstand the imperial British who had dangerous firearms.

---

[150] J. H. Hertz, *The Pentateuch and Haftorahs*, 2nd edition (London: The Soncino Press, 1937) 638.
[151] Afigbo A., *Ropes of Sand* (Ibadan: University Press, Ltd., 1981) 31.

### Nwa dibia na onye amuma (doctor/seer-prophet)

I will not be able to define the term *dibia*, because in contemporary Igbo language the term's meaning is obscure. But I can show who the *dibia* is by describing what he does.

An Igbo *dibia* divines and 'sees', in other words he or she is a diviner and a seer. He also diagnoses illnesses and prescribes cures. Some *dibias* only divine. The Igbos see such a *dibia* as *dibia afa*, and the one that gives medicines to the sick, as *dibia mgborogwu* (doctor of roots/medicine).The Igbo *dibia* that divines is very similar with the person[152] hereinafter described: "Beforetime in Israel when a man went to inquire of God, thus he said ,Come and let us go to the seer. (1 Samuel 9:9)."

This kind of *dibia* is stationary, and people go to him or her for consultations, just like the seer in ancient Israel.

Also like the seer in ancient Israel, persons who go to him for consultations go to see him as his counter-part in ancient Israel was approached.

The Bible is very illustrative on this subject. Saul who later became king, and his servant were looking for some missing animals. When all their efforts failed they resolved to consult a seer, but Saul wondered how they could go to the seer as he had exhausted all the presents he left home with.

The servant answered: "Behold, I have in my hand the part of a shekel of silver, that will I give to the man of God, to tell us our way[153]."

---

[152]The Holy Scriptures, *Jewish Publication Society*, Philadelphia, 1955, (1:Samuel 9:9) 371.
[153]The Holy Scriptures, *Jewish Publication Society*, Philadelphia, 1955, (1:Samuel 9:9) 371.

Any Igbo going to consult a *dibia* would go with some *ego* (divination money). The procedure is to hand it over to the seer once the ceremony of sharing of kola nut *(oji)* had been dispensed with.

An Igbo *dibia* will divine from studying the kola nut that was broken for that purpose. Some will cast their cowrie shells on the floor, and divine from the patterns, i.e., from how they are lying on the floor. Still some were so developed that on seeing or sensing those who have come to consult them they will tell the visitors what they have come to consult him or her for, and tell them the solution to their problems. A good case of the last is to be found in Flora Nwapa's *Efuru*[154]. Abram Leon Sacher[155] who wrote on the Israelite version of the seer, using the example we used, places him as been being just a little in advance of 'the Assyrian *baru*' who interpreted the wishes of the gods by inspecting the entrails of specially slaughtered animals.

Very interestingly some of the peoples ('tribes') that surround the Igbos use the above-mentioned Assyrian method in divination.

Also visible in Igbo society were *ndi amuma* (Prophets).

*Ndi amuma* who prophesied in the Igbo society were still very much around when I was growing up. Childhood memory affords me a remembrance of how they looked. Their hair was almost always long and matted. They were invariably bearded. The wilds were their preferred places of residence. The wicked tried to avoid them most times, because of their sharp tongues. The biblical scholar will identify them with the portrait

---

[154] Nwapa, Flora, *Efuru* (Ibadan: *Heinemann,* 1966m) 25, 26.
[155] Sacher, Leon Abram, *A History of the Jews,* (New York: Alfred Knopf, 1930) 62.

of Elijah as drawn by Abram Leon Sacher in the following description. "He is harsh, severe, relentless, of the typical dervish type, intolerant of all the effeminate corruptions of civilized life[156]".

Nelson Ejinduaka, an Igbo musician who has died and three Igbo musicians; who are still alive; Moore Black Chi Mmadike, Morocco Maduka, and Ozoemena Nsugbe, are seen as prophets because they don't/didn't spare the religiousity without godliness of many Igbos. Also many of their predictions have come to pass. They, like the prophets of Israel, were also very much concerned about social justice.

Chinua Achebe[157] gave a graphic description of an Igbo prophetess at work in *Things Fall Apart*.

Another Igbo scholar, F.C. Ogbalu[158] who tried very valiantly to document Igbo traditions in Igbo language gave a brief account of prophesy among the Igbos. An Igbo prophet' or prophetess' career may start rather like that of the Biblical Samuel. If a child's parents had gotten him after many entreaties to Chukwu, they may send that child to live with, and serve under the priest who officiates at the place of worship of Chukwu, as an apprentice.

Such a child may remain only a priest, or he may combine priestly work with soothsaying and he may also prophesy.

Another way some Igbos became prophets and prophetesses is by answering a 'call' from Chukwu. The

---

[156] ibid, 50-51.
[157] Achebe, Chinua, *Things Fall Apart*, (Ibadan: Heinemann Educational Books, 1958) 70.
[158] Ogbalu, F. C., *Omenala Igbo*, (Lagos: University Publishing Co. Academy Press, 1979).

Igbos see the medium that God uses to call the prophets as *agwu* (divine summons).

This second method of becoming a prophet, which F.C. Ogbalu[159] wrote about is similar to Isaiah's 'call.' Isaiah saw the Heavenly Throne, and offered to carry God's instructions to Israel, as seen in Isaiah 6:1-8.

F.C. Ogbalu, situated an Igbo prophet as being in a similar situation. He receives orders or instructions from [Chukwu] and delivers to his kinsmen, clansmen and brethren.

---

[159] Ibid.

# CHAPTER TEN: Duties, Relationships, and Behaviours

## Respect for Elders and Parents

When I, the writer, was growing up, when Omenana still regulated the Igbos lives almost completely, even though many had converted out of the Igbo religion, respect for elders, male or female, was absolute in Igbo society. So this section is about 'respect in Igbo culture'.

In the Igbo families, kindred, and clans, which make up the Igbo society, the oldest man, the oldest woman, and the elders are always accorded respect. In fact the oldest is always the first among equals in the Igbo society. In gatherings, the younger must get up from a seat, for his elder, if seats are few, in other words, he must rise ... exactly as Israel was commanded to do by the following law: "You shall rise up before the hoary head, and honour the face of an old man, (Leviticus 19:32)."

G.T. Basden observed, "Among the Ibos reverence for old age was a very marked feature[160]".

Among the Igbos, the younger must respect his elder. This mandatory requirement extends to parents too. In pure and uncorrupted Igbo settings, where *Omenana* rules it could not be imagined that an Igbo would rise and insult his parents.

The following story, gleaned from John Munonye's novel, *The Only Son,* shows us the great surprise and dismay of an Igbo father when his son who had become a Christian rose against him. In the story, Idimogu's first

---

[160] G. T. Basden, *Niger Ibos* (London: Frank Cass and Co., Ltd., 1966) 421.

son Ibe had just joined the incoming Christian missionaries. When Idimogu, who like many Igbos of that era was wary of the Christian faith, tried to force his under-aged son to abandon the new faith; the following event, which he narrated, occurred:

"I tried to frighten my son... I held him by his two hands; and threatened I would tie his feet to his hands and leave him folded up on the floor overnight like a criminal. What did my son do in reply? He dug his teeth into my flesh. See . . . My own son did that. After that he threatened he would report me to the man who organizes them who in turn would report to the white man at Ania! Of course I was forced to leave him. He ran out of the house pouring out further threats on me, his own father[161]."

As could be seen from the quoted passage, especially from the ending words-'his own father," the Igbos saw disrespect to elders and parents as sacrilegious.

In recent times, due to forgetfulness and abandonment of *Omenana,* the practice of respecting elders is on the wane.

Yet in spite of everything, a careful observer would still notice that the Igbos have a strong tradition that demands that the elders must be respected. In practice this is reflected in the Igbo tradition that grants the oldest man present in an Igbo setting, the right to pray, because to a very religious people like the Igbos, the person who prays/the priest is accorded the most respect.

---

[161] Munonye, John, *The Only Son* (Ibadan: Heinemann Educational Books, 1966) 92.

## Children

Igbos have overwhelming love for children. This love starts from an overwhelming need to have children, and extends to the importance the Igbos attach to the care of children.

A childless (Igbo) marriage is a source of grievous disappointment. The Jacob-Rachel, and Elkanah-Hannah sagas parallelizes the Igbo positions.

The Igbos would not be happy with a childless marriage. However in *Omenana* a woman had a customary right to 'marry' (get another wife for the husband) another woman into the home, who would as a surrogate, enable her to produce her own children. Jewish custom parallels Igbo practice directly in the above respect. We could see the parallelism in what both wives of Jacob, the Hebrew Patriarch did with their maids.

The Igbos love to have children, and they love to care for them. Among the Igbos no sacrifice is too much for a child.

On care of children, G.T. Basden observed: "Sleeping accommodation for the babe is a share of the mother's couch. The Ibo mother thinks this is the proper place for her offspring. To suggest a crib would raise doubts of the woman's affection towards her child: it would be equivalent to treating the child as an object of little, or of no more importance than a common utensil[162]."

This work will eventually be expanded to a comparative study of the Igbos and their neighbours. This doting on children that I am discussing here is uniquely Igbo in Nigeria. In Nigeria we have cultures that can I say, tolerate the dehumanizing of children. Children as

---

[162] G. T. Basden, *Niger Ibos* (London: Frank Cass and Co., Ltd., 1966) 174.

young as three would be routinely sent away from home with one pretext or the other.

As the child grows, both parents lavish love on it. He or she is taught wisdom, inducted into the appropriate man/womanhood rites, employment, assisted into marriage at the right time, and prayed for so that he or she will not die young.

Igbo expectations for their children are so high. Igbo parents can go through fire to see that their children stay on the right course. And when the children disappoint by taking the wrong turns, the Igbos suffer heart-break.

The following Igbo story, which is culled from John Munonye's novel[163], never fails to elicit tears from the eyes of Igbo people:

"When he left Chiaku broke into tears, sobbing spasmodically. But the load in her heart was such that could not be washed out by tears alone. She opened her mouth:

"No, I should not weep in this life where every broad road seems to end in bush? My eyes, you are both dry with weeping. Even the spring that flows does dry at times. How much more the tears in a widow's eyes?"

"She folded her cloth into her lap. She ran her palm under her eyes."

"For ten good moons I bore him in my womb," she continued. "The child will be a boy, his father used to say. And I'm sure he will be my father."

---

[163] Munonye, John, *The Only Son* (Ibadan: Heinemann Educational Books, 1966) 88,89.

"What Okafo foretold did come true in a way. For the child that was born was a boy indeed. But not entirely true, as I've come to discover. For my husband's father lived well till the end of his life........"

"I've laboured and laboured to obtain our living. What did I not suffer from Amanze and his wives! That was the day they said my son was possessed. On that day I taught them what not to do to a widow's only child. That's the child that has gone mad now."

"The day I faced Amanze and his wives! That was at Umudioba from where we fled. And yet I had to bear everything because of my child. That's the child that has gone mad now."

"I fled to Nade, to my father's land. Here to start life afresh and live in peace. Suitors have come and I've turned them out. I tell them I have a son who is my husband. Just because I don't want to live away from him. That's the child that has gone mad now.

And already I've found him a wife. She is a good girl and the family is *obi*. What will they say when they hear about this (that her son had become a Christian)? Why do I live and not die at once?"

The reader must have seen in the moving lines above, which portray practical love and sacrifice the lofty and tender position that children occupy in the world of the Igbos.

G.T. Basden found it difficult to go away from this touching subject, because this subject plucks at the heart. He noted:"Great affection abounds, normally, between parents and their offspring[164]".

---

[164] G. T. Basden, *Niger Ibos* (London: Frank Cass and Co., Ltd., 1966) 188.

He continued: "One of the most pleasing characteristics of the Ibos is the bond of affection between mother and son. This bond may be strained, but it is never severed. The son, on occasions, may be unkind to his mother, possibly neglectful, but such conduct would always bring condemnation upon him: it would be utterly contrary to Ibo tradition.

Seldom, indeed, does a son treat his mother with anything other than honor and respect. In his affections, she holds the premier place, and to her he turns as being the most trustworthy receiver of his confidence. His first thought in times of danger is for his mother: she ranks before wife and children, because she alone is irreplaceable."

In other words, she alone can make the supreme sacrifice for the son. Note that I wrote this section one month after my mother's death (in 2013).

When my father, who was my best friend, passed on when I was in Law School, I was inconsolable because I remembered that the man and my mother almost dressed in rags, and almost went hungry so that I and my siblings would be clothed, and fed. However, when my mother followed him in 2006, a part of me died. This was because I practically shared her apartment with her for more than fifteen years. Her departure created a major vacuum in my life. Among other things when I travel home from Abuja there is no longer anyone around to inquire "What will you eat, my son?"

### Strangers

The Igbos would rather behave indecently to fellow Igbos, than to strangers. This is the rule. But the reader must be aware that the clan was the basic structure of Igbo socio-political structure. So an Igbo man from clan

'A' is a stranger in clan 'B' in the strictest traditional sense. And truly the clansmen and women of clan 'B' will give him kind and honest treatment; even in preference to fellow clan-members.

In the wider sense this applies too. A non-Igbo in the midst of Igbos must be protected. We saw this unwritten tradition in practice in 1966. As lorries, trucks, trains and trailers were steadily ferrying home to Igbo-land the corpses of Igbos slain in the anti-Igbo pogroms of 1966, the Igbo authorities gave safe passage to the kinsmen of the people who were killing the Igbos, i.e., to those of them living in Igbo-land, so that they could return to their homes. In contemporary Nigeria Igbos who have non Igbos in their midst while discussing important matters that may not directly be relevant to the non Igbos, will unconsciously lapse into the English language, so that the non Igbos would be carried along. The Hausa, Fulani, Yoruba, and other Nigerian groups will not do this. This is verifiable.

When considering the laws that most closely parallels Igbo attitude to strangers, one is inexorably drawn to:"You shall not abhor an Egyptian, because you were an alien in his land, Deuteronomy 23:7 and you shall not pervert the justice due the stranger.

...but you shall remember that you were a slave in Egypt." (Deuteronomy 24:17).

In other words you were oppressed, and thus knows the bitterness of oppression, so do not yield to the temptation to oppress others. Also you knew exile, so be kind to others that go into exile.

Clearly the above explains total Igbo revulsion for oppressing and colonizing alien peoples. The closest the Igbos came to colonizing other peoples is as described by G.T. Basden: "When abroad, they maintain close contacts, cemented and sustained by a strong tribal bond of union. Whatever the condition, the Ibo immigrants adapt themselves to meet them, and it is not long before they make their presence felt in the localities where they settle. It has been remarked, that they make 'good colonists.' This they do in a quiet, unobtrusive, but effective manner[165]". But to seek to rule over their guests, the Igbos never think of!

**Hired Labourers**

By tradition the Igbos must feed the hired labourer. People are usually hired to work on Igbo farms and building sites on daily basis. The rule is that the hirer must give them a meal, which is comprised of the food itself, wine and water. It is a custom. There is no apparent reason for it, because the labourers are normally hired to work for agreed wages, and the meal, *(nni oru)* is not part of it. Yet no Igbo will think of not feeding his workers *(ndi oru ya)*.

John Munonye[166] was indirectly talking about this custom, even though his case involved the peers of Nnanna, his protagonist's son, that worked for her, and not hired labourers.

By custom an Igbo would not think of oppressing a hired labourer, as God ordered in Deuteronomy 24:10.

Igbo practice is that they must be paid their agreed wages before sunset. Israelite parallel is found in Deuteronomy 24: 15.

---

[165] ibid., 189.
[166] Munonye, John, *The Only Son* (Ibadan: Heinemann Educational Books, 1966).

## In-Laws

An Igbo son-in-law has a life-long duty to support and help the family from which he married, i.e the family of his wife.

In ancient times this support and help came in the form of manual labour by the son- in- law, in the farm of his in-laws: The Igbos call this work -*oru ogo*, i.e., working for the in-laws. In John Munonye's book an Igbo woman lamented thus:"Who could have been a better son-in in-law than he? .... I have missed having an in-law who could have worked for me, and made me rich in crops[167]."

Igbos say 'ogo wu chi onye'; this means that one's in-law is too important, and almost indispensable to one.

In the Bible we find instances of Israelites working for their in-laws.

Jacob worked for Laban, and Moses for Jethro.

## Children Towards Parents

Igbo tradition requires that, in the case of a man whose children have grown and formed their own households, that all the children must assemble on one particular day, once a week, and work for their parents.

I have to rely on Chinua Achebe's *Arrow of God*. In the this book an Igbo father restated the rule thus: "Listen to what I shall say now.....tell them that tomorrow my sons and my wives and my son's wife work for me[168]."

---

[167] Munonye, John, *The Only Son* (Ibadan: Heinemann Educational Books, 1966) 47.
[168] Achebe, Chinua, *Arrow of God,* (Ibadan:Heinemann Educational Books, ) 14.

We see the twelve sons of Israel working for him, and Saul working for his father as well as David working for his father, while his brothers went to war.

**Less Fortunate Relatives**

G.T. Basden's description of the Igbo traditional attitude towards poor relatives is perfect. In his own words, "family law and tradition of the Igbos demands that help must be given to a brother or sister in distress, regardless of the origin of the trouble, whether domestic, financial, or otherwise[169]."

According to him: "Hence, there were, in past days no homeless vagrants in Igboland, the family being responsible for the less fortunate relatives[170]."

What comes to one's mind when one observes the traditional Igbo system is Deuteronomy 15:7; which prescribes: "If there be among you a needy man, one of thy brethren, within any of thy gates, in the land which the Lord thy God giveth thee, thou -shall not harden thy heart, nor shut thy hand from thy needy brother; but thou shall surely open thy hand unto him, and shalt surely lend him sufficient for his need in that which he wanteth."

Directly paralleling the Biblical prescription is the Igbo attitude to needy relatives as can be gleaned from Chinua Achebe's, *Things Fall Apart*:

Okonkwo the protagonist of the story cleared a farm, but lacked yams to plant on it. He approached Nwakibie, a rich neighbour, who helped out, because, according to

---

[169] G. T. Basden, *Niger Ibos* (London: Frank Cass and Co., Ltd., 1966) 189.
[170] ibid.,121.

him, Okonkwo deserved help on account of his tendency to work hard[171].

Standard Igbo practice can be deduced from their interaction: 'You must help your brother', subject to the rule: 'he should be hardworking.'

The Igbos also have the customs of *nkpa ji* and *ede nga*, which allow the poor to extract the leftovers, after harvests.

After the Igbos have harvested their yams and cocoyam, and have held the New Yam festival, two other minor feasts, called *Mkpa ji* and *Ede nga* are held. They signal that harvests are over, that henceforth people, particularly the poor, are free to move into the farms and fields and take leftovers, without their been being considered as thieves.

These Igbo feasts remind the Biblical scholar of Leviticus 23:22; which prescribes: "And when ye reap the harvest of your land, thou shalt not wholly reap the corner of thy field, neither shalt thou gather the gleaning of thy harvest; thou shalt leave them for the poor, and for the stranger."

**Towards Animals**

It is Igbo custom to treat animals with kindness. In traditional Igbo society every Igbo man and woman rears goats, sheep, poultry and some also have cattle.

One of the first chores Igbos undertake in the morning is *ije nni eghu* (to go and collect fodder for the goats), and *imeghe mpio okuko* (to open the chicken coop so that the poultry can go out to look for food); and *ikpupu*

---

[171] Achebe, Chinua, *Things Fall Apart* (Ibadan: Heinemann Educational Books, 1959) 14, 15.

*aturu na efi* (to lead out the cows and sheep to their grazing grounds). In the evenings the goats are taken in so that they would not suffer from the cold.

We have a saying which portrays the extreme kindness and responsibility that we have for our livestock, 'mma ha awu okenye no na uno eghu amu o na ogbu' (I will not be the elder/adult who was around when the goat that is in the throes of labour delivered with the tether still on its neck). This saying serves two purposes. It shows that Igbos would prepare for their animals birth processes, as they would their own. Also it is a reminder to adults that they would be held responsible if things go wrong during their watch.

If Igbos buy a new fowl, it is customary to domesticate it first: the way this is done is by tying a rope to one of its legs. This rope is tied to a little piece of stick. This is to prevent the fowl from wandering off too far away, and possibly getting lost. While the fowl is still in this familiarization stage, the Igbos would customarily be feeding it as it would not be expected to secure enough food for its sustenance. This continues till it is familiar with its owner's territory and can be relied on to go out, look for food, and return at the right time.

Unfortunately the act of writing effectively came late to us, and those who brought the modern writing techniques also taught the Igbos to hate Igbo history, and cultural practices by branding them pagan and primitive, so we were not able to have in written form a record of our practices. Accordingly in studies like this I have to rely on my memory, and observation. But for the present study help can still be secured from John Munonye's *The Only Son*[172].

He narrated a conversation between two Igbo ladies. One had fallen into despondency and had started neglecting her livestock. Her friend reminded her of her responsibilities with the following words: "I will go out and get new leaves for it" she left the shed. "I guess you've been feeding it on palm fronds alone for days. Goats are like human beings, in that they don't like to eat same thing day in day out, from morning till night. Give me a knife and I'll go into the bush."

She went and got some fodder for the goat, and when the goat started eating, she added "its cry nearly rent my heart."

I looked at Deuteronomy 5: 14, and I wasn't surprised at what came out of Israel: " ….nor thine ox, nor thine ass, nor any of thy cattle—shall work on the Sabbath." And J. H. Hertz explains the provision thus:

"Care and kindness to cattle are of such profound importance for the humanizing of man that this duty has its place in the Decalogue. The Rabbis classified cruelty to animals among the most serious of offences[173]."

From Israel Deuteronomy 25:4, also provides: "Thou shalt not muzzle the ox when he treadeth out the corn."

Igbos who are still close to Omenana feel pain when they see animals in distress and pain. In Abuja where I live it is common to see fowls whose legs are on the verge of being slowly worn off by threads which the

---

[172] Munonye, John, *The Only Son* (Ibadan: Heinemann Educational Books, 1966) 110,111.
[173] J. H. Hertz, *The Pentateuch and Haftorahs*, 2nd edition (London: The Soncino Press, 1937).

owners tie on their legs as identification marks. As the fowls grow, the thread cuts into their legs, and the ultimate result is that they slowly lose the legs. I regularly commission small children to catch the fowls, and untie the thread, for gifts of biscuits or sweets.

# CHAPTER ELEVEN: Treatment of Crime and Other Offenses

## Igbu Ochu (intentional homicide)

Two Igbo sayings: 'Ogbu mma ya ana na mma' and 'ogba egbe ya ana na egbe', which mean literally—'he who kills with the knife will be killed with a knife, and he who kills with a gun would be killed with a gun'—sum up the total attitude and feelings of the Igbos for the murderer. What the two sayings mean is that the murderer must receive the same treatment which he had bequeathed to his fellow human being.

The Igbos view murder as a most grievous and heinous offence against man and Chukwu. When homicide occurs intentionally in traditional Igbo society, the typical Igbo reaction, which may be expressed in the following words is-*a kwafuru obara* that is that 'blood has been spilled or shed.' It is not very easy to transmit the feelings behind the few words, but the feelings are close to those expressed in Genesis 4:10-11, when God remonstrated against Cain's shedding of his brother, Abel's blood[174]. As Igbos utter the words, their faces would be contorted in grief, as if the worst calamity had occurred. And indeed by Igbo tradition, a committal of murder is calamitous, because murder, which is known as *igbu ochu* is an abomination: (*aru*) in Omenana Igbo.

Igbos believe that murder is so heinous that the land or country in which it was perpetrated or carried out had been soiled by the act; that such a land or country needs to be purified in order for it to be fit for habitation

---

[174] Hertz, J. H., *The Pentateuch and Haftorahs*, 2nd edition (London: The Soncino Press, 1937) 14, (Genesis 4:10-11).

again. One of the measures deployed to restore normalcy by the Igbos is resort to what is known as *lex talionis*, that is the murderer will be served the same measure which he had served his victim.

G.T. Basden observed that the Igbo approach is distinctly similar to the Israelite approach in Deuteronomy 19: 21: "Life shall go for life, eye for eye, tooth for tooth, hand for hand, foot for foot[175]."

He stated: The demand of "life for life" is a predominant feature in Ibo customs.

After the offender has been killed the land still has to be purified. A section of this book is on purifications so I will not go beyond mention of it here.

With all the foregoing it can be stated categorically that the Igbo people viewed murder as utterly reprehensible, odious, abominable and bad, and as an act that should be blotted out by very drastic means in order to ensure the survival of the society.

It can also be said that Igbo society has a parallel in Israel as far as utter revulsion for murder is concerned.

**Manslaughter**

What distinguishes the man-slaughterer from the murderer is that the former terminated someone's life unintentionally; while the latter plotted to do so, and carried it out.

To the Igbos any shedding of human blood, intentionally or unintentionally, is a serious matter. But the Igbos don't view or treat the man-slaughterer as they treat the murderer. They recognize that his offence was committed unintentionally. Accordingly his life is not

---

[175] Basden, G. T., *Niger Ibos* (London: Frank Cass and Co., Ltd., 1966) 415.

forfeit. But he is also not allowed to escape total punishment. He must go into exile for seven years. He must escape from the scene of the offence, and he is not impeded from doing so. After he had escaped all his property that he did not escape with are to be destroyed.

The practice of the Igbos is for such unfortunate victims to flee to their mother's kinsmen, and abide with them for seven years, which is the prescribed period for 'igba oso ochu' (fleeing after killing unintentionally).

Chinua Achebe[176] bequeathed to us one of the few recorded cases of this tradition in practice. The tragic hero of his novel Okonkwo killed a kinsman inadvertently, and had to flee to his mother's clan, and abided there for seven years. His experience is closely paralleled by that of Absalom, King David's favourite son, who killed his brother, albeit intentionally, even though he had a genuine grievance as Amon had violated his sister, and he fled to his mother's brother, Talmai the son of Ammihud, the king of Geshur; his grandfather. (II Samuel 13: 34-39).

Interestingly we find Chinua Achebe's Okonkwo's reprieve approved by Deuteronomy19 :4, which made the following call: "And this is the case of the manslayer that shall flee thither and live: who so killed his neighbour unawares, and hated him not in the past."

In Okonkwo's flight to his mother's kindred, he took a path that Absalom took thousands of years before him.

Some Igbos, from the present Ebonyi state, Igbo-land, insist that they have some towns set aside for the manslaughterer to live in till his period of exile ends.

---

[176] Achebe, Chinua, *Things Fall Apart*, (Ibadan: Heinemann Educational Books, 1958).

This claim has not been verified by me, but it may not be strange if such exist because we found Deuteronomy 4:41-43, setting aside three cities for such persons to flee to.

For the Igbos after the manslaughterer had fled his family members still have to carry out purification rites in order to expiate his great offence (shedding of blood).

In the discourse, as in the study on murder, it cannot be over-stressed that the similarities and parallels with Israel are more than compelling.

## Ikwu Udo (suicide)

Committing of suicide (*ikwu udo*), which means to take one's own life by hanging, is an act that every family in Igbo-land prays that its members will never do. Suicide is a very serious abominable act to the Igbo. If an Ozubulu man commits suicide, you can expect Ozubulu people to declare: 'O meru aru' (he committed an abomination). The Igbos handle the case with extreme caution. The body of the man or woman who hanged himself or herself is left untouched, because to the Igbos it is profane; and should not be touched lest it soil or profane anybody that touched it.

Also because the deceased had committed an abomination against Chukwu he must not be mourned. With haste a priest of Nri extraction is sent for. As soon as he arrives, he carries out purifications. When he does that, the body can then be cut down, and without ceremonies of any type, it will be bundled up and out, to be deposited or flung into the forest. The body is not buried, because the Igbos believe that the offender's defiled corpse has defiled the land, and rendered it polluted. To fully understand the Igbo psychology on this the reader has to study the section that deals with the similarities between *Omenana* and Judaism again. So, not having been buried, the corpse will be swiftly eaten up by carrion eaters. But back at home, all the property in the immediate vicinity in which the crime took place is forfeit. A reasoned guess is that the reason for Igbo strictness against suicide is to discourage people from treating life with levity.

And interestingly it is noteworthy that Israelite Law regarding hanged persons closely resembles Igbo custom relating to suicide by hanging.

In Deuteronomy 21:23 we find the charge: "For he that is hanged is a reproach unto God; that thou defile not thy land which the Lord thy God giveth thee for an inheritance."

For those interested in reading more about this, Chinua Achebe's *Things Fall Apart* can be helpful.

**The Witch/Wizard and Witchcraft: Ita Amonsu**

It is not easy to prove that witchcraft and wizardry are of foreign origins, that is that they infiltrated Igbo practices, but such suggestions have been made. And truthfully the presence of witches was not keenly felt by Igbos until many Igbos joined some churches that stage daily campaigns agains witches and wizards. Igbo hatred, fear and scorn for *ndi amonsu* (witches and wizards) was so great, that among the Igbos one of the greatest insults one could hurl at his fellow is *amonsu*.

A witch may be defined as someone, especially a woman, supposed to have magical powers used usually, but not always, malevolently.

No Igbo even in this present stage of the Igbo people had dared to call himself or herself a practicing witch, white or black. With 'modernization' of the Igbo society, and the infiltration of foreign religions some Igbos have however started coming out to 'confess' that they WERE witches and wizards. G.T. Basden likened the Igbo abhorrence for witches to the Israelite revulsion for witches and wizards. According to him; the Igbos would not hesitate to "ill-treat, drive away, or even kill" witches[177]. He parallelized it with Israelite Law, which called witchcraft an abomination which must not be allowed in Israel. Exodus 22:17 provides "Thou shalt not suffer a sorceress to live."

## Onye Asiri, Igba Asiri (gossiping)

To the Igbo people the tale bearer and the slanderer are as bad as the murderer. He is called 'onye na aku asiri' (a gossip). The Igbos believe that to slander somebody or spread false tales against him is worse than killing him. Thus the Igbos say 'nkwuto nwa ogaranya ka ogbu gbu ya' (the slandering or scandalizing of the rich man is worse than murdering him). From the position of Rabbi Solomon Ganzfried, translated by Hyman E. Goldin, it appears that Israel views tale-bearing and slandering equally seriously: According to them: "It is written (Leviticus 19:16): "Thou shalt not go up and down as a talebearer among they people.....it is a grave sin which may cause the death of some people in Israel[178]".

Jews view *Lashon Ha-ra* (gossiping) as a very serious offence.

While the Igbos viewed the offences as equivalent to, or even worse than murder, Israel views it is as capable of instigating murderous feelings.

---

[177] Basden, G. T., *Niger Ibos* (London: Frank Cass and Co., Ltd., 1966) 422.
[178] Ganzfried, Solomon, and Goldin, Hyman E. trans., *Code of Jewish Law and Customs (Shulhan Aruch)* (New York: Hebrew Publishing Company, 1961) Chapter 30, p. [97].

The similarities between both positions are striking.

## Insubordination to Parents and Dishonoring of Parents

Among the Igbos the son who would not respect his parents did not deserve to live. The saying 'ekweghe ekwe na ekwe na ute ekwere' is always applied to such sons. It means that the insubordinate, stubborn, rebellious and bad person ends up in the mat that is to be used as his 'burial' shroud.

But one observation needs to be made at this stage. It is noticeable that such Igbo customs that threaten harsh reprisals for crimes such as the one in discussion seem to be deterrents. For example in traditional Igbo society it was extremely rare to see an Igbo son disparaging his parents. There might be quarrels, but they were quickly resolved, and would not degenerate to anything near to what we found in other surrounding cultures: people having the courage to go around broadcasting that their parents and ancestors were evil people. Such people if they were to arise among the Igbos world not be allowed to live, because they are a corruption in the land. G.T. Basden stresses:"The ancient Ibo method of dealing with similar unsatisfactory characters also resulted in violent ends for the culprits[179]."

They are like the stubborn and rebellious son in Israel, that will not hearken to the voice of his father, or the voice of his mother, and though they chasten him, will not hearken unto them. (Deuteronomy 21:18.)

---

[179] Basden, G. T., *Niger Ibos* (London: Frank Cass and Co., Ltd., 1966) 422.

### Thieves/Armed Robbers

Igbo custom demands death for the thief, or the armed robber as he is called in modern times. If this crime can be dignified with the tag –vice, then an Igbo can argue that it was a vice that infiltrated Igbo- land after contact with Europeans, and other neighboring African peoples had been made by the Igbos. Before the contact, the customs served as enough check on the people. People were really afraid of polluting the land by violating *(imebi) Omenana*. And definitely robbery was acknowledged to be one of the acts that would defile the robber and the *ana* (the land). Some Igbos who were unfortunate enough to steal in the era before Westernization and 'civilization' gained ground were tainted and blighted forever because *nke zuru ohi* (the one that stole) was associated with them, and their descendants forever.

Even in these modern times the Igbos occasionally go after all known thieves. This has been done in several *boys o yee* campaigns (Traders group themselves as a mob and go after thieves). The Bakassi Boys did the same too.

The Igbos believe that the thief has forfeited his life. Comparison can be made between the Igbo conviction that the thief should be killed with Exodus 22: 1, which provides: "if a thief be found breaking up, and be smitten that he die, there shall be no blood shed for him."

# CHAPTER TWELVE: Igbo Revulsion for Irresponsible and Unnatural Sexual Behaviours

**Adultery**

The Igbos have no word for adultery in their language. Traditionally Igbo revulsion for adultery is total. And to prevent its occurrence the Igbo people developed so many measures that could forestall it.

Traditionally the Igbo society was both monogamous and polygamous. An average man could have a wife, or up to three wives. Some had up to ten or more. All things been equal it is difficult to see that man whose ardour would not be assuaged by the attention of five or six women. Also while our records do not show us strict sanctions that existed to punish adulterous men, yet we know that they were not regarded as responsible people. Perhaps that was enough in a society that every man believed that he was as good as or better than his fellow. Accordingly no person would like to be seen as irresponsible.

But for the women-folk the case is different. If a married woman commits adultery it is regarded as an abomination, and she could be killed for that. But strict proof of her guilt is required. Records do not exist as to how this penalty was carried out, and by whom, i.e., if it was ever carried out. The woman who was suspected of adultery is taken to the central place of worship of the entire clan /community. There she was administered an oath that is akin to the oath drink /bitter waters of the Israelites. In Ozubulu survivals of this rite is to be found in *ita oji ana* (to eat kola from off the ground). A kola nut is prayed over, and kept on the ground, in front of the *okwu Chi/ /ana*, and the woman is asked to pick up the kola with her lips and eat it if she was not guilty of adultery.

Flora Nwapa mentioned another procedure in her book. The words of the woman who was suspected of adultery is set out in the following passage: "... should kill me if since I married Eneberi any man in our town, in Onitsha, Ndoni, Akiti or anywhere I had been, had seen my thighs[180]."

Igbo custom demands that immediately a woman becomes betrothed to a man that she ceases to have intimate or sexual relations with any other man; and that is if she had been having sexual relations at all, a situation which is looked at with disfavour if it happens outside marriage.

The Igbo marriage covenant appears to be effective from the betrothal. But there is a pre-betrothal engagement, violation of which is also viewed with all seriousness and concern. A woman/girl who had entered into the pre-betrothal engagement with a man by accepting a coconut ritually from him, is expected to reject the sexual advances of all other men. Should she stray, from that moment till the betrothal *(ime ego)*, she is expected to confess her indiscretion at the *isa ifi* (confession) ceremony. Her punishment is loss of respect from her husband and his family. The offending man or men are required to pay certain fines to the offended man. Such a girl is described as *onye a no ho na uno* (she that was not found at home), i.e,. somebody

---

[180] Nwapa, Flora, *Efuru* (Ibadan: Heinemann Educational Books, 1966) 220.

that is sexually loose. Chinua Achebe's works on this in *Things Fall Apart* and *Arrow of God* are very helpful.

While comparing Igbo custom and Israelite law, G.T. Basden pointed out that Israelite law prescribes the death penalty for the man who commits adultery with a married woman. Leviticus 20:10, Deuteronomy 22:22.

It is a fact that Igbo tradition prescribes death for adultery, but as I have stated earlier, no records exists that tells us how this penalty is exacted, and if it was exacted.

**Premarital Sex**

As has been stated severally the Igbo society is a conglomeration of hundreds of clans, existing in total independence of each other, yet all are intimately related by traditions as the Igbo people.

This factor (decentralization) is very useful to a researcher who is in search of Igbo values and morals. As the clans are independent, Igbo culture is better preserved in some than in the others. If the Igbos are centralized this may not be easy. I made the foregoing comment, because I observed that some Igbo clans remember, and still observe some traditions of the Igbos that some other clans have forgotten. A case in point concerns the Umuawulu clan. This community, which lies less than thirty kilometres north of Ozubulu, has a tradition that "na ha ada ho anu nwanyi na afo ime" (A woman should not be made pregnant before she is bethrothed or married). In other words pre-marital sex, even between intending couples must be avoided. But they (Umuawulu people) have forgotten why they have that belief. All they know is that it is a carryover from their ancestral practices. Perhaps we can find a key to the puzzle in a Biblical case that has some similarities to the Igbo position.

In Genesis 34:2, we found tension between the sons of Israel and the Shechemites, because one of the Shechemites had had sexual relations with their sister by force. The Shechemites were prepared to heal the injury by marrying the girl, and were also prepared to make themselves acceptable to the Israelites by circumcising themselves. All these however did not assuage the anger of the sons of Jacob, because according to them "Should one deal with our sister as with a harlot?" In other words, that having had sexual relations with the girl, that the man of Shechem had treated her like a harlot. That marriage to the girl should have preceded the sexual union.

I see a similarity between the Umuawulu position and the Israelite position here. To the Igbos sexual activity should be primarily for procreation. And to the Igbos, as we will see shortly, procreation should only be within marriage. Also, to the sons of Israel, their sister should not be united sexually to a man who had not married her.

I will now deal with the major reasons why Igbos would shun pre-marital sex traditionally, and prefer sexual relations to be only within the bounds of marriage.

Igbo conviction is that the number one reason that should impel humans to have sexual relations is the need for procreation. This is stated expressly in Igbo lore, and a scholar who is listening intently to the Igbos can deduce it from Igbo sayings about related concepts: for example Igbos say 'ife eji anu nwanyi wu maka nwa' (the reason for marrying is for the purpose of procreation)

On the first saying they have company with the Jews who describe the purpose of marriage as consisting of: "The duty of building a home and of rearing a family (Genesis 1:28 'be fruitful and multiply') figures in the Rabbinic codes as the first of the 613 Mitzvoth of the Torah[181]."

One might expect a people like the Igbos who want to be "be fruitful and multiply," or who see sexual intercourse as useful primarily for procreation, to be sexually irresponsible.

But they are not, because their traditions came to their rescue. Igbo traditions encourage Igbos to be sexually active, but the sexual activity has to be between a lawfully married couple. Igbo traditions reserved a place far from honour for children born out of wedlock, so Igbo men and women strive to bring in children into the world, who would not start off with some disadvantages.

But as every society has its renegades; what happens if an Igbo girl that is unmarried becomes pregnant, and the person responsible for the pregnancy refuses to marry her?

A dilemma is here. From available evidence the Igbos understood medicine in ancient times. They could induce abortions if they wanted to, but they would not take that option in the ancient and traditional era, because then they understood that *igbu ochu* (murder) was too heinous, defiles the land, and earns the community the anger of, and punishment from Chukwu.

But as the Igbo society is organised to exclude, or at least to deny honour to children born out of wedlock,

---

[181] Hertz, J. H., *The Pentateuch and Haftorahs*, 2nd edition (London: The Soncino Press, 1937), p.931, (additional notes on Deuteronomy).

how do the Igbos get out of their dilemma, since they would not stain their hands with blood; and the incoming child would be treated exactly as described in the following passage:

"A bastard shall not enter into the assembly of the Lord, even to the tenth generation shall none of his enter into the assembly of the Lord."(Deuteronomy 23:3).

The following remedy is used to ensure that nobody is born as an illegitimate child. If a young girl becomes unfortunate and headstrong enough to become pregnant while she was not married to any man, obviously her value has decreased. The young men would not be interested in marrying her. Igbo custom and practice saves the situation. Older men who are on the lookout for a wife are contacted and they are informed of the situation, and they marry her with the pregnancy, thereby the child in the womb escapes from being born a bastard; because among the Igbos an illegitimate child (*nwa enwe ho nna*)—(bastard) cannot enter the assembly of the 'Lord.' Such a child cannot be an *aka ji ofo* (priest by position of being the oldest man) when he becomes the oldest man in the community. Is it not ironical that the Igbos whom some European scholars described as 'primitive', recognized more than those Europeans the need to guard against development of a class of disadvantaged people?

As promised, I will deal briefly with the subject of harlotry. Along with Igbo zeal to guard against anybody coming into the world with a social disadvantage, goes the zeal to prevent the formation of an underclass like prostitutes.

G.T. Basden categorically mentioned that; "harlotry, as a profession, was unknown in the Ibo country prior to the impact of Western influences[182]."

Thus while striving to ensure that the incoming child has a father, the mother is also given a husband, so that she can have a fresh start in life.

**Homosexuality and bestiality**

Same-sex relationships were not known by the Igbos until the modern era. But bestiality had been heard of. Even though its occurrence was so rare, yet I have heard it mentioned in Igbo lore about how an Igbo had had sexual intercourse with a sheep in his farm. He was seen during the act by a clansman who was on top of a palm wine tree, and was reported to the clan, which without hesitation declared that what he had done was *aru* (abomination).

The story is that a certain Igbo went to his farm, and the evil inclination took hold of him. He saw a sheep and caught it. He looked east, west, north and south, and seeing no prying eyes he mounted the sheep, but in his bliss he did not look up. And up there was a palm wine tapper who saw everything. The tapper did not keep quiet until the gentleman had finished, but he raised an alarm, as required by tradition. By Igbo tradition anybody who sees evil must report it, possibly while the evil deed was still in progress. The clan gathered. He narrated what he had seen. The community took a decision. *Aru* (abomination) had been committed. And to cleanse or purify *(ikpu aru)*, the land of the abomination which had been committed, a cow; a large animal, was required. The pronouncement having been

---

[182] Basden, G. T. *Niger Ibos* (London: Frank Cass and Co., Ltd., 1966) 239.

made, everybody went home. The culprit knew and understood the customs. *Aru* (abomination) defiles the land, and has to be cleansed from the land, because if not cleansed the land would definitely vomit (*gboo*) the inhabitants, by taking a toll through premature deaths, poverty, disease, etc.

But the clan could escape the repercussions by separating itself from the culprit, whose family, as well as he, be shamed unless they purify the land which he had defiled because "ife onye metar,' oburu na isi ya" (whatever a man sows he shall reap).

The culprit's family complied in haste. The Israelite law in Leviticus 18:23 directly parallels Igbo custom and it declares: "And thou shall not lie with any beast and defile thyself therewith; neither shall any woman stand before a beast, to lie down there to; it is perversion. Defile not ye yourselves in any of these things; for in all these the nations are defiled, which I cast out from before you. And the land was defiled therefore I did visit the iniquity thereof upon it, and the land vomited out her inhabitants."

Not only do the Igbo and Israelite parallels have striking similarities, but the thoughts of both peoples move in the same direction. Israelite idea is that a defiled land 'vomits out.' The Igbos believe and say that 'na ana na atu madu' (the land throws up somebody). Also the Igbos say and believe that 'ana na agboputa ndi mmadu' (the land vomits out people).

# CHAPTER THIRTEEN: Land Matters

## Igbo-land

The most striking and noticeable feature of Igbo-land is its smallness- when compared with its neighbours. In a Nigeria of nearly four hundred different ethnic groups the Igbos constitute one of the most populous. But an interesting paradox presents itself: the Igbos have less land than groups who have far less than their population. In fact some groups whose populations are less than one-fifth that of the Igbos have more land than the Igbos. I conjecture that what made the Igbos to have a small land vis-a-vis their population is the belief and conviction that they were/are given or granted what they have by Chukwu, (the Supreme Being), the Being that they cannot fight against. Also that the Igbos have through long practice grown used to being contented with what they believe that they were allotted by Chukwu (God), and lastly that the bonds of brotherhood between the Igbos is so strong that the Igbos lived/live close to each other. All these factors do in my opinion account for the smallness of Igbo-land.

Israel's history about its right to Canaan offers an interesting parallel. I know of only one nation, Israel, that asserts that it had/has a divine right to its land, and that had the boundaries of its land set out in its most sacred book (Numbers 34). This factor naturally inhibited the Israelites and the modern Israelis from seeking to annex land that they had no historical/divine claims to. The Igbos, at least as of today, have not found written records that set forth their rights to their land or its boundaries. But, like the Israelites whose claim on their land is based on the record of their ancestors' interactions with God, we find the Igbos exhibiting the same or similar traits. In a land dispute in which adjudication would be based on *Omenana*, great weight is attached to 'ife nna m gwar'm' (what my father told me).Israel has persistently based its claim on the Land of Israel on what his Father (God, Exodus 4:22), and fathers (the Patriarchs and Prophets) relayed to him.

As already stressed in the social organization section of this book, all the Igbos never came under a single central political authority. What we have as the Igbo society are hundreds of large families which have total independence from each other. Igbo-land, or the land of the Igbos, is divided between these clans /families, and owned by them. Every clan/family/individual has its own land, and is in effective ownership and possession of it. Land boundaries are clearly known because records have been preserved orally. Only very rarely do fights occur between the families over land

Robert Collis observed the absolute division of Igbo-land and the smallness of the land in his comment:"here 9Igbo-land) the land has been so subdivided that the average is less than half an acre per family[183]."

Collis observation reminded me of the Israelite division of the 'land' (Deuteronomy 3), and requirement for further divisions and subdivisions after each feast of Jubilee.

Another distinguishing feature of the land is that no portion of it is free of ownership. Every single portion of land in Igbo-land is owned by an individual, or a family, or the clan. If a man trespasses on his neighbours land, he is called to order quickly. Among the Igbos removal of another person's land mark is an abomination.

---

[183] Collis, Robert, *Nigeria In Conflict* (Lagos: John West Publication, Ltd., 1970) 415.

Removal of the landmark of one's neighbour is also legislated against in the Tanach (the Hebrew Bible).

Also it is interesting that as Abraham used livestock to cement a pact in which Abimelech acknowledged that a piece of land in dispute belonged to Abraham-(Genesis 21:27-28), so do the Igbos seal a transfer of land traditionally with the ritual of *igbu eghu ana* (slaughtering of the goat for sale of land). In this ritual an *mkpi* (male goat) is provided by the buyer, and it is slaughtered, and cooked, and both buyer, seller, and their witnesses partake of its meat.

## "The Land" and the Feeling of Being in Exile

The social anthropologist, of Swiss-Israeli extraction, Daniel Lis, who is also researching on the Igbo-Israelite relationship had posed the following question to me:

'Remy, do the Igbos have the feeling that they are in exile from the Land of Israel?' My response took a long time to come. We need not rehash or recount the relationship that exists between the children of Israel and the Land of Israel, because the following statement tells it all."There has never been a time when our people did not feel something special about this Land, something sacred[184]."

There is no evidence yet that the Igbos have a feeling that they are in exile-away from the Land of Israel, but there is widespread concern for happenings in the Land of Israel, by and among the Igbos. The Igbo is yet to be found who is informed, and who has the equipment to follow the news coming out of the Land of Israel: about the fighting between the Israelis and Arabs, who is not

---

[184] Rossel, Seymour, *Covenant People, Covenant Land* (New York: Union of American Hebrew Congregations, 1995) 9.

concerned, and who does not feel disquiet. This feeling has been a feature of Igbo life for as long as any living Igbo can remember.

This was the much I could tell about Igbo feelings about the Land of Israel. I communicated my findings to Daniel Lis. But then I asked myself; do the Igbos living outside Igbo-land not feel that they are on exile from Igbo-land? Clearly we do. In the section on rituals of death I took care to mention that one of the greatest misfortunes Igbos could think of was to have their loved ones buried outside Igbo-land. Also no matter how bad the economic situation gets in Nigeria, the Igbos consider it a duty to visit 'home' (Igbo-land) from time to time. I was drafted into my clan's constitution drafting committee in 2000. As the lawyer in the committee it fell on me to find documents that paralleled what we had in mind. I got the constitutions of ten other Igbo clan unions in Abuja. In all ten, the Igbos copiously referred to their clans as 'our home'; just as the Jew of Europe or of America or Canada recognizes that he has an ancestral 'home'-the Land of Israel. In the Igbo case my conviction, born out of my present research findings, is that the Igbos have adapted and accustomed themselves to the idea that Igbo-land is their 'home', i.e., the 'Land.'

# CHAPTER FOURTEEN: Ritual Cleanliness

**Ikwo aka na isa ihu uchu (washing of the hands and face in the morning)**

By Igbo traditions the first act that a person must perform when he or she wakes up from sleep is to wash the hands and the face. The Igbos call this ritual *'ikwo aka ututu, na isa ihu uchu.'* If these words or lines are translated they can only help marginally, because the key word *"uchu"* has no meaning in contemporary Igbo, at least in my part of Igbo-land. But I will try to unlock the reason behind this ritual washing of the hands and the face, which many Igbos alive may not know why it is done. If the Igbos say to someone *'uchu so kwa gi'* (let *'uchu'* follow you), it is not seen as a friendly or good wish. At the very least it is viewed as a wish for bad luck. And the same *uchu* is the element that the Igbos want to wash off their hands and faces in the morning. A safe conjecture can be drawn that *'uchu'* is something bad, or at least not welcome.

Jewish tradition seems to suggest that there is something that is bad on the hands of a person who just woke up that needs to be washed off. I noticed the suggestions of the foregoing in the quoted passage, which is from the *Shulhan Arukh*:"When rising from sleep, the unclean spirit departs from the entire body, except from his fingers and does not depart until one spills water upon them three times alternately[185]."

---

[185] Ganzfried, Solomon, and Hyman E. Goldin, trans., *Code of Jewish Law and Customs (Shulhan Aruch)* (New York: Hebrew Publishing Company, 1961) 3.

As ready mentioned *uchu* is at least a bad wish to the Igbos. Thus it can be approximated to the unclean spirit that has to be ritually washed off in Jewish tradition.

In Igbo culture, you can expect a wise mother to call to her the children in the morning 'ikwoo na aka ututu, saa ihu uchu?' (Have you washed your hands and face in order to get rid of *uchu*?)

An Igbo writer mentions "the very elderly ones begin (prayers) with ablutions[186]."

**Perception of Exposed Faeces as an Eyesore**

Igbo customs regard it as abominable in a minor degree for human faeces to be exposed to public viewing. Igbos are also incapable of staying around faeces. In this modern time, when all controls are collapsing, the young may leave faeces lying about, and what you will hear the elderly say is 'jee flushi a nya wu toilet, na mmadu na nsi a da ho ano' (please rush and go and flush that toilet, because humans and faeces cannot abide or cohabit). In olden times the reaction to exposed faeces was stricter. Whoever saw exposed excreta felt so bad, and was always moved to exclaim loudly 'anya a fuo m aru' (my eyes have seen an abominable thing). He or she immediately seeks for an egg, breaks it, and smears his or her eyes with it, to remedy the injury 'caused' to the eyes due to the (abominable matter) which it had seen. The Igbo tradition abhors hearing or seeing abomination.

Meanwhile the victim's exclamation, would have been loud enough to attract neighbours, who would gather, and the culprit would be identified. On identification he

---

[186] Ade Adegbola, E. A. *Traditional Religion in West Africa* (Ibadan: Sefer Books, 1983) 8.

or she would remove the excreta, and perform minor purification.

Jewish custom and law strictly forbids the exposure of excreta, and I use the following passage as an authority: "Thou shalt have a place also without the camp, whither thou shalt go forth abroad. And thou shalt have a paddle among your weapons and it shall be when thou sittest down abroad, thou shalt dig therewith, and shalt turn back and cover that which cometh from thee," (Deuteronomy 23:13,14).

## Iza Uno Na Iza Ezi (sweeping of the house and compound)

There is hardly any activity in the life of the Igbos that is devoid of religious implication. There is no distinction between the secular and the religious in Igbo life. Accordingly places that would just be secular places to other peoples are more or less treated like sacred temples by the Igbos.

An Igbo man expects his house to be swept by his children in the morning. Ordinarily a man's living quarters are not expected to be treated like a temple, but that expectation is not applicable to the Igbos. A woman having her menstrual flow cannot approach his *obi* (his personal quarters/personal synagogue[187]).

His *obi* as mentioned before must be swept as soon as day breaks.

In the book; *Arrow of God,* Chinua Achebe told the story of how an Igbo man waited for his *obi* to be swept in the morning; but he did not know that his son had gone to the stream. At a point he summoned one of his wives to

---

[187] Nwapa, Flora, *Efuru* (Ibadan: Heinemann Educational Books, 1966) 25.

explain why his *obi* was not swept. Her explanations only earned the following retort from him- : "The abomination all you people commit in this house will lie on your own head[188]."

Even in jest the Igbos only use the word abomination sparingly. The man employed it here to emphasize the seriousness that tradition attaches to cleanliness in the household and community.

Achebe poignantly captured Igbo attachment for a clean compound in another episode in the same book. A strong Igbo man had just suffered one of the worst and most dreaded calamities to the Igbos-- his children dying during his life-time. Like a typical Igbo parent, Ezeulu lost his sanity temporarily, but he was not too far gone to disregard cleanliness, and Ezeulu then makes the following comment: "People will soon be here,' he said weakly 'and the place is still unswept[189]."

The corpse was still before him as he spoke. One can say that it was habitual reaction at play. Only very careful observation can reveal that Israelite custom has parallels to the foregoing Igbo practice. Citing Ganzfried-Goldin at length, we have the following:

Cleanness of places used for holy purposes—using Deuteronomy 23:14 -15 as their basis the authors argued:"from this Rabbis, of blessed memory have deduced that whenever the Lord our G-d walks with us, that is, when we are engaged in a holy task, such as the reading of the Shema, a prayer, the study of the Torah, or the like, then the place must be holy, so that no excrement may be found there, and that nothing

---

[188] Achebe, Chinua, *Arrow of God* (Ibadan: Heinemann Educational Books, 1964) 124-125.
[189] ibid., 228.

unseemly should be visible to any one who worships[190]."

The Igbo man prays in his *obi*, receives visitors there, breaks kola nuts for offerings there. And his family altar (*okwu Chi/Mmuo*) is also situated in the compound.

## Washing of The Hands Before Eating

Most of the Igbo practices that I have mentioned in this study are still practiced even now, but what Igbos have lacked are written records in which they are set out.

As children all Igbos have it drummed into their ears that they must wash their hands before they eat. Expectedly nobody would think much about this, making it to seem merely a *general* or *universal* hygienic requirement, but it only makes sense when one begins to study it during research and when one compares what the Igbos do and what some of the peoples who share boundaries with the Igbos do, and their attachments or lack of attachment to this practice, and to general hygiene. I was able to see this practice mentioned only once in a book. Chinua Achebe recorded Igbos washing their hands before eating[191].

Among the Igbos it is universally practiced and has become so ingrained in the Igbos' mind that they are loath to eat unless they have washed their hands. This can be seen in how they eat bananas. No part of the pulp is touched. The Igbos gently pull off the peel gradually and keep on biting off the pulp, till the very last morsel is absorbed without touching the pulp. All this care is

---
[190] Ganzfried, Solomon, and Hyman E. Goldin, trans., *Code of Jewish Law and Customs (Shulhan Aruch)* (New York: Hebrew Publishing Company, 1961) chap. 40.
[191] Achebe, Chinua, *Things Fall Apart*, (Ibadan: Heinemann Educational Books, 1958) 99.

taken because Igbos who may want to eat bananas may not settle down to wash their hands before eating this fruit, as they would do before eating regular food. Among the Igbos the first item that must be brought to a dining table is water for washing hands *(mmiri aka)* or *mmiri ikwo aka.*

Israel has a direct parallel to the Igbo practice. Ganzfried-Goldin stipulates:"Before eating bread over which the benediction *Hamotzi* (who bringeth forth) is said, one must wash his hands first[192]."

But would Jews eat any food without saying benediction?

Igbo attachment to the practice in discussion is seen and understood better when Igbo practice is compared with the practice of some of their neighbours. For example Igbos are repelled when Igbos see people touching the pulp while eating bananas with unwashed hands.

**Nwanyi i No Na Nso (menstrual seclusion)**

Traditionally the Igbo woman having her menstrual flow is secluded; because 'o no na nso'. *Nso* is an Igbo word which can mean sacred or holy or forbidden. But it doesn't mean unclean or impure, or *unyi* (the Igbo word for dirty) as the English language presents the state of having a menstrual flow. Because of her state she will desist from cooking for grown men while having the flow.

Some more rigidly religious Igbo men such as seers[193] may even forbid a woman having her menstrual flow

---

[192] Ganzfried, Solomon, and Hyman E. Goldin, trans., *Code of Jewish Law and Customs (Shulhan Aruch)* (New York: Hebrew Publishing Company, 1961) chap. 40, p. 9.
[193] Nwapa, Flora, *Efuru* (Ibadan: Heinemann Educational Books, 1966) 25.

from coming too near to them. Olaudah Equiano mentioned that a special hut was reserved for his mother whenever she entered her period of menstrual flow[194].

It goes without saying that a people that would not eat food cooked by a woman because she is having her menstrual flow, will not have sexual relations with her during her period of menstruation.

G.T. Basden's work on this is delightful. It is set out below:"There are corresponding laws in respect of the menstruation of women. During the time of her period, the Ibo woman must dwell apart; she is forbidden to enter her husband's house until after her menstrual cleansing. The woman moves to a neighbour's, and abides in a corner near the entrance[195]."

I have had cause to listen to distinguished women on the subject of women having their menstrual flow being restricted in ancient Igbo and Israelite societies. Most are put off by the suggestions found in English translations of the Bible, which suggests that women are dirty because they go through a natural process. I noticed that a prominent Jewish scholar, Rabbi Harold S. Kushner, shares their concern too, as I do. Below is what he added to the debate[196]:

"English translators of the Bible are frustrated at trying to translate the traditional Hebrew term for a menstruating woman. They inaccurately render it as 'unclean' or 'impure'. The Hebrew word has no such connotations of being dirty or bad. It more nearly has

---

[194] The Interesting Narrative Of Olaudah Equiano or Gustavus Vassa the African. In: Ilona, Remy and Eliyahu, Ehav, *The Igbos: Jews In Africa*, (Abuja: Mega Press, 2005) 62.
[195] G. T. Basden, *Niger Ibos* (London: Frank Cass and Co., Ltd., 1966) 417.
[196] Kushner, Harold, *To Life* (Boston: Warner Books, 1993) 63.

connotations of being touched by the holiness of the life force so strongly during those days, and also after giving birth, that a woman is unapproachable in normal ways."

An Igbo would make exactly the same comment that Kushner made. In Igbo language *i no na nso* (being in nso) connotes and denotes being in a state that warrants temporary separation from her, and does not imply a dirty or impure state.

**Igbo Reaction to Leprosy**

Like the rest of humanity the Igbos do not know the cause of some diseases.

But they know the causes of some. For example the Igbos know that *iba* (malaria fever) is caused by *anwu nta* (mosquito bites). But there are some sicknesses which the Igbos do not know what the causes of them are. They view or believe that such sicknesses are caused by spirits, and they call them *ahu mmuo*[197] (sickness caused by spirits.)

In this one can see that the Igbos share with the Jews the tradition of distinguishing between what Joseph J. Williams[198], S.J. called *diaboli* and *daemonia*.

Leprosy is one of the diseases which the Igbos believe that it is caused by spirits. Nevertheless, they view it as deserving of eradication, and one of the primary weapons which they deployed against it was quarantining of sufferers.

Robert Collis observed the following: "There were between 30,000 and 40,000 lepers in that part of the

---

[197] Achebe, Chinua, *Arrow of God* (Ibadan: Heinemann Educational Books, 1964) 216.
[198] Williams, Joseph J., Hebrewisms of West Africa: From the Nile to the Niger With the Jews (New York: Biblo and Tanen, 1928) 99.

country-fear was the order of the day. If a leper passed along the highway he had to ring a bell. People meeting him fled.[199]"

This suggests that the Igbo practice of quarantining and other treatments worked.

Also the remedy of quarantining is found to be Israelitic: Leviticus 13:45-46 expresses: "And the leper in whom the plague is, his clothes shall be rent and the hair of his head shall go loose and he shall cover his upper lip and cry: unclean! unclean! All the days wherein the plague is on him he shall be unclean. He is unclean and he shall dwell alone; without the camp shall his dwelling be."

From the rigorous efforts Israel made to separate the leper from his kinsmen till he is healed, we can understand why he had to use a bell to warn his kinsmen of his presence among the Igbos, so that other persons could avoid infection.

---

[199] Collis, Robert, *Nigeria In Conflict* (Lagos: John West Publication, Ltd., 1970) 50.

# CHAPTER FIFTEEN: Dietary Matters By Remy Ilona and Ehan Ever

### Distinction Between Clean and Unclean Animals

The line was/is not clearly drawn here, but there are glimmers of light which can lead a researcher to the realization that the Igbo people knew that meat from some animals could be eaten, while some were to be avoided.

We can glimpse the validity of the above statement from some established positions of the Igbo people. For example to the Igbos *ezi* (pig) is the epitome of filth and dirtiness[200]. Before the intrusion of the Europeans, there were no pigs in Igboland. When I was growing up in Ozubulu, I used to hear about a pig farm belonging to one Amechi in the neighbouring Ukpor clan. There was none in my own, and other surrounding clans. The one in Ukpor was a novelty, that people from afar heard about. Instructively, there are no Igbo breeds of swine, as there are *okuko Igbo* (Igbo chickens), *eghu Igbo* (Igbo goats) and *efi Igbo* (Igbo cattle). The breeds that are in Igbo-land are the breeds brought by the Europeans. Interestingly many of the non Muslim ethnic groups in Nigeria rear pigs traditionally. We do not need an extensive discussion about the position of pork in Judaism. Pork meat is regarded as non-kosher meat by Jews. Also instructive is that for no 'meaningful' or reasonable, apparent reason, some Igbo clans shun the meat of some animals. For instance the people of Nnewi would not touch the meat of *ewi*—a small rat-like

---

[200] Munonye, John, *The Only Son* (Ibadan: Heinemann Educational Books, 1966) 121.

rodent, which falls into the category of forbidden meat in the Bible. And they have no coherent reasons why they should not eat it.

Moreover very importantly, G.T. Basden observed that in earlier times, by tradition pregnant Igbo women must not eat *ejuna* (snail), *nchi* (a rodent), and pig (*ezi*[201]). Basden also did not find out convincing reasons why the Igbo pregnant woman would not eat the mentioned meats.

It is certainly worth looking into that dog, and vulture meat, and meat from all the aforementioned animals, save the *nchi,* are not the popular and favoured meats by the Igbos. Igbos that eat the flesh of dogs and pigs nowadays are mocked and viewed derisively. It is unthinkable that an Igbo would touch vulture meat.

The Igbos would shun meat from animals that died of sickness, or old age. Besides fear of whatever took the life of the animal, they would also feel uncomfortable with eating meat which has undrained blood in it.

**Nni (Igbo food)**

Is it not funny that some neighbours of the Igbos have described the Igbos as grass eaters?

To those neighbours whose diet did not contain much vegetables, if any at all, the great love the Igbos have for vegetables seemed strange. Well before Western education came to Nigeria, and Nigerians or the people living around the Igbos benefited from its teachings on the advantages of including green vegetables in their diets, the Igbos had been eating vegetables. In fact most of the Igbo diet is vegetable-based. Robert Collis, a

---

[201] G. T. Basden, *Niger Ibos* (London: Frank Cass and Co., Ltd., 1966) 169.

British colonialist, while discussing the peoples of Nigeria wrote:"They (Igbos) only had one one-sixth to one-tenth of the land that the average family had in the West (Yoruba land and environs) yet they were living better. There was less protein malnutrition there also because they were using green vegetables in their diet[202]."

The fact was not only that there was less malnutrition, but that there was no malnutrition and no abject poverty in Igbo-land, in the era that preceded the contact with Europe.

As Collis observed rightly the Igbos ate much vegetables.

A particular Igbo meal-*ji afifia nni* or *ji akwukwo nni* (yam mixed with vegetables) is a study in dietary advancement. This meal which is actually mixture of yam slices, vegetables, oil bean seeds (*ukpaka*), palm oil (*mmanu*), pepper (*ose*) and salt (*nnu*), is very rich in nutrients. But surprisingly most Igbo children do not relish it. Children, for reasons no one has been able to understand, do not find vegetables tasty. To make sure that the children have the proper nutrients, an Igbo mother keeps a cane beside the plate of *ji akwukwo ni*, in order to ensure that her children eat their portions; otherwise the children will pick out the yams, eat them and throw the vegetables away (smile).

Another is cassava fermented and sifted to produce what the Igbos call *akpu ayoru ayo*. This, after it is boiled and pounded becomes *utara akpu*, and is eaten with soup. The Igbo soup is mainly vegetables with some of the aforementioned condiments.

---

[202] Collis, Robert, *Nigeria In Conflict* (Lagos: John West Publication, Ltd., 1970) 45.

Even maize flour (*nni oka*) is eaten with vegetables. With all the foregoing one can understand why the Igbos were described as eaters of grass by neighbours who did not know the value of eating green vegetables.

Now, if we are to accept the Biblical account of the origins and beginnings of man as authentic, and we must say that we have yet to see other accounts that approach it in meaningfulness, then we have to admit that the Igbo preference for vegetables and vegetarian diets certainly merits serious consideration due to the following reasons:

Stating that the Bible sprang out of Israel is stating the obvious. The *Torah, Neviim* and the *Kethuvim* (Teachings, Prophets and the Wise sayings)— collectively called the Hebrew Bible is indisputably the work of Israel. It would be deducible then that the Israelites knew about the accounts that were eventually recorded in the Bible. It should not be strange then if Israelites tend to adhere to traditions or stipulations that are found in the Bible, that require adherence to some rules and regulations that God stipulated, even before the people of Israel started to exist. For example from Genesis 2:16 we read: "And the Lord God commanded the man, saying: "of every tree of the garden thou mayest freely eat."

According to many classical Jewish Bible commentators, this means that God's original plan was for mankind to be vegetarian, and that God later gave permission to man to eat meat because of man's craving for meat. However, others argue that people may eat animals because God gave Adam and Chaya (Eve) dominion over them. Some prominent rabbis have been vegetarian, among them the first Chief Rabbi of pre-state Israel, Abraham Isaac Kook, former Chief Rabbi of Israel

Shlomo Goren and former Chief Rabbi of Haifa She'ar-Yashuv Cohen.

Other important rabbis have argued otherwise: former Chief Rabbi of Ireland, David Rosen, considered: "the consumption of meat as halachically unacceptable" and made a strong case for Jewish vegetarianism. Several Talmudic statements support this opinion. Some believe that halakha encourages the eating of meat at the Sabbath and Festival meals, and some Orthodox Jews who are otherwise vegetarian will nevertheless consume meat at these meals.

Kabbalistic teachings, from Talmudic and medieval sources, restrict the consumption of meat to only those who are spiritually highly developed. Others suggest that all Jews except the spiritually highly developed can eat meat. The soul of an animal is more complex than that of a vegetable, so requires a correspondingly complex soul to consume it. Conversely, eatingmeat has often been seen as luxuriously indulgent, and, therefore, the highly spiritual would abstain from it as a form of self-denial.

It is in such a light that I see that the Igbos mainly vegetarian diet as similar to the position of various parts of the Jewish community on the same issue.

Very interesting too is the presence of two very bitter herbs *utazi* and *onugbu* in the Igbos diet. Jews eat bitter leaves as part of their food during the Passover and Unleavened bread feasts.

It is also noteworthy that the Igbos did not extract animal milk nor did they drink milk traditionally, even though they ate meat. Also remarkable is that the Israelites are forbidden to eat milk and meat together. Is it not puzzling that the Igbos who knew that the various palms had wine 'couldn't have known that cows, sheep and goats which they had have milk'? I think the Igbos may have avoided milk simply to avoid eating milk and meat together.

## Igbu Anu (slaughter of animals)

Even though the Igbo diet is mainly vegetarian, the Igbos still eat meat. Their choice meats are goats, poultry, sheep and some rodents.

By Igbo traditions these animals must be slaughtered in a particular way. Assuming that the people want to eat a goat, the person that will slaughter the animal will get his knife ready by sharpening it (*iso mma*)..

While writing this section in the early parts of 2006,I conducted an extensive investigation to find out how the Igbos slaughtered animals traditionally, to confirm if it was in line with the way I slaughtered animals myself. I was surprised to hear that the Igbos washed the necks of animals that were to be slaughtered. Two members of my congregation; Chikwelu Attah, and Oliver Asogwa, whose fathers were strong in *Omenana*, up to the time that this work was written confirmed that Igbos washed the necks of animals that were being prepared for slaughter. At the time of writing the ritual of washing of the animal's neck was no longer common, so I had to check and confirm. At the time of the slaughtering in the Igbo tradition a hole is dug in the ground, to receive the blood. The hind legs of the animal are lifted up and held firmly by one or more strong persons. The animal's throat is then placed over the hole, and according to Eric Udoji, an Igbo attorney, a brief prayer which goes like this is uttered: 'Chukwu, we are not killing the animal for sport, but for food, so may we be forgiven'. The slaughterer will then seize the animal by the horn and kill it with a single slash across the throat. The head/throat of the animal is held over the hole until all the blood is drained into the hole, after which the hole is covered with sand. The Jewish practice of Shechitah[203] has some parallels with the Igbo model, as can be seen below.

"The animal's neck is first washed thoroughly to remove any sand particles in the fur, which could cause a nick in the knife during slaughter. The shochet's hand must be very steady, and he must employ one continuous movement, carefully avoiding the spine. This cut only takes a few seconds and is a much more humane method of killing an animal than are such common practices as smashing the head, shooting the animal or scalding it while it is still alive. Following the slaughter, the carcass is hung upside down so that the blood can drain properly[204]."

In Devarim (Deuteronomy 12:17) 16 G-d commanded that the blood of animals that are slaughtered is to be poured away "Like water upon the earth." The Torah records the prohibitions against consuming blood as being incumbent upon Noah and his family as well as the Israelites. It is my belief that the Torah is the root of the Igbo custom of draining the blood. It is also interesting to note the method of slaughter that was common amongst the Beta Israel (Ethiopian Jews):

"The Cahen (Kohen, i.e., Ethiopian Jewish priest), or another specially trained community member, slaughters the animal by making an incision on the neck. The animal's head is turned towards Jerusalem,

---

[203] Wikipedia Online Encyclopaedia, Article on Kosher, http://en.wikipedia.org/wiki/Kosher
[204] Shechita. In: Eidlitz, Eliezer, Is It Kosher? Feldheim Publishing; 1992. See kosher/quest.org/bookhtml/SHECHITA_THROUGH_BUTCHER.htm.

and before striking the blow, the Cahen recites a special blessing to God, which includes the Ten Commandments.

The initial flow of blood is channeled into a trench in the ground, where it is covered. The blood, which remains is drained in a special manner. After skin and arteries have been removed, the carcass is cut up into extremely small parts. These chunks are immersed in salt water and the juice of dough or some other liquid, and are washed thoroughly. The pieces are then hung up to dry out any remaining blood. An alternative method is to pour boiling water on the meat a number of times[205]."

G.T. Basden, making reference to Vayikra (Leviticus 17:14) and Devarim (Deuteronomy 12:14-16), suggests very strongly that the ideas behind the Igbo draining away of the blood is the same with the Israelite demand that the blood be discarded. Basden wrote that- "There is an inherent belief among the Igbos that the 'blood is the life[206]."

The next step taken is to carve up the carcass. The way that the component parts of the carcass are separated remind me of the provisions in Vayikra (Leviticus 7:30). The Torah states that the "chest area where the heart resides" of the slain animal is to be for Aharon (Aaron) and his sons the Kohanim and Levites. In the Igbo case the "chest area" is referred to as the *obi anu* i.e. (the heart of the animal), which is normally reserved for the elder who served as the priest in our time. Vayikra (Leviticus 7:32) states that the right thigh shall be given to the Kohen as a "free will offering." The fore-arm in the case of Igbos, i.e, the *aka anu* goes to the presiding priest; the *aka ji ofo* (the family elder). A similar process

---

[205] Ibid.
[206] G. T. Basden, *Niger Ibos* (London: Frank Cass and Co., Ltd., 1966) 420.

and treatment can be found amongst the Igbo in terms of their elders and priests.

Interestingly, these portions of Leviticus quoted earlier are from a portion of the Torah that deals with the ritual slaughter in relation to the Mishkan (Tabernacle), yet they resemble Igbo slaughtering practices as a whole. It is striking that the Igbo and the Israelite methods of slaughtering have various practices in common.

Existence contains four distinct levels: inanimate, vegetable, animal, and man. These levels are not only physical, but spiritual as well; every aspect of the created universe possesses a spiritual essence. All these elements are locked in a mortal struggle with each other, for each strives to rise to the next level, and thus become closer to the source. The sages taught that the only time when all of these basic forces are rectified and in harmony with each other is in the Holy Temple. For in the Temple service, all four aspects of creation unite together in the service of God, and thus reach their full potential in fulfilling His will and sanctifying His name. The priest who offers each sacrifice represents humanity; the animal offered, the animal kingdom; the flour, frankincense, libations etc. represent the world of plants; and even the inanimate level is represented... for salt must be a part of every sacrifice. Thus when the Temple stands, all of creation functions in harmony. This is one aspect of how the Temple brings peace to the world, "and in this place, I will grant peace, says HaShem of Hosts" (Haggai 2:9).

It is quite remarkable that the Igbo and the Israelite methods of slaughtering have many ideas in common. For example Jewish law prohibits making an animal to suffer before dying. Thus the knife to be used has to be extremely sharp. The same reason underlies the words, 'biko so kwaa mma esoo ofuma' (please really sharpen the knife very well) before Igbos commence the slaughter of animals.

As I was growing up, it was usual for my father to send for one man to slaughter animals for our family during marriages and funerals. Now I can remember that this man offered the same service to other families; just as the *shochet* (slaughterer) does in the Jewish community.

# CHAPTER SIXTEEN: Similarities Between Igbo and Semitic Manners of Dress

## Igbo Attitude to Clothes

I will start working on Igbo dressing by stating one factor that is striking: Igbo attitude to clothes or dressing.

To the Igbos there are clothes for men and clothes for women. And a man must not dress like a woman; neither should a woman dress like a man.

G.T. Basden observed: "Deuteronomy 22:5 states that 'the woman shall not wear that which pertaineth unto a man.' This is a very strict law among the Ibos and very strong feelings used to be aroused at such an indiscretion[207]."

Basden mentioned that Igbos felt chagrined and horrified when a (British) colonial official's wife started moving around them (the Igbos) in "land-worker's kilt." He observed that it was in her favour that she didn't hear the uncomplimentary comments that the Igbos made about her, and that also her husband was criticized for allowing such a gross misconduct.

## Fringed Garments

As for the Igbo men, their dressing is similar to Israelite dressing in more than one respect. From the distinctive Jewish use of the *'tallit'*; the fringed garment that Jews are commanded to wear all the time, to others. The

---

[207] Basden, G. T., *Niger Ibos*, (London: Frank Cass and Co., Ltd., 1966) 414.

Igbos wear this tallit. We call it *akwa mmiri*, because the cloth from which the Igbos make it; a linen type material is called 'akwa mmiri'.

As with some customs of the Igbos, the reason for wearing a fringed garment, was forgotten with time. It became merely an article of dressing for the Igbos. As I was growing up towels had started replacing *akwa mmiri*. Now in most areas of Igbo-land, its use is extinct, but it struggles on in some parts.

I find the following quote from a Jewish source as a good basis for further research on why the Igbos wore, or wear *tallits*:

"In ancient times, Tallits had a blue thread in the fringes; its dye came from a now-extinct rare snail from the West coast of Africa[208]."

West Africa is the region that the Igbos reside in now.

**Caps and Wrappers**

Also quite distinguishing is the Igbo man's usage of a red fez for religious or ritual purposes. Only Igbos who take a religio-social title can wear a particular red cap. Those who have not taken the title can wear our black fez. It would be strange and mysterious to someone who has not studied Igbo culture, that when an Igbo adult male puts on the red cap an aura of dignity, respect and holiness descends on him. One instinctively avoids playing pranks around him, and he too instinctively behaves well. I think that what is responsible for this is that traditionally, it is responsible Igbo people that are admitted to the society that its members wear the red fez.

---

[208] Dr. Danny Ben-Gigi, *First Steps in Hebrew Prayer. Living Israeli Hebrew*. (Scottsdale, Ariz.: www.hebrewwworld.com, 1998), 86.

Even though I have not been privileged to know exactly the dresses the ancient Israelites wore, it is safe for me to conjecture that the ancient Jews must have dressed very decently. From the Scriptures it is discernible that immodest and immoral behaviours, which can be reflected in the dressing modes of a given group, were repugnant to the Israelites. Myriad rules were given to the people to enable them to be holy. As I have done occasionally I use the present to understand the past of the Igbos. Truly I have not seen the full dress of an ancient Hebrew woman so that I can compare it to the dress of the Igbo woman, but I can use 'modesty' to connect the two. We can see the typical dressing of married Igbo women reflecting modesty. In Nigeria women tie wrappers around their waistes. The Yoruba women tie one wrapper. A married Igbo woman ties two wrappers. This ensures that the sensitive and erogenous parts of her body, like the buttocks, thighs, and calves are not exposed to public viewing, through her clothing.

An Igbo Jewish man named Nduka Igbo narrated a fascinating story to me. His family lived in Kontagora in the 1960s- an era when most Igbos still lived by Igbo morals, and the Igbo community was still very cohesive and strong. According to Igbo, his mother who was cooking one day ran out of a particular condiment, and had to run to the market, which was nearby to purchase the item. Because the lady was not prepared or dressed to go out she was dressed casually. The casual dress was her under-wears, a half-semi, a wrapper, and a blouse. At the market when the woman squatted to examine what she wanted to buy, the wrapper which was the outer-most of the three garments that the woman was wearing tore, and the under-ears were exposed. She suspended what she was doing, and began to rush home, but not before some Igbos who were in the market had seen what happened. The Igbos alerted the Ibo State Union, and all the Igbos began to gather at my friend's house; to deliberate on the grave happening. To cut this story. They fined my friend's father, and warned him to ensure that his wife did not expose herself, and the Igbos again. It is remarkable that the Igbo woman's dress does not put her in a cage, which is what the religious dressings of some other Nigerian groups do. Neither is her body exposed to the public. The dress ensures that she is just dressed, decently.

Numerous other Nigerian peoples copied this Igbo mode of dressing. The peoples living to the south of the Igbos, some in the near west, and some in the near north, borrowed this style of dressing from the Igbos.

This is the one-time oldest man of Ozubulu, an Igbo Hebrewist (onye ogo Mmuo/Chukwu), with a *tallit*-like garment traditionally worn by the Igbos.

# CHAPTER SEVENTEEN: Parallels Between the Igbo and the Hebrew Reckoning of Time

### The Igbo Week And Seventh Day Sabbath

The Igbos have the following revolving market days *Orie, Afor, Nkwo* and *Eke.* This has made some people to say that the Igbos have a four day week. We have not seen evidence that the above stands for 'week'. But as we have not been able to see from available evidence that the Igbos have a strong enough consciousness of the regular week-days, and this is understandable because Sunday, Monday, Tuesday, Wednesday, Thursday, Friday and Saturday, are Greco-Roman in origin, and the Igbos were not influenced by the Greeks and the Romans. That said, serious effort has to be made to show that the Igbo concept of time is the same as or similar with to the Hebrew concept, in which a week is seven days. I will say from the outset that I have done only the scantiest of works on the Igbo concept of time at this point.

The Igbo calendar year is divided into thirteen lunar months, each of which has twenty eight days.

Each of those months is made up of seven weeks, each of which is made up of the four market days.

The first revolving 4 days in an Igbo month is called *izu nta* by the Igbos, while the following one is called *izu ukwu*.

It would be very beneficial to discuss a peculiarity that is to be found in these Igbo days. The Igbo people observed a day in the *izu ukwu* as a day when nobody must do any work.

In other words the first four days, i.e., (the *izu nta)* are treated normally, i.e., every day in it is for work. The first and second days of the next four days *(izu ukwu)* are treated similarly, but on the third day, in the evening, as the sun sets, the rhythm changes. The communities assume a festive air, community members that were in their farms in the wilds return; and the next day there is feasting galore. Nobody works. In Ozubulu, specifically the Eziora sub-clan, even till the present day work in the farms is prohibited on the *Eke* days that fall within the *izu ukwu*. Interestingly many of the people do not know why they rest on the *eke ukwu* day. All that they know is that their fathers rested on that day. I singled out Eziora, not because the custom of resting on a particular day was peculiar only to it in Ozubulu, but because only Eziora still retains and respects the tradition absolutely. My sub clan, Egbema, had the *nkwo oru* day during which work was prohibited.

It is remarkable that the Jews observe the seventh day as a day of rest.

## Day Begins at Night

It seems also that the Igbos believe like the Jews[209] do that the day starts when the sun sets, and ends when the sun sets the following day. The Igbo month is called *onwa* (moon).

Through the ritual of *igu aho* (counting the year), the Igbos observed the seasons. This was done by the chief

---

[209] Hertz, J. H., *The Pentateuch and Haftorahs*, *2nd edition* (London: The Soncino Press, 1937) 2.

priests watching out for the new moon. When they see the moon they herald its arrival by beating of their *ogene* (metal gongs) which signals to the community that a new moon has arrived[210].

Contrasted with the following, we find some similarities with Judaism. "Judaism, blessings upon it and us, did not abandon observed time despite the development of the calculated calendar. The importance of ancient moon-watching reflected in the quite exciting material of *Mishnah Rosh ha-Shanah*, Chapters 1 and 2 persists in the ceremony of *Kiddush ha-Levanah* or *Birkat ha-Levanah*[211]."

In Igbo culture and traditions major offerings[212] are made to [God] on the full moon. 1 Chronicles 23:31 records that in ancient Israel, sacrifices were made on the new moon.

When the moon fills the world with its benign light the Igbos start their famous moonlight games. It is the aforementioned beating of the *ogene* (gong) that announces that the games can begin. Once it sounds, children and young adults troop out of their houses. Everywhere people raise their voices and greet the moon thus: "Ooo, otu ibe ji zuru oha onu, anya m jiri hu gi akpokwala m. Onye di, ibe ya diri, ma onye si ibe ya adila, ya buru okuko uzo lakpue ura," (live and let live, may anyone who wishes that his neighbour not live, not see the next day himself). Meanwhile wrestling, dancing, athletics, etc, will be going on.

---

[210] Achebe, Chinua, *Arrow of God*, (Ibadan: Heinemann Educational Books, 1964) pp. 1-2.
[211] Siegel, Richard, Strassfeld, Sharon, and Strassfeld, Michael, *The First Jewish Catalogue*, (Philadelphia: Jewish Publication Society, 1999) 97.
[212] Interesting Narratives of Olaudah Equiano or Gustavus Vassa the African, Ilona, Remy, and Eliyahu, Ehav, The Igbos: Jews In Africa? Vol 1 (Abuja: Mega Press, 2005), 60,61.

# CHAPTER EIGHTEEN: Joining the Igbo and Jewish People and Leaving Them

## Nnabata Na Nsupu (Igbo and Jewish conversion and excommunication)

Because so much is already known about how one becomes a member of the Children of Israel or a member of the Igbo people, I will not talk exhaustively about them here. However there is a need to address the issues, even if not exhaustively.

Principally the Children of Israel are the descendants of the twelve sons of Jacob, and other peoples or persons that joined them in totality, thus becoming part of them. Presently this family of Jacob's generally still go by 'Hebrew' the title of their Patriarch, Abraham. They are also Israel, the name that God gave Jacob, and 'the Jews' ('Yehudim'), a word derived from the name of Israel's fourth son Judah (Yehudah). Judah was the 'tribe' that survived exile better than the other eleven tribes.

A stranger who joins himself or herself to this family in totality is said to have converted to Judaism, which is the term used to describe the most influential Hebrew way of life presently. The Abayudaya-an African people in Uganda have done this. Around three hundred of them converted to Judaism in the late twentieth century, and today many Jews regard them as kin.

An Igbo is someone who is a member of an Igbo clan, and who has ancestors that can be traced to the first father or mother of the clan, who invariably would be traced to the figure or figures who fathered the people known as the Igbos now. It should be mentioned here that the people have also been known as the Ibo, Ebo, Ibi, Heebo, etc.

It is important to note at this stage that the Igbos never developed a notion of common Igbo nationality. Traditionally even today, I Remy view myself as onye Ozubulu (Ozubulu person), more than I see myself as 'onye Igbo' (Igbo person). An Ozubulu person sees an Nnewi person (nearest community, and just as Igbo as Ozubulu), as *onye mba* (a non native). Thus an Nnewi person who wants to join a family in the Ozubulu community would to a certain degree be expected to go through what a Moabite who wanted to join ancient Israel would go through, or what an Italian who wanted to become a Jew would go through.

Even though it is not common, people (from my experience ,Igbos) who did not originally belong to an Igbo clan could join one, and become full members of such a clan, with full rights, except on a few minor issues, like becoming a family priest by virtue of becoming the eldest man in the clan or family.

Below is a very brief account of the procedural steps that the Igbos use to accept *ndi mba* (strangers) into their communities. Afterwards I will also talk about how the Igbos ex-communicate people. I will also do a very brief comparison with the Jewish procedures.

This particular study serves the purpose of letting us know how one who was not born Jewish becomes an adherent of Judaism, and consequently becomes a part of the People of Israel. And it also throws light on how one who was not a member of an Igbo clan by birth becomes a member of an Igbo community/clan through some traditions provided in *Omenana*. Doing this we can see similarities between the two ways of life that I have been comparing.

Also I used the study to introduce how one is excommunicated from the Jewish and Igbo communities.

Only very long and serious reflection on some Jewish practices makes a researcher to recognize their Igbo equivalents and parallels.

## Nnabata (conversion)

Various Jewish writers have stated that the Biblical Ruth who was the daughter-in-law of Naomi was a convert to Judaism. They explained that the episode which saw her insisting on following Naomi back to Israel, offering to join Naomi's people, and accepting Naomi's God, was a conversion process. But does the process which I just described resemble a conversion process of any of the Jewish movements? I would say it does, but only to an extent though. I will discuss this in more detail soon.

If Naomi had been Igbo, and Ruth had been a non-Igbo wife of her deceased son, Ruth would still have been retained in the family of Naomi, if she wished to be retained, even though she hadn't yet gotten a child for her late husband. This is because in Igbo traditions a wife becomes a member of the husband's family. And the death of a spouse does not terminate her rights as a family member. And we can see that Ruth's right as a wife in the Elimelech family was not terminated when her husband died. I don't think that Ruth's case is a *locus classicus* as far as conversion to Judaism is concerned. Even though the story deals with some steps that are taken to effect a conversion, it deals more precisely with the practice of levirate marriage in ancient Israel. And with the conversion process among the Igbos it connects only faintly, but more seriously with the retention of a wife in the family through the process of *inye okuko* (levirate marriage). By Igbo traditions Ruth would have been required to become a wife to a near kinsman of her late spouse. It is observed that Ruth eventually became a wife of Boaz, her late husband's near kinsman. But it could be seen that Ruth actually took an extraordinary step to remain one with her mother-in-law's people, after Naomi had decided to return to Israel. She pledged to have the God of Israel as her God, and to abide by Israel's cultural norms. This entailed renunciation of her own gods, and her culture are steps that a convert to Judaism takes. That is where the aspect of conversion came in. But among the Igbos we do not know if she would have been required to renounce her own culture, because we did not envisage that an Igbo would marry foreign women.

But if an Igbo man wants to join an Igbo family or clan that is not his, the Igbo practice of *nnabata* would surely be activated. Nnabata means "to admit." I witnessed *nnabata* as an adolescent in my clan Ozubulu. Two men belonging to one kindred group had a serious quarrel. One was a well-to-do man. The other was poor. The well-to-do man used his influence and wealth to ignore a basic Igbo tradition: "Never invite the police (outsiders) to intercede in a problem between you and your brother." He used the police to harass the poor man so much. So many times he had him detained in Nigeria's police stations. At a point the poor man got fed up. He could no longer tolerate such treatment from a kinsman. He gave up his right as a member of that kindred group, and sought to join another kindred group which he felt could protect his interests and rights more effectively. They admitted him through the process of *nnabata*. This happened over twenty years ago, and he is still a member of the kindred group that he joined.

Admittance involves a process known as *oriko*, which entails the person who wishes to join a group, agreeing to start conforming to the rules, regulations, morals and laws of the admitting group. And sharing a ritual meal called *oriko* with the members of the group he wishes to join. Literally *oriko* means 'eating together.'

It is also right for me to deal with how an Igbo could leave the Igbo Community.

## Nsupu (excommunication)

I have read so many Jewish books that have given me a basic and sound knowledge of Judaism, from the rabbinical perspective; but I read Rabbi Harold. S. Kushner's, *To Life*, to understand that the Igbo *nsupu*, which literally means 'to ostracize', means, and has the same effect as an excommunication in Judaism.

Harold Kushner, a Jewish rabbi/scholar wrote in his book *To Life*:

"But in Judaism, excommunication does not cut you off from God. It separates you not from communication but from community. The reprobate Jew who has been excommunicated can pray to God every morning and every evening if he wishes, but none of his Jewish neighbours will talk to him, buy from him, or sell to him."

When Igbos 'supu' (excommunicate) or ostracize someone or a group, what Kushner described applies with exactitude.

Mathew O. Orji described how an Igbo who stole a widow's chattel was ostracized (excommunicated), very succinctly. The remarkable words used are:

"I am now saying that Nweke be ostracized from our community which means in effect that right from now onwards, no one is to exchange greetings with him. He will not be allowed to enter anybody's house. Whether in the stream, farm or on the road, nobody will assist Nweke in lifting heavy loads on to his head. He should not be allowed to enter anybody's kitchen to fetch embers of fire. If he dies under this condition nobody will mourn him. He would be denied honourable and decent burial[213]."

Igbo excommunication only came up to this point, and never beyond it.

---

[213] Orji, Mathew O., *The History & Culture Of The Igbo People* (Nkpor: Jet Publishers (Nig.), Ltd., 1999) 28.

# CHAPTER NINETEEN: The Igbo Society

## The Igbo Clan

The clan is the biggest/highest unit in the Igbo society. The Igbo clan is really a collection of extended families. The Igbos, unlike their neighbours, never coalesced into a kingdom. They did not gather into a state, or even a federation of clans. The members of each of the various clans are however aware that they are related by blood and culture to the members of the other clans.

The clans are completely autonomous of each other in every important matter. None of the clans rule over another. None conquered and subjugated another.

The clans have as their leaders; the elders (*ndi okenye*), the chief priests (*ndi eze Mmuo*), titled men and women (*ndi nze na ndi lolo*), with the Umu Nri priests (the Levitic-like Igbo priests from the Nri clans), and *ndi amuma* (the prophets) as the guides/advisors of the leaders. These persons ensure that the clans are administered well. The clans do not have regular armies and police forces. Every member of the clan is a police and army officer; in an informal way. They police themselves, and guard their clan from internal and external predators. They have the *mmonwu* (the masquerade societies) which could be used for entertainment, and as secret services. They have a judicial system that in effectiveness and fairness is far in advance of any other system that I am aware of, because its primary goals are to find out the truth, and to reconcile, and not to bestow 'victory'. The clans have everything that 'normal' states have or should have. The youth organizations known as 'age grades' (*otu ogbo*) ensure that the clans' territories are kept clean and neat. That the streams and rivers are cleaned periodically. In my locality this activity is called *igwo mmiri*. And that graves are dug when deaths occur in the community. In economic matters the same autonomy is noticed. Each clan has its own markets. And makes rules that ensure smooth running and effective operation of the markets. No clan tries to impose itself on other clans. This extreme autonomy of the Igbo clans, i.e., independence from each other is remarkable because all the Igbos are of one stock, and were expected to have joined together to form a single entity. One might think this way because all the immediate neighbours of the Igbos produced kingdoms, and had even in some cases conquered some of their neighbours and gained empires. While some scholars have tried to reason that the impulse that impelled those neighbours to form centralized entities was the need for common defense, such scholars have generally been unable to understand why the Igbos failed to respond to the same *stimuli*. After all the Igbos were faced with the same threats or dangers that the Bini, Yoruba, and others faced. In this study we would be able to get into why the Igbos did not coalesce into kingdoms, but only peripherally.

I examined ancient Israel and found what could pass as a very near facsimile of what I see the Igbos having as their society. Painstaking perusal of the Bible reveals that individual Israelites had utmost personal freedom, and individual Israelite clans were for the most part virtually autonomous in the early period of the biblical times. This tends to happen when power is not centralized. Power was quite remarkably decentralized in ancient Israel. People identified much more with their families than with any other authority or authorities during the earlier periods of Israelite history. We can glean evidence of this by 'listening' to statements like the following: "Am I not a Benjamite, of the smallest of the tribes of Israel? And my family the least of the families of the tribe of Benjamin?" That was Saul responding to Samuel. (1 Samuel 9.)

We can better understand what Saul was saying by looking at the Igbo society. Like an Ozubulu man who knows that he is an Igbo, but would see himself first of all as an Ozubulu man, Saul knew that he was an Israelite, but his attachment to Benjamin was, I would say, more intense. I observed that identifying more with the tribe, than the nation of Israel was the rule rather than the exception in those very early periods.

We can glean from the book of Joshua that many of the campaigns for the conquest of Canaan were fought by individual tribes of Israel; though with occasional help by their brother tribes.

An argument can be made that clans were more or less the primary units of authority in Israel then. And we can try to prove this by enumerating more than a few prominent Israelites whose identification then was by their family/clan names.

We had Joash the Abiezrite (Judges 6:11). Strongly in support of my position too is the Shechem and Abimelech saga (Judges 9). Shechem which was just an Israelite clan saw itself as a distinct entity with a distinct interest and agenda in Israel.

Continuing, we had Jair the Gileadite (Judges 10:3). And Jephthah the Gileadite (Judges 11:1).And Ibsan of Bethlehem (Judges 12:138). As well as Abdon the Pirathonite (Judges 12:13). Just as in ancient and modern Igbo-land we would have had, and in fact as we have, Remy Ilona of Ozubulu.

Considering what I just narrated, the following will be helpful. An Edomite, or an Ammonite, or a Midianite stalwart in the contemporary period would more likely than not be addressed as a Midianite in those days. His family, and clan affiliations might not have been deemed very important. For example all we knew about Goliath is that he was a Philistine. We did not know his clan or his family. One might try to argue that this is so because the document that gave us information about these historical figures is Israelite, and that that is why it gives much more details about the Israelites. However the argument is not convincing. This is because we can find that the same tendencies that we find in relation to the Israelites and their peers are also to be found in relation to the Igbos and their Nigerian peers. A typical Yoruba or Hausa man in Nigeria is likely to identify more with the empire or kingdom or metropolis that he came from or that is closest to his place of birth, while the Igbo man would more likely than not identify himself just with his clan. This is because states tend to subjugate or suppress the entities that make them up. The Yoruba and the Hausa came from centralized autocratic entities. Nigeria will serve as a good example of what I am saying. Many mighty peoples make up Nigeria, and those peoples are fighting to be seen and heard, because the centralized sovereign (the state) wants to corner all the allegiance and fealty. Nigerians have gradually been robbed of their individuality and uniqueness. One found expressing pride in his ethnic origins is denounced and derided as a tribalist.

In early Israelite history individual clans did to a great extent conduct themselves like independent entities. We would see the uniqueness of what I am trying to convey by comparing the ancient Israelite society with its peers, and the Igbo society with its peers. The Bible shows us Edom as already an established kingdom in very early times. In Genesis we are told that numerous kings had reigned in Edom. Kingdoms, like empires, tend to submerge the entities that make them up. Accordingly we can assume that all the entities that made up Edom had by this stage coalesced into one kingdom. Around the period in discussion the Israelites were still a collection of tribes that acted quite autonomously.

Around the Igbos we have the Bini Kingdom, (Edo), the Yoruba kingdoms which were at a point absorbed by the Yoruba Oyo Empire, the Idoma Kingdom, the Igala Kingdom. And staying side by side with them were the Igbo clans.

F. K. Buah, an African historian, while acknowledging[214] that the Igbo society is an uncommon one, because of the socio-political structure, had attempted to explain its peculiarity by suggesting that the forest region in which the Igbos live could have precluded them from forming centralized states, but he gave up midway, offering that centralized states were formed in those same forests too.

## The Structures of the Igbo Clans

All Igbo clans have the same basic structure, so for the sake of convenience I will use Ozubulu clan in the present Anambra State; Igbo territory, Nigeria; as a case study. I am a scion of Ozubulu.

According to oral traditions, a man migrated from across the River Niger, traveled to the present site of

---

[214] Buah, F. K. *West Africa and Europe*, (London: Macmillan Educational Books, 1966) 137,138.

Ozubulu, and resettled. And while he was there he married and had several children.

The settlement that the man founded became known as Ozubulu. Oral traditions say that the man had several children. The descendants of the afore-mentioned children are the people who identify themselves as the people/children of Ozubulu today. Oral traditions mention that the man met some people when he arrived, and that some other people attached themselves to his four sons' descendants too, but we are not going to concern ourselves with that at this stage.

For convenience I will concentrate on the 'son' from whom I (the writer) descended. I descended from Egbema.

As his brothers; the other sons of Ozubulu, Egbema, the writer's ancestor had his own children, among whom was an Uruokwe. Uruokwe in turn had his own children among whom was an Onyia. Onyia's sons included an Ezeanike. Among Ezeanike's children was an Enendu who had Igwerionwa, Efogwo and Nwosu, among others, as his sons.

Efogwo had children who bear the name Umu-Efogwo. One of those children was Ezeanyaezughu, who in turn had several children among whom were Ilona, whose titular name was Ezeofido, and another son, Nzom.

Ilona in turn had many children among whom was Anekwe, who was also named Joseph.

Anekwe also had many children, among whom is Chukwukaodinaka who is also named Remy, and who is the writer.

A careful trip up the ladder, from Anekwe to Ozubulu reveals that I, Remy, is related by blood to the thirty-nine to fifty thousand or so persons that view Ozubulu as their ancestor.

Three or four other classes of persons are also parts of this family of Ozubulu:

Umu-Nri who are resident in Ozubulu. The Umu Nri are Igbos from a clan/group of clans that remind the biblical scholar of the Levites. The Umu Nri settle among other Igbos and carry out certain priestly/ritual functions; such as purifications when abominations are committed by their hosts.

There is also another class of people who are Ozubulu people. They are *ohu*, i.e., they were (of slave origins).

These people that other Ozubulu people view as having emanated from slave origins more than probably acquired that status from a situation akin to what is presented in Deuteronomy 15:22, in which the Hebrews were enjoined by Moses to deal fairly with any fellow Hebrew who through strained circumstances found himself or herself sold into slavery to them. I am forced to use this most hateful word 'slave' here, so that I can describe acutely this category of Ozubulu people. Ancient or traditional Igbo society knew slavery, but Igbo slavery was quite dissimilar in almost all respects to the Arab and European concepts of slavery and [slave trade].

Another people that are Ozubulu people are the *osu*. Modern Igbos, out of negligence I must add, simply borrowed the term that the foreign scholars who delved into Igbo Studies applied to this class of people, 'outcasts.' The descendants of the *osu* are bona fide Igbos who sought refuge with Chukwu Abiama (the God of, probably Abraham) in ancient times, and as Igbo custom provided they became inviolable. Their status was identical to the status of the Israelite that sought refuge in the sanctuary or any other place that the God of Israel had a shrine in, in ancient Israel.

Lastly there are Ozubulu people who migrated from Arochukwu and Arondizuogu, and settled in Ozubulu. Both are Igbo clans too. Their scions like the Nri migrated to other clans in ancient times, but retained strong ties to their original clans.

All the above-mentioned are children of Ozubulu. All will describe themselves as Umu Ozubulu or Ndi Ozubulu, i.e., children or people of Ozubulu.

What I have just presented is a description of an Igbo clan. All Igbo clans would fit into the description which I have proffered.

I can now move to the next issue which is how the various organs of the Igbo society such as the nuclear and extended families, the kindred group, the sub-clan and the clans which are the highest units of the Igbo society, operate or work. In other words, how they are administered.

**How the Igbo Society Works**

My starting point must be to reiterate that the Igbo clans are totally free, and independent of each other, and the level of independence between them is perhaps as much as the one between the United States and Canada, or Nigeria and Ghana. There are friendly ties between clans for sure, which emanated from inter clan marriages, friendships, and the knowledge that they are Igbos, etc, but they are just what they are – completely independent entities. They never deteriorated or developed to the extent of one clan interfering in the internal affairs of the other.

As I had mentioned the Igbos did not centralize and evolve kingship systems. The kingship system is antithetical to real democratic values. Entities/nations/peoples are or become or evolve into kingdoms due to a variety of factors; ranging from custom, dictatorial inclinations, need for strong rulership, etc. Similar tendencies, including greed and acquisitive inclinations lead entities to embark on empire building too.

In addition, as I also mentioned, the Igbos are surrounded by peoples that have centralized entities atop which sat semi-divine kings. Some circumstances of some of those peoples were/are similar to those of the Igbos. For example they and the Igbos have inhabited the same stretch of forests near the coast of the Atlantic Ocean for as long as we know. Yet the Igbos failed to evolve into centralized entities as they did. This point may indicate that the Igbos did not centralize and form kingdoms because the customs of the Igbos did not allow for such. I had to go to ancient Israel to find those customs that very likely prohibited the Igbos from centralizing and evolving into kingdoms.

Israel at its early stage was seriously decentralized. And as we can see readily, Israel at its earliest stage was a theocratic egalitarian entity. The King of Israel is God, Who was represented by authentic men and women of God, like Moses, Joshua, Caleb, Deborah, Samuel, etc. However as history revealed to us Israel eventually bowed to the tendency to centralize power by evolving into a monarchy. But however when we look at the monarchy that Israel got we would see that what it had in common with 'normal' monarchies like the Gentile monarchies of ancient and even modern times is just the word 'king'. That whereas kings and queens among the Nations were seen as divine and semi-divine, that the Israelite monarch was seen as just a little above a first among equals among the Israelites. Whereas among the neighbouring peoples the king was a god or at least the representative of God to his subjects, whose word was divine law; that among the Israelites the king was subject to the Law of the God of Israel, just as, or even more than, the ordinary Israelite. My extensive portrayals of Israelite society is deliberate, because it is actually the society that I am looking at, albeit from the Igbo perspective.

In the early part of this essay I mentioned the various persons and groups that run Igbo affairs in the various Igbo clans. Now we can proceed to how the Igbo society is organized and run.

A distinctive feature of the Igbo society is the fact that every Igbo individual, be he a man or a woman, is actively involved in running the affairs of the clan.

**The Nuclear Family**

At the level of what I will call the nuclear family, an Igbo man is expected to present any important case to his wife and children, and the decision on such a matter is reached by consensus.

I have personal experience of this as I was growing up in my father's household. Even as an adolescent my opinion was compulsorily sought on any matter that would affect me and the family.

Igbo culture presented to us through literature Igbo practices on this matter. In Chinua Achebe's *Things Fall Apart* highly authoritarian Igbo men such as his character Okonkwo[215] would not think of deviating from this unwritten rule and tradition; that decisions affecting a family as a whole have to be reached by consensus.

In the story we learn that Okonkwo's two daughters grew up into beauties when the family was in exile. Suitors were coming for them. Okonkwo would have preferred them to marry when they returned home, after the years of exile would have passed. As an authoritarian person he could have tried to have his way, but Igbo custom on this is that the girls must be heard, and that their say is very important. Okonkwo knew the tradition. That the girls must have the last word on their choice of husbands. He followed Igbo custom; i.e., he opted for the Igbo way. He called aside his favourite among the two girls, Ezimma, and spelt out his desire in just a few words. She agreed with him. Her agreement/consent was necessary and essential.

What I just described is an example of how an Igbo family is run.

**The Extended Family**

The extended family, which I will use the Ezeofido-Ilona family as an example of; is run on similar lines too. I will refer to this unit as the Igbo extended family. In all important matters, and these may range from birth of children, to marriage, to worship of Chukwu (God), to funerals, etc, every adult member of this unit is consulted.

In Igbo language this unit may be called *umunna* (children of the fathers), literally.

---

[215] Achebe, Chinua, *Things Fall Apart*, (Ibadan: Heinemann Educational Books, 1958), p. 122.

In Igbo extended families if a child is born, the whole family is informed, and everybody joins in the rejoicing because the child belongs to every member of the extended family.

If a bride is coming in, the same thing applies. In fact Igbos believe that the bride is married to the family. Her husband has exclusive rights to her only on sexual and actually intimate matters. Igbos convey this idiomatically by saying 'ofu onye a da ho anu nwanyi'(a wife doesn't belong only to her husband, a wife belongs to the family).

And on social, and other matters, every extended family has an *obi*; just as every adult Igbo man has. I am sure that the *obi* serves the same purpose in all Igbo settings, so whatever I present here can be taken as applying to every other unit of Igbo society.

To the Igbos, the *obi* is the equivalent of the synagogue to the Jews.

On several occasions Igbo extended families perform worship related matters together. The men do so in the *obi*; the women outside the *obi*, but in its environs.

Traditionally an Igbo family meets every week, i.e., on the Eke ukwu day in Eziora, Ozubulu, the seventh/eighth day. The men meet separately and the women meet separately. Communal worship takes place at the meetings. A brief service called *ikpe ekpere oji* or *igo oji* always come before meetings commence. Also important family matters are discussed and resolved at such meetings. Every family-dues paying adult male has a right, and is in fact required to be present and contribute his voice to the resolution of any outstanding matter. The decision of the men-folk are binding on the entire family. This meeting of the men-folk is called *nzuko umunna* (congress of kinsmen).

That of the women is called *nzuko umu nwanyi* (congress of the women).

Still another group that is involved in running the affairs of the extended family is the *umu okpu* (the daughters that have married). They have periodic meetings too; where they deliberate on matters that affect their kinsfolk.

As we leave the family unit, and go to the extended family unit, and continue upwards to the other units, the bond of brotherhood starts to get less and less intimate. For routine matters only the elders of each family may meet, unlike at the family and extended family levels where for even routine matters everybody must meet. But even at this distant level, for extra important matters everybody must meet.

At this stage I am sure that the reader must have realized that the family is the base of the society.

Igbo writer Matthew O. Orji[216] seems to be alluding to that in the following passage which I shall quote extenso:

"The communities (families) that made up one single town (clan) were each responsible to the town as a whole. The community was made up of many families and the families were each responsible to the community. But the responsibility of the community to the town and that of the family to the community were not total. This was because there were certain matters which the family had exclusive powers to deal with,

---

[216] Orji, Matthew O. *The History and Culture of the Igbo People (Before the Advent of the White Man)* (Nkpor: Jet Publishers (Nig.) Ltd., 1999) 10.

without referring it to the community. Likewise the community had authority to dispose of certain matters without reference to the town."

Even at this stage it is evident that authority and power were not centralized at any level. Individuals could exercise a measure of freedom, just as families could, as could kindred groups, right up to the individual clan which may only take its decisions collectively, i.e., without having to defer to one potentate.

However there is no real room for arbitrary conduct. Traditionally, and as mentioned by Mathew O. Orji, individual families were certainly barred traditionally from causing enmity with neighbouring clans as this would affect the entire clan. Also no community as he preferred to call the extended family /kindred group was allowed to engage in war with neighbouring clans without the knowledge and consent of the whole clan[217].

We have to refer to the other sections of this book, to see so many of the regulating and moderating rules that ensured that such a free society does not become anarchic.

I have drawn a framework of the Igbo society. I believe that it is expedient at this stage to put some flesh on the skeleton, i.e., to explain in some detail, how the society that has just been described works.

I will begin with a very important feature of the Igbo society, the representation of women.

---

[217] ibid., 11.

## Women's Representation in Government

From what I have presented so far it is clear that Igbo women were seen and heard. The wives and married daughters could rule on and influence policy at all levels.

Igbo writer, Humphrey Akaolisa[218] mentioned that the Igbos probably were the first people to evolve adequate women representation in the governing of the society.

I would say that the phenomenon is Israelite, that it is noticeable even in the times of Abraham, Isaac, and Jacob.

Sarah was more or less an equal of Abraham. She was the force behind the inclusion of Hagar in the family. She also forced her, and her son, Ishmael's, departure.

Likewise Rebekah. Even though she only connived with her favorite son in getting the choice blessings from Isaac, we could still feel her power and influence in the family. Also in the case of the mothers of the 12 twelve tribes, Jacob had to consult the Matriarchs before taking his leave of Laban's estate.

Dr J.H. Hertz, a Jewish scholar, beautifully comments on the following statement[219], "and Jacob sent and called Rachael and Leah to the field unto his flock" thus: "Another instance of the dignified position of women in ancient Israel. The Patriarchs do nothing without consulting their wives, whom they regard as equals."

He also explains Jacob's calling them aside 'to the field' to signify—'to speak with them in private', and is better

---

[218] Akaolisa, Humphrey, *Igbo Race, Origin and Controversies* (Awka, Buckstar Publishers, 2003) 23.
[219] Hertz, J. H., *The Pentateuch and Haftorahs, 2nd edition* (London: The Soncino Press, 1937) 113, (Genesis 31:4).

understood to mean that he had utmost respect for them and their positions'. This becomes very lucid when we juxtapose it with the Igbo reaction in equivalent situations.

In a similar situation an Igbo husband will call aside his wife or wives so that they will engage in what is called *igba izu*, which if translated literally would mean to whisper together, but which really means 'so that he will confer with her or them in quietude'. Similarly if an Igbo offspring needs to talk with any of the parents, and they are in a gathering, he or she must engage in *igba izu* with them. This activity expresses and implies that due to respect he or she will respectfully whisper or talk to them with a low tone, rather than just talk to them.

From the position of Israel as seen in the Bible, and the Igbo position as seen in the practice, we can sufficiently see that the women-folk are genuinely valued as pillars of the family, and the society. And as we have seen the Igbo family is merely a microcosm of the Igbo clan which is typically the Igbo society.

Using literature Chinua Achebe eloquently illustrates the ideal relationship between husband and wife in the Igbo society when in his *Things Fall Apart* he narrates how Ogbuefi Ndulue and his wife Ozoemena lived and died, in the following passage:

Okonkwo and his friend Obierika were chatting at Obierika's house when their friend Ofoedu arrived and announced that Ndulue, a one-time leading warrior of their clan had joined his ancestors. As is required by custom, the drum (*ikoro*) ought to have been beaten to announce his passing, but it hadn't because according to Ofoedu, Ndulue's first wife Ozoemena also died shortly after hearing that her husband had died.

Chinua Achebe was at his best in the narration of how it happened:

"When he died this morning, one of these women went to Ozoemena's hut and told her. She rose from her mat, took her stick and walked over to the *obi*. She knelt on her knees and hands at the threshold and called her husband, who was laid on a mat. 'Ogbuefi Ndulue', she called three times and went back to her hut. 'When the youngest wife went to call her again to be present at the washing of the body, she found her lying on her mat, dead[220]."

The three men went on to discuss that the great warrior took decisions only after consulting his better half.

The story above was, and to a great extent still is, the Igbo standard as far as spousal love is concerned.

Before departing from husbands and wives as equals in Igbo society, let us ponder over one issue. Why did the Igbo society, so free, maintain such great stability even without the existence of one strong leader? I hope that the answer will emerge from a consideration of all the evidence accumulated by the time I will have finished writing this section. But I the writer can take a risk by saying that it is the *Omenana* (religious tradition of the Igbos), which in Israel is called Judaism, which created the harmonious balance in Igbo society. But we must wait till the end of the book to understand and appreciate every case that we make.

This freedom in the society that is mentioned extends to the parental-children relationship.

---

[220] Achebe, Chinua, *Things Fall Apart*, (Lagos: Heinemann Educational Books, 1958) 47.

On parental, and children's relationship, Chinua Achebe using literature gave us a glimpse into the Igbo family of Ezeulu of Umuaro Clan. Achebe's words: "His youngest son, Nwafor now came into the *obi*, saluted Ezeulu by name and took his favourite position on the mud-bed at the far end[221]."

Not only did Achebe give us an insight on how an Igbo father relates to the child, but his words reminds us of the relationship existing between another 'priest', Jacob, and his then-youngest, Joseph. Joseph was close enough to his father as to become his spy against his brothers. Moreover we could see from the Bible that the other eleven sons of Israel were very close to him too, and respected, but did not fear him. From the Igbo side Nwafor at four years walked into his father's *obi* and saluted him by name (titular name), and moreover he had gotten so used to his father, that he had acquired a favourite position in the *obi*. Among some neighbours of the Igbos the whole scene would be quite inconceivable and incomprehensible. To some it would amount to pure sacrilege that the boy did not prostrate before his father-in a worshipful way. In addition the boy and his sister could even talk in the priest's' presence. And because their talk was quarrelsome the only punishment they got was "keep quiet there, you two." One's mind can't stop straying to how the earlier mentioned other 'priest'--Jacob--equally only told Joseph to shut up when he was narrating his dream.

I, the writer, in my own personal relationship with my parents, experienced what was akin to what Achebe was narrating.

---

[221] Achebe, Chinua ,*Arrow of God*, (Ibadan: Heinemann Educational Books, 1964) 4-5.

My late father, J. Anekwe Ilona, was a great man in all respects. He passed on when I was in my early twenties. I was in the Nigeria Law School then. By then my father had accomplished everything that a successful man should accomplish. He had married, and had gotten children, otherwise I wouldn't be here writing; acquired wealth, otherwise I wouldn't have become a lawyer, etc. Compared to him I was a small man. Yet I observed and noticed that my father treated me as an equal. His routine in the mornings as he passed my room, which was on the way to the washroom, was to stop, knock, open my door, look in, and say 'good morning Remy.' I would return, 'good morning Papa', and he would continue to the washroom. Among many neighbours of the Igbos what would have been traditional and proper would have been for me to leave my bed, and prostrate before my father.

My mother who passed on as I was revising this section extended the same or similar treatment to me. This is the standard in all Igbo relationships.

The closest parallel that we can find to this kind of parent-children relationship is in Israel. In Jacob's family everybody, including the children had a voice and could raise it, albeit respectfully. We saw this in the story of the children of Israel's trials in Egypt when their brother Joseph recognized them. Simeon having been detained in Egypt, and Joseph having 'died', in Jacob's mind, Jacob was unwilling to release Benjamin to travel to Egypt. And as is customary in Israel the sons could, and actually did argue forth and back with their father, on the need for him to release Benjamin to go to Egypt with them. Israelite tradition did not enjoin them to accept whatever their father said. They had the rights to contribute their opinions too, albeit respectfully.

Persons that live in Western lands that have become *pot pourris* of peoples and cultures will not easily understand the point I am making here, because the differences between cultures are not clearly distinct anymore in such societies. But someone in Nigeria will see my point easily, because he sees the differences in cultural practices daily: the Igbo saluting his father by greeting him with his titular name while bending slightly, albeit respectfully, and the Yoruba lying fully prostrate on the floor when saluting his father or king.

At this stage I must mention one curious observation or realization. I must point out that the past may not really be in the past. It may in fact still be present in the present. I have observed that so many ancient Igbo practices are still to be found in the behaviours of modern Igbos. And I realized that the same applies to ancient and modern Israel too.

I, the writer, in the recent past had an encounter with some modern Israelites that made me to confirm this. Their behaviours and reactions to my actions were typically Israelitic, i.e. they acted and reacted the way Jacob would have reacted if he had been faced with an identical or similar situation. So many years ago I had cause to take a position that was contrary to the position of Jack Zeller, who was the President of Kulanu then, on a particular matter. I expressed my views in a private letter to him, and I also sent a copy of the letter to Harriet Bograd, who was the Treasurer of Kulanu then. I must admit that I only acted in the circumstance because my culture conditioned me to do so, i.e., I shouldn't be quiet or muzzled in a matter that concerned me. As Kulanu's Nigeria liaison I felt that the issue in discussion concerned me, so I took the risk of opposing Zeller's position. I describe my stand as a 'risk' because their organization partly bankrolled the research that produced this book, deployed Ehav Ever, the anchorman of the project, and was providing much of the organization and resources for my own project of continuing a religious and cultural Renaissance of the Igbos. So it was with some trepidation that I went about my opposition to Zeller. Very surprisingly Zeller did not take offence at my opposition. Rather he proceeded to explain his position, even engaging in lengthy phone conversations with me. We were still talking when Bograd actively joined our discussion. She wrote me a very thoughtful, insightful and thought- provoking letter.

In summary the letter stated that it was not wrong, in fact that it was right and proper for me to have opinions and positions that may not accord with those of Kulanu, and Zeller's, and that it wasn't wrong also for me to express such opinions and positions of mine too, albeit respectfully, as I had been doing on the issue in question.

I had to get to this level of this research to understand what was at play. The religious traditions of Israel (Judaism) had conditioned Zeller and Bograd to accept respectful dissension from subordinates, while the traditions of the Igbos (*Omenana*) had conditioned me to offer opposition to my superiors if I felt that I had a good reason to do so, albeit with respect.

To a person living in the United States and other lands that have become egalitarian and democratic to some extent my experience with Zeller, and Bograd would not seem to be uncommon, but in societies like Nigeria, where ancient traditions are still alive in spite of modernity and legal enactments to the contrary, the encounter will strike a chord. Among many Nigerian groups subordinates must take instructions, and carry them out without question.

I am sure that the reader understands the necessity of bringing in anything and everything that can help us to see the similarities between ancient Israelite practices and their Igbo equivalents. But as we have been seeing the past is really not so much the past, as it is the present. The real problem has been that there has been laxity in studying, understanding, documenting, and transmitting the Igbos' way of life (*Omenana*).

I have devoted much time and effort to explaining the role of the individual Igbo, because the behaviour of the individual is but a mirror image of the behaviour of the family, clan and tribe.

Also part of my brief is to try to find resemblances and parallels in Israelite society. A possible advantage of this work to the Igbos is that it will give them a written code of their hitherto unwritten traditions. Moreover this work will open up some hitherto obscure parts of Israelite culture.

At this stage it is expedient, I think, for me to do some more work on the working of the Igbo family. And I must still use the Ilona household as my case study.

This family resembles Abraham's family to some extent. We know that at a point Abraham 'adopted' Lot. Very similar is Ilona's association with his much younger brother Nzom. Even though both men died over sixty years ago, their children, grandchildren and great grandchildren constitute one Igbo family, but as Abraham's direct descendants progressed to become the Israelites, while those of Lot went on to become the Moabites, so did the descendants of Ilona go by his name, while those of Nzom go by Udoji, Nzom's and Ilona's father's name.

Most members of this Ilona/Udoji family live together on the grounds of their ancestral *obi*. A few like the writer live outside, i.e., in 'Diaspora.' My father bought land outside the homestead and developed it for our use. We are described as 'ndi puru obi.' Translated into English this phrase means those who live outside the homestead. Interestingly this has not diminished our rights as authentic Ilonas at all. We have every right that the Ilonas who live on the grounds of the *obi* have to the use of certain communal properties. This reminds one of the perception of all the Jewish people as the People of Israel, and owners of the Land of Israel, even if they had/have the citizenship of countries other than that of the State of Israel, and live outside it. And very crucially and interestingly, even though it amounts to a digression, when my beloved father died, as his body was brought back to our present home to be buried, Ozubulu sages decreed that a detour had to be made into the Ilona ancestral homestead. A detour was made, and before the *obi* a twenty-four gun salute was fired in salute to "Ogo" (his nickname as a young football prodigy) who had gone to rejoin his ancestors, and his daughter Ngozi and son Chukwuma who predeceased him. At the cessation of the cannon shots Ozubulu sages cried 'ooo na na nu o', which if translated into English would result in 'he has returned' and which embodies the meaning: 'he has returned to his ancestors.'

What are we reminded of in all these? Did Jacob not cry and entreat Joseph: "But when I sleep with my fathers, thou shalt carry me out of Egypt, and bury me in their burying place."

Also, did we not see the body of Robert Maxwell, the late Jewish media tycoon's body fished out of the sea, put in a coffin, flown to Israel, and buried in the Mount of Olives, from where he, like other children of Israel, started his/their journey?

Did we not witness the removal of Theodore Herzl's remains to Israel many years after his death? So what do the Igbos do? In my opinion the Igbos are doing something akin to what the Jews do.

We go back to how the Ilona family works. To a large extent the members of this family do most things together. If a member's wife delivers a child, every other member has a duty to visit and rejoice with the lucky member. The child belongs to the entire family.

If a member wants to marry, the others have a duty to assist him from the very beginning; from the search for a suitable bride, to the duty to accompany him to the bride's house. Just as well the groom-to-be is compulsorily required to inform his kinsmen about his desire to get married. Custom has already stipulated in the areas that his kinsmen and their women folk should help.

There is a traditional duty for the members to train and educate any orphan in this unit of the family. Just as well the members ought to rally round and help any member that is slipping into poverty.

When a death occurs in the family even though the immediate/nuclear family of the bereaved bears the major cost of the funeral, the extended family has a duty to contribute certain amounts in wine, food and money, and also each individual member of the family has the duty to mourn with their bereaved member.

Now I must discuss the persons that run all these, in passing as I have glossed over aspects of them before.

The premier administrators of this unit of the Igbo society are all the taxable adult males. Their decisions bind all and sundry in the family.

A secondary bastion of authority are the women folk, i.e., the wives of the family. They have the right to rule on matters that exclusively concern the women. Occasionally, but rarely they may ignore the decisions of the men.

Another powerful group is the *umu okpu*. These are daughters of the family, who have married. If there are difficult cases in the family they can be summoned to adjudicate, or they may summon themselves. They are feared and respected and may even in rare cases overrule the men-folk. They are unique. In case of death they are chief mourners.

Still another influential group is the *ndi ikwu nne* of an individual or individuals (one's mother's kinsmen). We can understand more about this group by mentioning, and talking about their parallel in Israel. Laban is *nna ochie* (maternal uncle) of Jacob and Esau, i.e., Laban is *onye ikwu nne* (a member of the family of the twins mother) of Jacob and Esau. This relationship is an important one among the Igbos. And the *ndi ikwu nne* may influence the workings of the family of their nephew, but there must be general consent from the other members of the family that are not related to that uncle before they can step in. In other words Laban could have settled the rift between Jacob and Esau if he was invited, because he was well -positioned to intervene. To the Igbos he would have been viewed as a guardian to Jacob and Esau. And I think that we can see evidence of that in Israel's history. When Absalom slew Amnon his brother, he fled to *ikwu nne ya*, i.e. to the family of his mother's kinsmen, exactly to Talmai the son of Ammihud, king of Geshur. It is very interesting that as Absalom got total safety in *ikwu nne ya,* so would an Igbo. My favourite niece Uche is *nwadiana m.* Igbo custom gives her so much rights and privileges in the Ilona homestead, where her mother sprang from. She cannot be insulted, humiliated or treated badly while she is there. The Igbos say that 'nwadiana wu eke', i.e., that a child of a married daughter of the family is inviolable.

In the same vein in the Igbo worldview a *nwadiana*, i.e. what Jacob and Esau were to Laban, could also go to the house of his *nna ochie* and settle disputes if he is invited. The aunts are *nne ochie.*

A question that must arise at this stage must be how these 'governments' take a decision since I have not presented any single person as a sole person in authority since I started describing the Igbo socio-political structure.

There are first among equals in all these 'governments' that I have described. For the *umunna*, i.e. congress of the men of the family, their first among equal is the oldest man in the family. In the Ilona family/the Igbo society he is the *aka-ji-ofo* (the possessor of a staff, akin to the staff of Aaron). He opens all meetings and important discussions by praying, and ends all discussions by speaking last, after all the others have spoken. He more or less aggregates the views of his brothers, refines them, removes unlawful and immoral suggestions in them, and politely expresses the remainder as the decision of the family. Dissent is allowed, in which case more talk is allowed until a consensus is reached.

For the purposes of this study, we would see this eldest man (*aka-ji -ofo*) as the elder of this family, because it is the oldest man that holds the *ofo*. The closest facsimile to this that I could find was the person that Dr. J.H. Hertz, a Jewish commentator on the Bible had in mind when he explained: "In primitive times, the head of the clan or the first-born acted as the priest[222]."

Remove the primitive times and he could have been talking about the Igbos. But we need to throw more light on Hertz' efforts. Which people was he talking about that had their first born sons acting as priests? Can't we conjecture that he was referring to the Hebrews' ancestors, since his work was on and about the Bible?

My late father was an *aka-ji-ofo* of the Ilona/Udoji family. He was a priest while he was the *aka-ji-ofo*. When he died, his younger brother Igwegbe took over his position as the *aka-ji-ofo*. Both my father and his successor had and have the right to lead in religious affairs in the family as their fathers did.

Professors J.B. Webster, A.A Boahen and Mr. H.O. Idowu, threw more light on this personage (*aka-ji-ofo*) and the elders, when they were explaining that among the Igbos the elders' opinions were respected and regarded highly not merely because of their age, but also because they acted as priests[223]. However, the image that always crosses, my eyes when I think of our *aka-ji-ofo* (elders) is that of Moses and the 'elders of Israel' in

---

[222] Hertz, J. H., *The Pentateuch and Haftorahs, 2nd edition* (London: The Soncino Press, 1937) 94, (commentary on Genesis 25:31).
[223] Webster, J. B. and Boahen, A. A., with Idowu,H.O., *The Revolutionary Years in West Africa Since 1800* (Bucks: Longman, 1967) 263.

Deuteronomy 27:1 commanding Israel to keep the commandments of the Lord.

There is also another person that deserves mention in the running of a typical Igbo family. This person is *nwa di okpara*. If translated into English this means the son of the first son. This position is hereditary; unlike the position of *aka-ji-ofo* which persons can succeed to, by becoming the oldest member of a family. To be more illustrative: The first son of a family is the *di okpara*. He is the legal successor of his father. His brothers are his equals, but he is the first among equals. When he dies, his son becomes the *nwa-di-okpara.* But if his son is older than every other member of the family he becomes also the *aka-ji-ofo* which his father had been. For an Igbo first born son to merit the position, one must have outlived his own father.

In purely Igbo family matters the *aka-ji-ofo* is the only person that is really deferred to, while his younger brothers are respected too, but to lesser degrees, according to their ages. But if the family has to go to meet the general clan the *aka-ji-ofo* may go with the *nwa-di-okpara* and other brothers that precede the *nwa-di-okpara*. The *nwa-di-okpara* could also be called *nwanonaobi*, i.e., the child that lives near and maintains the *obi*.

In the case of the women folk, the most senior wife in the family is the first among equals. She is the first to be married into the family among the surviving wives. Her position is one of honour. I find her position and role paralleled in the similarities found in the saga of Sarah vis vis-a-vis Hagar. Abraham allowed tradition to rule by allowing Sarah to discipline Hagar when Hagar became insolent.

Buchi Emecheta did a lot of good work on the position of the senior wife among the Igbos.

Agbadi who was one of the major characters in her book, misbehaved with his mistress to the hearing of his entire polygamous household and friends.

Agunwa his first wife fell ill as a consequence of Agbadi's misconduct. Shortly after she died. Addressing her son, Agbadi said.... : "I don't know who else will help me keep an eye on those young wives of mine, and see to the smooth running of my household[224]."

In the case of the *umuokpu* who are female members of a family that are married their oldest member is their chief. Her position is also one of honour.

As no socio-political group can function without money, it is pertinent to have a discussion on how the family raises the money that it uses to carry out its communal activities.

There is the *utu umunna*, i.e., family dues. Every adult pays these annual dues. In the annual payment the Igbos are not unlike the Jews who subscribe annually for their synagogue membership. This fund is normally saved for emergencies. Parts of it may be tapped to meet emergencies, for example it could be used for the burial of an indigent kinsman. Also the members of the family may borrow from it but it must be replaced as soon as it can.

Dereliction in paying these dues is not viewed with much sympathy by Igbos. Family members are encouraged to always be up up-to to-date in paying up. Deliberate shirking of payment of it invites censure

---

[224] Emecheta, Buchi, *The Joys of Motherhood*, (Oxford: Heinemann Educational Books, 1979) 21.

from the family. However because blood is thicker than water no Igbo family would fail to bury its dead even if the deceased shirked paying his dues. I have seen Igbos who saw their membership in alien social and religious clubs, as an impetus to disregard the *umunna*, and when they died, the foreign entities could not cope because the deceased was not a family member of theirs, and their corpses would have rotted in the streets, but for their kinsmen (*umunna*) who had to rush in and save the situation, because the Igbos believe that 'ozu siwe isi, enyi ka nwanne agbaa oso'; this means that when the corpse starts to smell, the friend who is more close than the brother takes his leave. Also dereliction in payment never results in ostracism.

The women folk have their own dues too.

The *umuokpu* have annual dues too.

There are some businesses at the sub clan and clan levels as well. Some dues are collected at these levels too. At times matters that may concern the clan or sub clan at large may arise. If it is a serious matter, every taxable male adult is required to attend. But if it is a routine matter the head of each family attends. All that I have described is replicated in all the strata, or extended families, which it may be convenient to describe as sub-clans, sub-sub-clans, sub- sub- sub-clans etc, of Ozubulu. The unit after the unit that follows the Ilona family unit has an organization colloquially known as *age grade*. This organization or group is made up of people who are not adolescents and not yet middle-age. They are in charge of digging graves whenever a death occurs in the sub-sub clan. They also repair roads. They run their affairs with annual dues that each member must pay. They meet, but not very regularly as in the nuclear or extended family units.

Every clan has a chief priest, who may be appointed, or whose position may be hereditary. They are in charge of service to Chukwu in the clan. They also teach *Omenana*. They are influential and are respected and their advice is rarely disregarded.

Titled men also exist. The clans' people may respect them, because almost always they are elderly and successful men. But respect to them is not automatic or traditional.

At this stage I must begin to wind down this discussion on the socio-political structure of the Igbo society. But before I finally draw the curtains I need to highlight a few things.

The following stand out in this study:

The sense of community is very strong in Igbo society.

There is much regard for individual freedom.

There is a conspicuous lack of opportunities for authoritarian figures to arise.

There are abundant checks and balances in the system.

There is no standing army.

There is no regular police.

There is no prison.

In the beginning I pointed out that Ozubulu people believe that all Ozubulu people are descendants of one man, plus a few friends and allies who attached themselves to Ozubulu in olden times. The descendants of these friends and allies fully identify themselves as descendants of Ozubulu also. I feel that this feeling of a common ancestral root helps to nurture the feelings of brotherhood and kinship. Interestingly from the definition of the Jews by Joseph J. Williams S. J., the composition of the Jewish people is strikingly similar to the formation of the Igbo people of Ozubulu.

In William's words: "The minimum requirement would seem to be descent through at least one line of ancestors from one of the sons of Jacob or from some individual who in the past was incorporated into the body of Jews so as to imbibe their spirit and adopt their practices[225]."

As already pointed out, probably the feelings of having originated from a common ancestor accentuates the community spirit in the Igbos, and the place we found the strongest parallel to this feeling was in Israel.

A few instances of such parallelism in Israel might be helpful.

From the Scriptures, Abraham was Lot's uncle but we saw him referring to Lot as his brethren in Genesis 13:8 because both men had the same ancestors.

Similarly Eliezer in Genesis 24:27 followed his master's example in addressing Bethuel, Abraham's distant cousin as Abraham's brethren. In Genesis 24:48, Eliezer directly calls Bethuel Abraham's brother. This tendency was also found with Jacob. In Genesis 29:12 he refers to Laban his uncle as his brother. In less close knit societies Laban would have been referred to as Jacob's uncle.

It is easy for the writer as an Igbo to understand why these fellows who shared common ancestors, but were not 'brothers' in the strict sense view themselves as

---

[225] Williams, Joseph J. S.J, Hebrewisms of West Africa: From the Nile to the Niger With the Jews (New York: Biblo and Tanen, 1928) 158.

brothers. It was a core essence of their (Semitic) tradition.

In Deuteronomy 15:12, the fostering of community feelings continued relentlessly. In that section the language was so grand and explicit in the quoted passage: "If thy brother, a Hebrew man, or a Hebrew woman ..."

A deceased Igbo singer, Sir Warrior, could have been quoting that section when he released a song entitled, *Anambra na Imo wu nwanne*. The song was released when the Igbos were divided into Anambra and Imo states. Warrior simply viewed the people of both states as brothers, and the import of his song is that the inhabitants of the two states must never forget that they are one.

I received an inadvertent lesson in Igbo feelings of kinship from one Nigerian film entitled, *Not with my Daughter*. An Igbo lady had stubbornly got involved in an inter- tribal marriage, i.e., marriage with a non-Igbo man against custom and tradition and against advice from her family. At a point she couldn't fit into her husband's family and tradition. But before then she had been advised by an Igbo whom she had just met to rush back to her roots. She ignored him, remonstrating that all humans are the same. He went his way, after all the implication of her comment is that there was no special relationship between them. But when she felt threatened, she rushed to that Igbo 'stranger' and compelled him to aid her to escape, at great risk to himself... He did; on the ground that, as she insisted, he is her 'brother.' By Igbo tradition she was not wrong. We did/do not know about the designations 'cousin', 'uncle', 'aunt', 'nephew', 'niece', etc. All we know is brethren or brother or sister. And as can be seen from the few examples that I have offered Israel too knew only brothers and brethren.

I do not think that it is necessary to add anything to the Igbos great respect for individual rights and freedom. And allied to this feeling or desire not to be shackled, is the Igbos' total abhorrence of authoritarian leadership. In Chinua Achebe's book[226], some European missionaries; themselves subjects of kings and or queens, and being well acquainted with the monarchical societies that surround the Igbos, requested to see the king of an Igbo clan. But the clans-people responded that 'there is no king here!' The Igbos went further to state what they have as rulers; "the chief priests and the elders."

One needn't go far to spot the similarity with Israel. At all points and times in Israel's' long history the priests, prophets and the elders were evident. In the aforementioned Deuteronomy 27 the Bible poignantly captured the position with the following statement: "And Moses and the elders of Israel commanded the people . . . " while in verse 9, it was "Moses, the priests and the Levites."

Israel was a theocratic democracy, and I put forward the argument that all the evidence that I have marshaled presents the Igbo society as such too. And as in all human societies, where decay is almost inevitable, but can be prevented by vigilance, when Israel deteriorated, it slipped down to what could at worst be described as a theocratic-constitutional monarchy, with the democratic spirit still very much alive. King Saul still continued to view himself as subject to Samuel, the man of God, as the Law required. And unlike 'real kings' in

---

[226] Achebe, Chinua, *Things Fall Apart*, (London: Heinemann Education Books, 1958) 105.

ancient or modern times, he did not even have a palace or capital, but lived in his own house in Gibeah. Also he did not accumulate many many wives and had no standing army. His successor David respected/deferred to Nathan the prophet. Also as a *bona fide* Israelite he recognized that he was still no better than any other because he (David) was the king, so stoically he absorbed and endured the insults of Shimei, the son of Gera in II Samuel 16:5, at Bahurim. Youthful, uneducated advice was that the insulter should be killed, but David, thoroughly schooled in the traditions of Israel refused and took the insults, and that was something that no real potentate, in ancient or modern times could take or tolerate.

Continuing further to even some of the less tradition minded kings; Ahab, in 1 Kings 21, had to remonstrate with, and accept the refusal of a common citizen to sell his vineyard to him, even though the refusal distressed him greatly. His evil wife Jezebel had to ingenuously devise a plan to get rid of Naboth and then gain possession of the vineyard. This encounter reveals much about the Israelite society. In the society, just as in the Igbo society, every individual was entitled to a portion of the 'Land', unlike in most other societies where all the land was vested in, or belonged to, the sovereign.

And as I have stated before, in Israel as well as among the Igbos, citizens knew their rights. Citizens in both societies were ever ready to exercise their rights.

In Israel, Rehoboam, against good counsel, addressed Israel as if he had become a potentate. As a society in which everybody including the king had a voice, when Rehoboam had finished speaking Israel spoke also, and because what the king said was contrary to the laws and traditions of Israel, the people refused to accede to his demands. I added enough evidence to show that in Igbo society everybody was and is given a voice to contribute to how he or she is governed.

I have written repeatedly that ancient Israel did not maintain a standing army. The Igbos also did not maintain a standing army. Both societies depended on their citizens to defend the society when necessary.

As well in both societies, there were no regular police forces. The entire citizenry policed themselves. Repeatedly the Lord urged Israel to "blot out the evil from your midst." Among the Igbos too, in the traditional society, it was not uncommon to find seers cum doctors who would broadcast the names of any evil person who came to seek their assistance to eliminate their opponents.

Just as well boycotts and ostracism of malefactors were sufficient deterrents against evil people. There were no prisons. Repeatedly God warned that evildoers would be cut off from Israel. The Igbos adopted same measures of cutting off from evildoers. For example the Igbos in the past, on foreseeing that the approaching colonial authority with a new ideology, religion, tradition and set of laws would divide the society, and weaken it, simply warned Igbo clansmen not to have anything to do with it, and those that persisted were ostracized. They were not killed or imprisoned or harmed physically.

# CHAPTER TWENTY

# Not a Conclusion

By the time I got to this chapter I had begun to think about drawing this study to a close. But I asked myself, is it wise to draw this study which a knowledgeable Jew described as the beginnings of the Igbo Mishna and Gemara to a close, rather than to leave it open, and add new information as I get it? With this in mind I decided to refrain from having a formal conclusions section, but to discuss some unusual phenomena that lend credence to the theory that the Igbos moved from Israel to West Africa.

**Thought-provoking Phenomena**

*Igbo Folk-lore*
Curiously many of the lore of the Igbo talk about droughts and famines and hunger and relief when the rains began to fall, in ancient times. Chinua Achebe, Africa's greatest novelist preserved one of those stories of severe droughts and famines that affected the Igbos in *prehistoric times* in his classic *Things Fall Apart.*

Every Igbo child knows the story of the tortoise and the birds. About how the tortoise fell from heaven, and his shell broke into pieces, after the birds had refused to lend him feathers to fly down to the world, after they had gone to heaven to go and plead for rainfall to save them from the severe drought, and accompanying famine that was ravaging their land.

What we are describing here; droughts and famines affecting the Igbos raises questions. The Igbos live in the rain forests of Nigeria where the real worry is about flooding and erosion, and are thus not expected to have stories of droughts stored in their lore. Most parts of Igboland have heavy rainfall for up to eight months every year, and irregular rainfall for the remaining four months. At the time that I was writing this in late 2012 large parts of Igbo-land were submerged by flood water. Accordingly, that droughts and famines became ingrained in the collective memory of the Igbo people is certainly thought-provoking. And careful examination of the stories of droughts and famines lead a researcher to observe that the stories are intended to teach a lesson. So, one can safely surmise that the Igbo people must have passed through experiences that were remarkable and compelling enough to make them to save stories of droughts, and famines in their lore. Based on the foregoing, and other circumstances which I will bring up hereafter, we can say that those experiences that made such an impact on the Igbos were not likely experienced in the Igbos present location, but in a place where droughts and famines occur.

**The Lion Story:** Also very significant in Igbo lore is the lion known as *agu* in the Igbo language and which is known as *eze umu anumanu* (the king of the animals) is always talked about in Igbo *iho* (folklore). This should elicit surprise! The lion could not have entered Igbo lore if the Igbos had not known the lion or about the lion [in ancient times]. And the Igbos could not have known the lion if the Igbos had always lived in the rain forests (where the Igbos live presently). The lion's natural habitat is the grasslands, and the semi-arid Savanna. No part of Igbo-land is grassland. There are no lions in Igbo-land. There are no accounts that are reliable that show that any Igbo has seen a lion in Igboland. The locations nearest to Igbo-land where lions could have roamed and thrived are several hundred kilometers away, starting from the areas presently called Northern Kogi and Plateau in the middle of Nigeria. Yet there (in Igbo stories) they (the lions) always are, lording it over the animals, including the wisest, the tortoise. So where did the Igbos have contact with the lion? I feel confident enough to say that they did, in an earlier home. Somewhere drier! We can decisively rule out a problem that may arise here. Presently among the Igbos there is confusion about whether *agu* stands for the lion or the leopard. The correct position is that the lion is *agu*. To the Igbos *agu* epitomizes strength, majesty and power. The Igbos have never thought that the leopard could be the king of the animals. So we can say definitively that it is the lion that entered Igbo lore, and as the Igbos could not have saved memories of what they had never seen, we can say that they had the lion as a neighbour in a former home that is drier than where the Igbos live presently. Also it must be pointed out that these folktales were Igbo, well before many Igbos began to settle semi-permanently outside Igboland and to have steady and sustained contacts with their non Igbo neighbours in the forests of West Africa.

Lastly I find it very interesting that the Hebrew word for young lion is *gur*, and the Igbo word for the large cats is *agu*.

So much information is saved in Igbo sayings and lore. Igbo memory is very strong about experiences with droughts and famines.

Igbo lore are very ancient Igbo folk-tales passed from generation to generation. In the good old days, the young children in every family use the story telling time to while away the one or two hours between dinner and bed-time.

**Igbo and Israelite farming practices**

In addition the farming practices of the Igbos point to the Igbos having lived in a very dry region. I have studied Igbo farming practices. I also did a cursory study of the farming practices of the Ebira, Idoma, Igala and other neighbours of the Igbos'.

To the west the Igbos have the Ishan, Bini, Ijaw, Isoko, and Urhobo peoples, as neighbours. While to the south and east are the lands of the Kalabari, Ogoni, Ibibios, Efik, Ogojas, etc.

The Western neighbours of the Igbos practiced the system of agriculture known as monocropping and mixed farming; i.e., in the first instance if they earmark a piece of land for farming in a particular year, they would only plant a particular type of crop on it. On inquiry they responded that that was their tradition. Most kept a few poultry and ruminants; goats, sheep, and poultry, and many also kept pigs. In most cases their animals roamed.

The situation was the same in the other neighbouring zones. Monocropping, and in a few cases some of their members, especially the ones that share boundaries with the Igbos will have a mixture of mono cropping and mixed cropping farms.

## Chapter 20: Not A Conclusion

In Igbo-land the situation became markedly different. It was the rule to use mixed cropping, i.e. to plant many different types of crops on one field. It is good to make a point here. Samuel Taddesse, PhD, Ethiopian Jewish scholar, had suggested to me to examine Igbo farming and storage practices. His feeling was that traces of Hebraic practices might be found in them, if indeed the Igbos originated from Israel. A study of the Bible suggests that mixed cropping might have been a Hebraic practice, until Mosaic reforms outlawed it. It was probably resorted to because of the infrequent rainfall in Canaan, so any fertile piece of land had to be maximally used.

As a rule too, Igbos practiced mixed farming by keeping poultry, goats, sheep and a few cows, but the Igbos never kept pigs traditionally. As mentioned earlier, to the Igbos *ezi* (the pig) is an epitome of filth. Remarkably the Igbos' animals lived with the Igbos, as part of their community. Igbo ruminants do not roam. Igbos keep them at home, and feed them as humans.

The Igbos also have a unique kind of shifting cultivation: If a particular crop like yam is planted in a field in a given year, if that same land is still to be used the following year, yam would not be planted on it, but cocoyam might replace it as the basic crop, with the accompanying crops as usual.

I decided to find out why the Igbos use the mixed cropping method, in contrast to their neighbors who use mono cropping. I held extensive discussions and consultations with the following people; Ekama Elogbo Ekinya, then of the Faculty of Agriculture, University of Uyo, Akwa Ibom State, Nigeria. She is Ogoja by tribe. The Ogojas are one of the south eastern neighbours of the Igbos. Arinze Osegbo, an Igbo man, then a bureaucrat of the Nigerian Building & Road Research Institute; Science & Technology Ministry Abuja. He has a B.Sc in Industrial Chemistry, and a Post Graduate Diploma in Environmental Sciences. Samuel Ozoekwe, also Igbo, an economist and accountant. Lastly Mazi Nnacheta Obudulu Nwokike, a priest of Nri Clan, Igboland. I discussed separately with all the aforementioned persons, including U.A. Okonma, an Igbo farmer in Abuja.

Miss Ekinya, the agriculturist, posited that her Ogoja tribe mainly practices mono cropping, but in a few cases practice mixed cropping. She also posited that she knew that Igbos use mixed cropping exclusively. Then she yielded a fortuitous information; which is that the Igbos could only have adopted mixed cropping as their method of crop farming as a custom or tradition, because even though mixed cropping is the option most likely to be used in a place of land scarcity, the Igbos were known to be practicing mixed cropping even in the ancient times when land was abundant and plentiful. But then I reasoned, have the Igbos always had plentiful land? Was Erez Yisrael a large enough piece of real estate with enough water? Was it not likely that Igbos acquired the habit of managing scarce land when they lived in Israel as Israelites?

I continued with the agriculturist. She pointed out that in her corner of Eastern Nigeria, conditions were more or less the same as in the Igbo areas, yet the rule was monocropping, with mixed cropping an exception. I encouraged her to find out why there are those that went against the rule. She shocked me with her response-"those people who use mixed cropping have the connection of marriage with Igbos or were those believed to have descended from the Igbos."

I took up this question with the two Western educated Igbos; Arinze Osegbo and Sam Ozoekwe. Their opinions were more or less identical. Our effort to blame present land hunger for the practice fell flat on its face when we recalled that Nigerian tribes that had even less land than the Igbos, like the Ebiras, who really live atop rocks, practice monocropping. I decided to approach Nwokike who is a more traditional Igbo man. When I sought for his opinion on why the Igbos practice mixed cropping, he was tempted to blame contemporary land hunger. I pointed out to him that land hunger was not an issue in the past; and he said that perhaps the Igbos were afraid of kidnappers in the past, and therefore avoided risk by planting all their crops near their homes. I pointed out to him that the communities that were neighbours of the Igbos could not have been immune to abductions too. He laughed and answered, of course not. Why then did the Igbos farm differently, I continued to press on? His answer was 'customs and traditions'. I asked him then, who are the Igbos, where did they come from, who handed them the customs? He answered, Israelites, Israel. I decided to continue searching. This man is one of the priests of Nri Clan, and always had the opportunity to talk one -on- one with visiting Israeli tourists.

I went back to Abuja, Nigeria's capital in Northern Nigeria. There I interviewed several Igbo farmers. Hereafter is what I discovered from one of them, Mrs. Uche Modesta Okonma. This lady is from Enugu State, Nigeria. Of Igbo stock; she had a sizeable farm and in it she planted yam, maize, beans, okra and vegetables- a really mixed crop farm. Her neigbours who are not Igbos practiced mono cropping, i.e. one crop per field. I questioned her relentlessly to explain why her method of farming is different. To her it was her tradition and custom. Who taught you this custom? "Our ancestors," she responded. Who are your ancestors? I asked her, "In my hometown we were told as children that our ancestors were Israelites", she responded.

Mention must be made of Igbo mixed farming. A typical Igbo farmer would keep poultry, goats, sheep and sometimes one or two cows. A typical example of a successful Igbo farmer was Janet Nwazuonu Nwosu, my late maternal grandmother. She had various fields—all with mixed crops. She also kept poultry, goats, sheep and a few cows. She never kept pigs and I cannot recall any of her neighbours who kept pigs. I tried to find out why Igbos have an aversion to pork. The generally known reason was that it was dirty alien meat introduced by Europeans.

**Family Trees**

Also when we study Igbo family trees the evidence we see is that the Igbos have not stayed for a very long time in their present location. From the founder of my clan to myself I cannot get up to ten persons. And my clan Ozubulu is one of the really old Igbo clans.

Why do we describe the Igbos as The Largest Diaspora?

We said that the Igbos constitute the largest Diaspora of Israel. We said so because the Igbo people are by far the biggest single group of Israelites. Twenty to thirty five millions are estimated to be Nigerians presently. Also from the Igbos of Nigeria there are millions of persons who are presently Sierra Leoneans, Liberians, Afro-Americans, Canadians, Caribbeans, South Americans, Haitians, and Europeans.

# An Igbo Rhyme That Is Also a Jewish Rhyme (Had Gadya), Translated from Igbo by the Author

**Igbo Version: What Happened to the Tortoise?**

What happened to the tortoise?
The tortoise, the tortoise
A breadfruit fell on the tortoise
The tortoise, the tortoise
What happened to the breadfruit?
The tortoise, the tortoise
A stake pierced the breadfruit
The tortoise, the tortoise
What happened to the stake?
The tortoise, the tortoise
The termite ate up the stake
The tortoise, the tortoise
What happened to the termite?
The tortoise, the tortoise
A fowl ate the termite
The tortoise, the tortoise
What happened to the fowl?
The tortoise, the tortoise

## Chapter 20: Not A Conclusion

A hawk carried the fowl

The tortoise, the tortoise

What happened to the hawk?

The tortoise, the tortoise

A gun shot/killed the hawk

The tortoise, the tortoise

What happened to the gun?

The tortoise, the tortoise

Fire burnt the gun

The tortoise, the tortoise

What happened to the fire?

The tortoise, the tortoise

Water quenched the fire

The tortoise, the tortoise

What happened to the water?

The tortoise, the tortoise

The ground soaked up the water

The tortoise, the tortoise

What happened to the ground?

The tortoise, the tortoise

God (Chukwu Abiama) created the ground

The tortoise, the tortoise

What happened to Chukwu Abiama?

The tortoise, the tortoise

Nothing happened to Chukwu Abiama

The tortoise, the tortoise

**Jewish Version:** *Had Gadya*

A father bought a kid for two zuzim;
A cat came and ate the kid;
A dog came then bit the cat;
The dog was beaten by a stick;
The stick was burned by fire;
Water quenched the fire;
An ox drank the water;
A *shohet* (ritual slaughterer) slaughtered the ox;
The *shohet* was killed by the Angel of Death who in punishment was destroyed by God.

# Acknowledgments

Many fine individuals and groups helped me in so many ways as I carried out the research that enabled me to write this book. I will however be able to acknowledge only a few of them because of space.

First and foremost I want to thank Kulanu Inc., the dedicated Jewish group, with which I spent countless hours discussing Igbo and Jewish histories and cultures and which made available to me a research grant.

I must also acknowledge individually the officials of Kulanu, and some of their friends and associates who gave me much support.

There were:

Rivkah Lambert Adler who took her Jewish culture and Jewish people-hood seriously enough that she found my work fascinating enough to introduce me to Jack Zeller, the founder of Kulanu.

Jack Zeller, who examined my programme, found it worthy, and asked Kulanu to include it in their own. He also gave me a lot of valuable information which helped me to understand Jewish culture more.

Ehav Ever, whom Jack Zeller asked to work closely with me as I began to study Jewish culture, and who did exactly that. He gave me my first Torah and my first Tanakh.

Harriet Bograd who surveyed my work, discovered very early that I had the necessary enthusiasm for the task, and gave me every assistance that enabled me to develop the necessary research skills.

Karen Primack, who was always ready to answer many questions that I had.

Aron Primack, who also helped in clarifying knotty issues. Carol Carter, who used her skills as a copy-editor to improve the book.

Gladys Schwarz, who taught me new skills that enabled me to read the Tanach (the Hebrew Bible) with more understanding.

Herman Storick, who not only gave me major financial support, but scoured the bookshops in his country, selecting rare books which he sent to me. His, and his wife Cecilia's assistance to me was very vital.

Peter Persoff, who read the book, edited it for grammar and content, thereby greatly enriching and improving it. Uche Onwumelu Umeokolo, who gave me financial assistance, and helped by refreshing my mind on Igbo customs and traditions.

Teddy Luttwak, who helped when I needed financial assistance.

Andria Spindel, who took a healthy interest in my programme, and untiringly supported me.

Rabbi Howard Gorin; the spiritual leader of Tikvat Israel Synagogue, Maryland, U.S.A, at the time I began to write the book; who visited Nigeria three times, and spent valuable time discussing *halacha* (Jewish Law) with me. With members of the Social Action Committee of Tikvat Israel such as Danny Siegal, and others assisting, he carefully selected, and sent thousands of books of Jewish interest to me.

Jeffrey Davidson, who visited Nigeria over fifteen times, faithfully served as Kulanu's Nigeria representative, in the capacity of which he not only supported me financially, but also shared his knowledge of Jewish Law and customs with me.

Daniel Lis, Swiss-Israeli social anthropologist, who visited Nigeria for weeks, toured Igbo-land with me, during which he began to investigate the Igbo-Israelite story, and who read and reviewed the book when it was nearing publication. His own study of the Igbos and the connection to Israel which is ground-breaking will make waves in the world when he releases his book, *Imagined Kinship? Nigerian Igbo in Israel and the Question of Belonging*. Among other things Lis discovered that some important Jewish rabbis in Europe, in the early nineteenth century wrote letters referring to the Igbos as possibly their brothers.

Gil Amminadav, who encouraged me to continue writing about the Igbos, with the following words: "publishing saved us (the Jews) when our communities all over the Diaspora were falling apart."

His wife, Elana Amminadav, who worked with him to improve my program. Their generous support, which encompassed both financial and educational help, was vital and crucial.

Thomas Timberg, who spent many years in Nigeria, and who helped me in my research.

Evan Green, who has visited Nigeria many times, and who has untiringly continued to support me.

Judith Helzner, who has also visited Nigeria, and has supported my work financially.

Marc Wishengrad, who has also visited Nigeria, and has been a benevolent friend.

Hartley Springman, who has also visited Nigeria, and has given me support.

Rabbi Jacques Cukierkorn who gave me and my community fifty copies of his book, *Accessible Judaism*. Igbo-Israel musician and activist Moore Black Chi Mmadike who has given me a lot of financial and other material support.

Rabbi Capers Funnye, who joined us in the debates of the ibo-benei-yisrael@yahoogroups.com discussion group and shared information with me and other Igbos.

Rabbi Leo Abrami; whose interest in my research was very encouraging.

Joel Levitt, the young Jew who used his *bar mitzvah* as an occasion to raise support for me, and his mother Kay Klass who stood by him as he performed the *mitzva* (good deed). Barbara Shair, who sent very important and educational Judaica to me.

Susan Schorr and Katie Rosenthal; who as assistants to Harriet Bograd very kindly played roles that enabled me to do my work with a settled mind.

Orit Regev, who tried to get Israeli academic support for me.

Morris Bear Squire, the founder of the Forest Foundation, who with assistance from Kulanu opened a 'Moishe House' in Abuja which I lived and worked in, for one year. Rachael Aron, David Cygielman, Brady Gill, Isaac Zones, and Levi Moses; my friends in the "Moishe

House" programme whose friendship I enjoyed while the program lasted.

Michael Ophir, my dear friend who gave a lot of support to me.

Donna Halper who was very supportive.

Irene Orleansky; Russian Israeli musician who has given me a lot of material support and encouragement, and has also visited the Igbos in the course of her work to integrate Igbo-Jewish, and the music of other re-emerging and emerging Jewish communities into the music of world Jewry.

Rabbi Brant Rosen with whom I spent a full month touring Igbo-land, other parts of Nigeria, learning about the Igbos and the Jews.

Carolivia Herron, who used her technical know-how to turning the manuscript into a book, and who has published it.

Avraham Van Riper, this knowledgeable man who has helped me in many important ways.

Ikechukwu 'Mobi' Amobi, who has been a very kind benefactor, brother and friend to me.

Miriam Lindenberg, my kind friend who has helped me in many ways.

From the Igbo/Nigerian community: the Igbo priests/chroniclers from Nri Clan who are my friends; Obudulu Nnacheta Nwokike, Nze Onwa, Nze Chitoo, Nze Akunne, Elder Nnalue, Elder Okpuzor, Nze Obaegbuna and Mr Samuel Ozoekwe.

The many friends whose letters, words of encouragement, gifts of books, etc., were very important and morale-boosting: Favour Ifezue, Yhoshua ben

Yisrael, the departed Rabbi Moshe Cotel, Daniel Boone, Michael Pinion, David Elleff, Jim Michaelson, Rabbi Alon Asefovitz, Yohannes Zeleke, Sam Taddesse, Yekutiel Gershoni, Samuel Klausner, Jonathan Sarna, Daniel Benlolo, Barbara Weiser, Irwin Berg, Saul Issroff, Shepard Wahnon, Hadassah Har El, Emeka Nwokedi, Rabson Wuriga, Dean Malik, Le Rico Richardson, Daniel Bernadin, Yehiel Yisrael, Chaim Klein, Roger Froiken, Rabbi Barry Leff, Rabbi ben Tzion Saloff, Joshua Cane, Isaac Mozeson, Edith Bruder, Terry Hess, Charlie Radin, Carmine Caifano, Yehudah Tochukwu Shomeyr, Jack Goldfarb, Raymond Keen, Philippe Assouline, Cajetan Iwunze, E 'Dilic' Elobi, Harry Rozenberg, Edward Rensin, Nathan Katz, Okey Nwabueze Godson, Cliff Pinto, Jeff Lieberman, Michael Freund, Sar Elkanah, Teresa Kemp, Charity Dell, Judah Moshe, Dumisani Washington, Anthony Edwards, Chaimae Mechtaly, Nathan Devir.

Also, Emma Okika, Ernest Kemakolam, Richard Chime, Armstrong Isiocha, Sidney Emezue, Jonas Ahazuem, Christian Madubuko, Chinyere Gbugu, Caliben Ikechukwu Okonkwo, M Osita Nwaneri, Ike Nwachukwu, who helped to expedite the re-establishment of diplomatic ties between Nigeria and Israel as Nigeria's Foreign Minister. Dozie Ikedife; former president-general of Ohaneze, Peter Nnabude, Rochas Okorocha, governor of the Igbo Imo State at the time of publishing of this book, Uche Eni, Habila Na'aya, Onyekwulusi FBI, Kelechi Deca, Ingram Osuigwe, Sule Ahmed Gise, Obinna Njaka, Randie Dikeukwu, Cletus Amaraegbu, Anayo Nkamnebe, Odera Mmadike, Charleston Okafor, Uche Odinaka Nnadi, Larry Okey Ugwu, Kenneth Awele Maduabuchi Okafor, Eunice Okpala, Remigius Agubuonu, the departed Charles Nwosu, Valentine Chukwudi Iwuchukwu, Emmanuel

Ojukwu, Justin and Monica Malizu, Kenneth Ilona, Chukwudi Ilona, Dick Onwuamegbu, Azuka Ogbuka'a, Emeka Okeke, Anayo Osuji, Chioma Osuji, Izuchukwu Onuchukwu, Festus Okenyi, Perez Chikwelu Attah, Obinna Nwobi-Obinwanne, John Okiyi Kalu, Victor Ogbonnaya, Ikechukwu Uchenna Osuji, Avi Kraft, Reuven Kossover, Shai Afsai, Alexander Umeokolo, Afikpo Chic, Zion Lexx, Maria Ude Egwu, Mac Jossy, Ethel Obiakor, Adaobi Uchegbu, Irene Uzoamaka Okoli, Chima Onyeulo and numerous others that I can't mention now.

From my home front, my wife Irene Malizu-Ilona, who recognized that this subject is dear to me, and supported me. And my son Daniel and daughter Aliya who enriched the work in no small way, by bringing excitement and joy to the enterprise.

The publisher, Street to Street EpicCenter Stories sends a special thanks to funders of this publication: Drs. Jack and Diane Zeller, Kulanu, Inc., Mark and Mona Berch, the Social Action Committee of Tifereth Israel Congregation of Washington, DC.,

# Words of Praise for the Author

When I got *The Igbos and Israel*....... I said to myself as I was about to open it 'another history book.' Alas! It wasn't so. Reading the book, 15,000 kilometres away from Igbo-land, was like reliving the Igbo way of life. Remy Ilona produced a work that will make it possible to write the Igbos accurate history. He recorded the Igbos way of life accurately. Very importantly he worked as an eyewitness; telling our story the way it should be told. That is why I call him the Igbo Josephus, and his book 'Living History'. I would say, Ilona is the Igbo writer that has succeeded in documenting and interpreting our culture, and presenting it accurately. Every Igbo man/woman can relate to the context in the book. Besides, some of the 'outdated practices therein are not of the remote past...but are practices that can still be observed among the Igbos.

-------------Moore Black Chi Mmadike, University of Adelaide, and Flinders University, Australia.


This cultural study has by far presented the strongest parallelism in Judaism and Igbo tradition, the emphasis on language is a most needed bonus! The traditions are beyond similar, so many things I can re-count that stood out, such as the prayer wall, the true meaning of Omenana, and most important the festivals that correlate to sukkot and passover, such as Oriri Achicha, and Ima ntu (Sukkot). The book is greatly detailed and offers a lot of insight into Igbo and Yisraelite concepts.

-------------Lerico Richardson, USA

The book is impressive. It clearly explains the striking similarities between Igbo culture and Jewish culture. This wonderful book makes me to see how my beautiful Igbo culture derives from Judaism, and helps me to understand Igbo history.

------------Okey Nwabueze Godson

I have just finished reading "The Igbos and Israel: An Inter-cultural Study of the Largest Jewish Diaspora" by Remy Ilona - (Publisher - EpicCenter Stories.

Jewish Igbo scholar Remy Ilona beautifully describes Judaic rituals, beliefs and concepts as they are practiced in the Igbo culture of Nigeria. His book is written with the understanding that a very significant part of the Igbo people identify the origin of their customs as emanating from the ancient Israelites, and this Jewish identification has been an integral part of the Igbo life experience for many years.

Religious practices of the Igbo Jews include circumcision eight days after the birth of a male child, observance of kosher dietary laws, separation of men and women during menstruation, wearing of the tallit and kippah, and the celebration of holidays such as Yom Kippur and Rosh Hashanah. The Igbo communities have also adopted holidays such as Hanukkah and Purim. Mr. Ilona informs us of the astonishing fact that 30% of the Nigerian population are of Jewish descent!

## Praise for the Author

In 2002 Remy Ilona began to seriously investigate the origins of the Igbo people of Nigeria who have also been known as "Ibos", and during the Nigerian Civil War as "Biafrans." Remarkably, then, Mr. Ilona has thought, worked and written on this subject for more than 10 years, and the result is this amazing book. I highly recommend Remy Ilona's book, which links Western and African culture in a most profound way - through the heart and mind of Jewish religion and culture.

--------Raymond Keen, USA


Remy Ilona's "The Igbos and Israel: An Inter-cultural Study of the Largest Jewish Diaspora" is a brilliant, ecstatic book for individuals who are willing to inquire about the biggest Jewish Diaspora in Africa. It provided cultural, philological and trustworthy evidence of the Igbos connection with Yisrael. Igbo families across the world are seriously advised to include this wonderful book in their library, because the book is a masterpiece that will bring Igbo people together. It is obvious that is Omenena which this book deals extensively with that is the catalyst for restoration of unity and pride in the Igbo society.

As an Igbo Jew, Ilona's research helped me to understand the qualities of Igbo culture, and the similarities between Omenana and Judaism, with his excellent analysis of our cultural practices that are manifest in the Torah. He also enunciated with clarity how Igbo people performed traditional Omenana. Ilona's narration included a detailed rendition of Igbo rituals and traditions; such as Oriri Achicha (Passover and unleavened bread) and Igbu Aja (Atonement and Yom Kippur).

Ilona is the only Igbo scholar whose work can encourage Igbos to begin to revive Igbo faith in Igbo culture and language. In addition, the book can also help young Ndi Igbo to understand the importance of Igbo culture, because of its detailed detailed comparison with the Jewish tradition which provided an easy approach to understand Omenana.

Finally I'll say that Ilona is on the verge to become a phenomenal scholar/philosopher whose works can help Jewry to preserve Jewish interest in Jewish culture.

--------Ken Awele Maduabuchi Zechariah Okafor, U.K

Author Remy Ilona does a masterful job with scholarly attention to detail. "The Igbos and Israel: An Intercultural Study of the oldest and Largest Jewish Diaspora" provides cultural, linguistic and anecdotal evidence of the Igbo connection to Israel. Mr. Ilona follows in the tradition of 18th century African abolitionist and author Olaudah Equiano, in uncovering the mystery of the Igbo Israelite community. He is a wealth of knowledge, and shares the fruits of his labor with humility and grace. And it is the abundance of examples paralleling the Igbo and the Israelite that is precisely why the book is so effective.

For those of you familiar with Jewish law (Torah) or history, consider if you will the following quotes: "If a girl likes a poor man, who in turn likes her, and both families agree that their children can marry, the young man may elect to pay for his bride by working for her family for a number of years. That was what Jacob did for Laban his future father-in-law for seven years for the matriarchs of Israel, Leah and Rachel. Some Igbo oral traditions state that in Igbo traditions that it is also for seven years."

"In my clan, Ozubulu, and in Igbo-land generally, we believe and say: "na ana na atu/ na agbo onye mer' aru" (that the land throws up/ throws out/ vomits persons/ people who commit abominations). Because of the consequences that followcommission of abominations Igbos take various measures to ensure that they give aru and its commission enough distance."

"The Igbo day starts from sunset, and ends on the next sunset. Quoting an Igbo scholar on this would be helpful: "Before the white man came to Igbo-land with his clock, a new day began at sun-set in Igbo-land. It was also observed like that by the Israelis. Even today for an example, the Sabbath day in Israel is observed on Saturday. But its observance begins on the evening of Friday".

I highly recommend this book for all who desire to know more about the Igbo-Israel community, and the African Israelite Diaspora in general.

Dumisani Washington, USA

Remy Ilona's book "The Igbos and Israel: An Intercultural Study of the Largest Jewish Diaspora" is a wonderful well-written resource for anyone who wishes to learn more about the largest Jewish Diaspora in Africa. It is nothing short of a research masterpiece about a group of people who have been called "the Jews of Africa" by their neighbors.

This book will be used by scholars of history and anthropology to trace the paths that God's Chosen people took after the destruction of the First and Second Temple in Jerusalem. Jews have migrated by choice and by force to remote parts of the world with the hope of one day being called home to the Land of Israel. I urge all, especially the descendants of Africans who were enslaved and brought to the Americas and Western Europe during the Transatlantic Slave Trade, to buy this book.

-----------Yhoshua Ben Yisrael, USA

Remy Ilona is a top notch scholar on Igbo History and origins as well as Judaism and Torah and unequivocally shows beyond the shadow of a doubt through his detailed and thorough first hand accounts and extensive research Jewish literature and Igbo lore that the Igbo are certainly portions of the lost tribes of Israel, that Igbos are Hebrews and Jews. He clearly demonstrates this most powerfully through comparing the laws, customs and cultures of the two and shows how they are in actuality one and the same. This is a powerful must have and must read book for any one interested in the Igbo or the Lost Tribes of Israel. It is a resource you will refer to again and again and read more than once. It is also a book, if you are Igbo or Jew, that you cannot help but share with your family and friends.

Yehudah Tochukwu ben Shomeyr (Kris Shoemaker)

This is a must read if you are genuinely seeking knowledge on the inter-link between Igbo culture and that of Israel. This book will take you on that journey of intellectual emancipation. It is scholarly written, mentally enriching, culturally liberating. I recommend this book to those at the echelon of Nigerian society and other professionals interested in African Studies.

------------Cajetan Iwunze, U.K

**Researcher's Researcher**

Remy Ilona is a researcher's researcher and his trail-blazing efforts will lead to the revitalization of Igbo Studies. The way he treated the topic of tithe in particular was an eye opener.

------------Remigius Chukwunonye Agubuonu,

University of Hull, England.

**Suggested For Further Reading:**

Daniel Lis: (forthcoming): Imagined Kinship? Nigerian Igbo in Israel and the Question of belonging.

Edith Bruder: The Black Jews of Africa.

Remy Ilona with contributions from Ehav Eliyahu Ever: The Igbos: Jews In Africa, Vol 1.

Remy Ilona: The Igbos: Jews In Africa: With Reflections on the Civil War and Solutions to the most critical Igbo problems.

Remy Ilona: A Short Story From Igbo Israel-republished as (Uri's Travels).

## 294  Praise for the Author

Remy Ilona: Introduction To The Chronicles of Igbo Israel, And the connections between Afro-Americans and the Jews.

# Map of Igboland 295

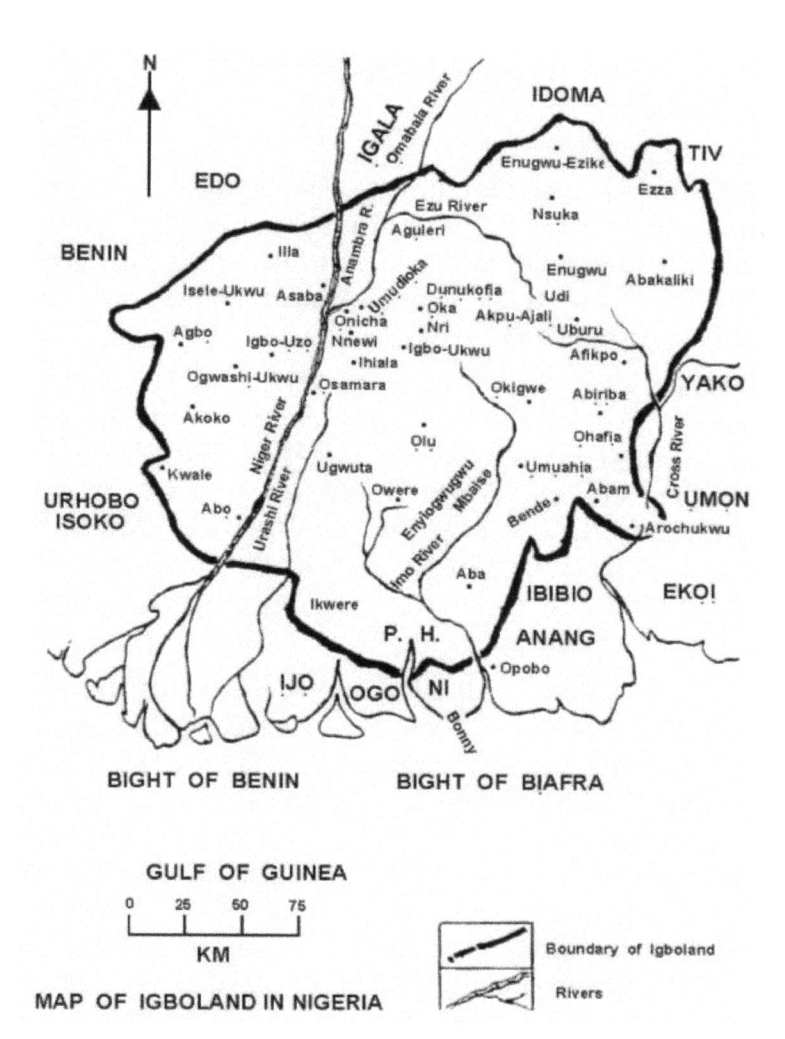

Map Reference[227]

---

[227] http://igbology.igbonet.net/docs/igboworld/detailed map.html

# About Remy Ilona

Remy Ilona is Igbo by ethnicity. The Igbos are said to be the Jews of Nigeria/West Africa. Remy was born in Ozubulu, Igbo-land, to Pauline and Joseph Ilona, both of Ozubulu. Presently he lives in Abuja with his wife Irene, son Daniel and daughter Aliya.

He holds a degree in Law from ASUTECH (UNIZIK). He qualified from the Nigeria Law School, and is an Igbo-Jewish scholar. His work on Israelite Africa helped to earn him an admission to study for a Masters in Near East and Judaic Studies at the Brandeis University, Boston, M.A, U.S.A, but he was unable to proceed to Brandeis due to ill-health. He is without question Nigeria's top Hebraist, and Bible scholar.

He practices law, and serves as the head of the Igbo Israel Union which he founded. He also helps to lead *Beth Knesset Siyahh Israel* which he also helped to establish. In addition he is a Nigeria liaison for Kulanu Inc', an American Jewish group, which searches for, and aids Israel's lost Diaspora. He serves as a field correspondent for the International Society For The Study of African Jewry (I.S.S.A.J). He is one of the facebook admins of the facebook groups: Igbo Israel International Music and Film Festival plus Book Fair, Igbo-Israel University and Odinala/Omenana (Igbo Culture) Defenders.

Besides the numerous essays and articles which he has written and published in traditional media such as the National Times, True National newspapers, and in online media like kulanu-list@yahoogroups.com,ibo-benei-yisrael@yahoogroups.com, the discussion forum of www.igboisrael.com, blog "voice of igboisrael," which can be followed at http://igboisrael.blogspot.com/ etc.; he has written and published *The Igbos: Jews In Africa Vol 1, The Igbos: Jews In Africa: With Reflections on the Civil War and Solutions to the most critical Igbo problems, Introduction To the Chronicles of Igbo-Israel- And The connections between the Afro-Americans and the Jews, A Short Story From Igbo Israel* which he will republish very soon as *Uri's Travels*.

Remy is working presently on a new book about transmigration which is entitled *Reincarnation* and he is also revising some of his books.

ABOUT THE BOOK

*The Igbos and Israel (An Inter-cultural Study of the Oldest and Largest Jewish Diaspora)* is essentially a compilation of Igbo cultural practices. A comparison of Igbo culture with Jewish culture, and somehow a commentary on the Tanach (Hebrew Bible), undertaken from an Igbo perspective.

Am I surprised that Remy took the turn he did? I'm not. As a scion of the Ilona family of Egbema Ozubulu, he is a descendant of priests and prophets. Also his mother's family produced many important Igbo doctors.

Emma Okika

Federal Polytechnic Oko, Anambra State, Nigeria.

## 298 About the Book

*The author can be reached as follows:*

Remy Ilona
Telephone +234-8065-300-351
Email: remy.ilona@gmail.com ,
Facebook: Remy Ilona
Twitter: Remy Ilona

*You can also converse with him at the following Facebook sites:*

Igbo-Israel University
Igbo Israel International Music and Film Festival plus Book Fair
Odinala/Omenana (Igbo Culture)
Igboville
Ndi Igbo
Andria Spindel
Ikechukwu Uchenna Osuji
Moore Black Chi MMadike
Igbo Israel International Music and Film Festival plus Book Fair 2012
IBSI (Institute for Black Solidarity with Israel)
Dumisani Washington
Zion Lexx
Rivka Lambert Adler
Irene Orleansky
Ruvy Kossover
Miriam Metzinger
Yehiel Yisrael
Dennis Tate
EWAO
Phil Riper

*View us on YouTube:*

http://www.youtube.com/watch?v=hTo5u9qb-0I&feature=youtu.be

**And at the following yahoogroups:**
Ibo-benei-yisrael@yahoogroups.com

www.kulanu-list@yahoogroups.com

**Also learn more about our work and purchase copies at the following websites:**
Kulanu.org
Kulanuboutique.com
EpicCenterStories.org
Carolivia.com
StreetToStreet.org

# References

Achebe, Chinua. *Arrow of God.* Ibadan: Heinemann Educational Books, 1964.

Achebe, Chinua. *Things Fall Apart.* Ibadan: Heinemann Educational Books, 1958.

Adegbola, Ade E. A., Ed. *Traditional Religion in West Africa.* Ibadan: Sefer Books Ltd, 1998.

Afigbo, A. *Ropes of Sand.* Ibadan: University Press, Ltd., 1981.

Akaolisa, Humphrey. *Igbo Race, Origin and Controversies.* Awka: Buckstar Publishers, 2003.

Buah, F. K. *West Africa and Europe,* London: Macmillan Educational Books, 1966.

Arazu, Rev. Dr. Father Martin. *Our Religion: Past and Present.* Awka: Martin-King Press, 2005.

Basden, G.T. *Among The Ibos of Nigeria* London: University Publishing Company, 1921.

Basden, G.T. *Niger Ibos.* London: Frank Cass and Co., Ltd. 1966.

Ben-Gigi, Danny.*First Steps in Hebrew Prayer: Living Israeli Hebrew.* Scottsdale, AZ, 1998. hebrewworld.com

Boteach, Shmuley. *Judaism For Everyone.* New York: Basic Books, 2002.

Collis, Robert. Nigeria In Conflict. Lagos: John West Publication, Ltd., 1970.

Van Crevefeld, Martin. "Build a Wall to the Sky" in *Newsweek,* April 1, 2002.

Cukierkon, Jacques. *Accessible Judaism.* Booksjustbooks.com, in cooperation with Solving Light Books, 2004.

Dunner, Joseph. *The Republic of Israel.* New York: Whittlesey House, 1950.

Eidlitz, Eliezer. *Is It Kosher?* Jerusalem: Feldheim Publishers, 1992.

Emecheta, Buchi. *The Joys of Motherhood.* Oxford: Heinemann Educational Books, 1979.

Ganzfried, Solomon, and Hyman E. Goldin, Trans. *Code of Jewish Law and Customs (Shulhan Aruch).* New York: Hebrew Publishing Company, 1961.

Hertz, J. H. *The Pentateuch and Haftorahs.* 2nd edition. London: The Soncino Press, 1937.

Ilona, Remy and Eliyahu, Ehav. *The Igbos: Jews In Africa?* Vol 1. Abuja: Mega Press, 2005.

Isichei, Elizabeth. *History of West Africa Since 1800.* London: Macmillan Education, Ltd., 1977.

Klinghoffer, David. *The Discovery Of God.* New York: Three Leaves Press - Doubleday, 2004.

Kolatch, Alfred. The Jewish Mourners Book of Why. New York: Jonathan David Publishers, Inc., 1993/96.

Kushner, Harold. *To Life.* Boston: Warner Books, 1993.

Munonye, John. *The Only Son.* Ibadan: Heinemann Educational Books, 1966.

Nwapa, Flora. *Efuru.* Ibadan: Heinemann Educational Books, 1966.

Nzeako, Tagbo. *Omenala Ndi Igbo.* Lagos: Longman Nigeria PLC, 1972.

Ogbalu, F. C. *Omenala Igbo.* Lagos: University Publishing Co. Academy Press, 1979.

Okere, T. I. *Religion in a World of Change: African Ancestral Religion, Islam and Christianity.* Owerri: Assumpta Press, 2003.

Orji, Matthew O. *The History and Culture of the Igbo People.* Nkpor: Jet Publishers (Nigeria) Ltd, 1999.

Potok, Chaim. *Wanderings – History of the Jews*. New York: Fawcett Crest. 1978.

Promoter, Show.(Nelson Ejinduaka). Igbo musician.

Rossel, Seymour. *Covenant People, Covenant Land*. New York: Union of American Hebrew Congregations, 1995.

Sacher, Abram Leon.*A History of The Jews*. New York: Alfred Knopf, Inc., 1930.

Saturday Sun Newspaper. Nigeria. sunnewsonline.com

Sayyed, Tashbih. *A Muslim in a Jewish Land*. 13 Kislev 5766 (14 December 2005), Aish.com.

Siegal, Richard, Strassfeld, Sharon, Strassfeld, Michael. *The First Jewish Catalogue*. Philadelphia: The Jewish Publication Society of America, 1999.

Talbot, D. Amaury. *Women's Mysteries of a Primitive People: The Ibibios of Southern Nigeria.* Original Publication, London: 1915. Reprint. Forgotten Books. n.d. 20?? Cited in Joseph J. Williams, *Hebrewisms of West Africa: From the Nile to the Niger with the Jews*. New York: Biblo and Tanen, 1928.

Telushkin, Joseph. *Biblical Literacy*. New York: Harper Collins Publishers, Inc., 1977.

Webster, J. B. , A. A. Boahen, and H. O. Idowu. *The Growth of African Civilization: The Revolutionary Years Since 1800 to the Present Day.* Bucks: Longman, 1967.

Williams, Joseph J. *Hebrewisms of West Africa: From the Nile to the Niger With the Jews*. New York: Biblo and Tanen, 1928.

Zeller, Jack. First president of Kulanu, Inc. Personal Communications.

<<<<>>>>

Lightning Source UK Ltd.
Milton Keynes UK
UKHW010734180322
400272UK00001B/218

9 781938 609008